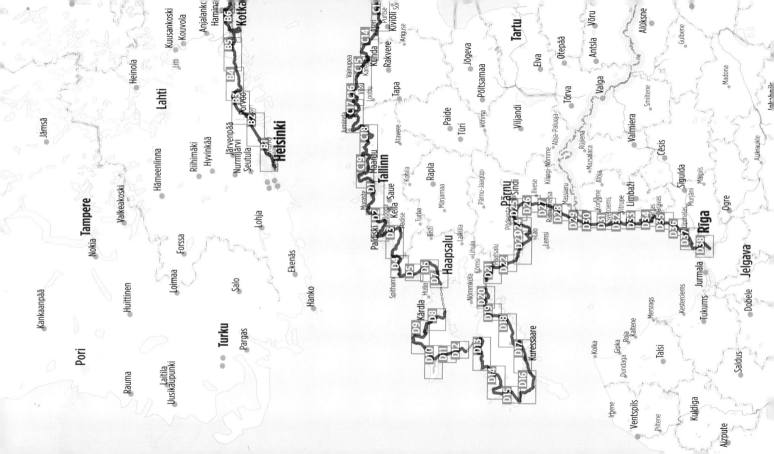

Iron Curtain Trial

Finland
Baltic Sea Coast

From the Barents Sea and from Helsinki to Rīga

An original *bikeline*-cycling guide

VERLAGESTERBAUER

bikeline®-Guide
Iron Curtain Trail 1
Finland • Baltic Sea Coast
© 2018, **Verlag Esterbauer GmbH**
A-3751 Rodingersdorf, Hauptstr. 31
Tel.: +43/2983/28982-0, Fax: -500
E-Mail: bikeline@esterbauer.com
www.esterbauer.com
2nd edition 2018
ISBN: 978-3-85000-745-0

Please quote edition and ISBN number in all correspondence!

Translation: Chris Lines

We wish to thank all the people who contributed to the production of this book.

The ***bikeline*-Team:** Birgit Albrecht-Walzer, Katharina Amon-Schneider, Beatrix Bauer, Michael Bernhard, Michael Binder, Veronika Bock, Petra Bruckmüller, Roland Esterbauer, Gabriela Fürst, Dagmar Güldenpfennig, Martina Kreindl, Nora Ludolph, Gregor Münch, Karin Neichsner, Carmen Paradeiser, Sabrina Pusch, Claudia Retzer, Petra Schartner, Sonja Schleifer, Isabella Tillich, Christian Thoren, Martin Trippmacher, Carina Winkelhofer, Martin Wischin, Wolfgang Zangerl

Cover photos: The river Narva with the two fortresses, Frank Wurft; The church in Grense-Jakobselv, Niklas Prenzel; The Museum of Border Protection in Raate, Roman Schulte-Sasse

Photo credits: Fabian Jaehn: 69; Frank Wurft: 118; Hannu Ojala: 62; Janis Humann: 35, 88; Jens Müller: 85, 101; Jürgen Ritter: 16; Knut Åserud: 24; Margo Märtsoo: 160; Martin Kozàk: 18; Michael Cramer: 14, 26, 30, 38, 42, 45, 54, 58, 60, 64, 65, 66, 67, 74, 76, 80, 84, 93, 95, 98, 104, 106, 116, 120, 122, 124, 128, 130, 132, 138, 140, 142, 144, 146, 151, 166, 169, 172, 173, 180, 183, 184, 185, 188, 190, 192; MTI Photo, Matusz Károly: 15; Niklas Prenzel: 48; Philipp Cerny: 187; Presse+Infoamt Berlin: 11, 13; Pyhä Luosto National Park Timo Newton-Syms under license CC BY-SA 2.0, flickr.comphotostimo_w2s: 36; Raitis Sijäts: 102, 109; Roman Schulte-Sasse: 22; Timo Setälä: 28; Visit Estonia: 154; Von Hedi Witter - Eigenes Werk, CC BY-SA 3.0, https://commons.wikimedia.org/w/index.php?curid=30459627: 50; Vyborg Museum: 90

Cartography created with *axpand*
(www.axes-systems.com)

Base Map 1 : 120.000 and Citymaps:
© OpenStreetMap Contributors

LIVE-UPDATES

 On our web page we offer an online-service, that provides updated information and current changes concerning this cycling guide. This information is brought up-to-date regularly and enables you, in combination with the current edition of this book, to plan your trip in the best possible way. The Live-Update for this book is freely available under:

www.esterbauer.com/db_detail.php?buecher_code=ICTN1_E

Have you noticed some changes or mistakes during your journey concerning the itinerary, the overnight accommodation or the tourist information along the route? Then you have the possibility to bring the bikeline-team up-to-date using the Update-section on our web page. We are looking forward to getting your information and say Thank You in the name of all cyclists.

 The latest bikeline GPS-Track for this book is freely available under:

tracks.world/?dir=fi/trk53do538

Preface

To properly live, breathe and experience history – that is the goal of the "Iron Curtain Trail". From the Barents Sea to the Black Sea, this guide takes you along the Western border of the old Warsaw Pact countries, all the way across Europe. The route does not just connect European culture, history and sustainable tourism but it also provides historically interested cyclists with some spectacularly beautiful and varied landscapes and unique habitats that were able to emerge in the former border strip, which is today the European Green Belt.

The maps in the revised edition are scaled larger at 1:120,000 from Helsinki to Rīga, and from Grense Jakobselv to Vaalimaa it remains at 1:400,000. This volume describes the 4,000-kilometre-long part of the route from the Barents Sea to Rīga.

Maps, route descriptions, extensive historical background information, references to the cultural and touristic offering of each region as well as practical travel and accommodation advice make this cycling guide a helpful companion on your journey to discovering the route along the former Iron Curtain.

Map legende

Cycling routes (Radrouten)

Main cycle route, low motor traffic
(Hauptroute, wenig KFZ-Verkehr)

──────── Paved surface (asphaltiert)

─ ─ ─ Unpaved surface (nicht asphaltiert)

┄┄┄┄ Bad surface (schlecht befahrbar)

Main cycle route, without motor traffic / cycle path
(Hauptroute, autofrei / Radweg)

──────── Paved surface (asphaltiert)

─ ─ ─ Unpaved surface (nicht asphaltiert)

┄┄┄┄ Bad surface (schlecht befahrbar)

Excursion or alternative cycle route, low motor traffic
(Ausflug od. Variante, wenig KFZ-Verkehr)

──────── Paved surface (asphaltiert)

─ ─ ─ Unpaved surface (nicht asphaltiert)

┄┄┄┄ Bad surface (schlecht befahrbar)

Excursion or alternative route, without motor traffic / cycle path (Ausflug od. Variante, autofrei / Radweg)

──────── Paved surface (asphaltiert)

─ ─ ─ Unpaved surface (nicht asphaltiert)

┄┄┄┄ Bad surface (schlecht befahrbar)

Other cycle routes (Sonstiges)

──────── Other cycle route (sonstige Radroute)

●●●●● Cycle route with significant motor traffic (verkehrsreiche Radroute)

▬▬▬▬ Cobbled street (Kopfsteinpflaster)

▭▭▭▭ Cne-way connection (Einbahnführung)

⊶⊶⊶ Ferry connection (Fährverbindung)

▬▬▬▬ Road surface unknown (unbekannter Belag)

━━━━ Tunnel (Tunnel)

▪▪▪▪▪ Dismounting recommended (Schiebestrecke)

╫╫╫╫ Train connection (Zugverbindung)

oooooooo Planned cycle path (Radweg in Planung)

xxxxxxx Closed cycle path (Radweg gesperrt)

▫▫▫▫▫ Cycle lane (Radfahrstreifen)

▬▬▬▬ Cycle path along road (straßenbegleitender Radweg)

× × × × Road closed to cyclists (Straße für Radfahrer gesperrt)

⇨ Described direction (Beschriebene Fahrtrichtung)

⑤ Waypoint (Wegpunkt)

Gradient / Distance (Steigungen / Entfernungen)

➡ Steep gradient, uphill (starke Steigung)

➡ Light gradient, uphill (leichte bis mittlere Steigung)

⌐2,4 Distance in km, rounded (Entfernung in Kilometern, gerundet)

Important cycling information (Radinformationen)

🔧 Bike workshop* (Fahrradwerkstatt*)

🚲 Bike rental* (Fahrradvermietung*)

🚲 Covered bike stands* (überdachter Abstellplatz*)

🚲 Lockable bike stands* (abschließbarer Abstellplatz*)

🔌 E-bike charging station (E-Bike Ladestation)

ℹ Information board* (Infotafel*)

⚠ Dangerous section (Gefahrenstelle)

⚠ Read text carefully (Text beachten)

▬ Stairs (Treppe)

🚲 Bicycle must be carried! (Tragestrecke)

✕ Constriction, bottleneck* (Engstelle*)

O17 Nodal point (Knotenpunktnummer der Wegweisung*)

┌┄┐ Town or city map (Stadt- /Ortsplan)

Symbols only in the city maps (Nur in Ortsplänen)

🅿 Garage* (Parkhaus*)

🎭 Theatre* (Theater*)

✉ Post office* (Post*)

♫ Pharmacy* (Apotheke*)

🏥 Hospital* (Krankenhaus*)

🔥 Fire brigade* (Feuerwehr*)

🛡 Police* (Polizei*)

* Selection (* Auswahl)

Scale 1 : 120.000
1 cm = 1,2 km

0 1 2 3 4 5 6 7 8 9 10 km

Scale 1 : 400.000
1 cm ≙ 4 km

0 4 8 12 16 20 24 28 32 km

Sights of interest / Facilities (Sehenswertes / Einrichtungen)

- ♿ 🏛 Church; Chapel (Kirche; Kapelle)
- 🏛 Monastery/Convent (Kloster)
- ✡ ☪ Synagogue; Mosque (Synagoge; Moschee)
- 🏰 🏯 Palace, Castle; Ruin (Schloss, Burg; Ruine)
- 🗼 🗼 Tower; Lighthouse (Turm; Leuchtturm)
- ⚙ 🗼 Watermill; Windmill (Wassermühle; Windmühle)
- ⚡ Power station (Kraftwerk)
- ⛏ ⛰ Mine; Cave (Bergwerk; Höhle)
- 🗽 Monument (Denkmal)
- ✈ Airport (Flughafen)

- ✳ Other sight of interest (sonstige Sehenswürdigkeit)
- 🏛 Museum (Museum)
- 🏺 🏛 Excavations; Roman site (Ausgrabungen; röm. Objekte)
- 🦌 🌳 Zoo; Nature info (Tierpark; Naturpark-Information)
- 🏞 Nature reserve/Monument (Naturpark, -denkmal)
- ❄ Natural sight of interest (sonstige Natursehenswürdigkeit)
- 🔆 Panoramic view* (Aussichtspunkt*)
- ℹ 🍴 Tourist information; Restaurant (Tourist-Info; Gasthaus)
- 🛏 🏠 Hotel, Guesthouse; Youth hostel (Hotel, Pension; Jugendherberge)
- ⛺ ⛺ Campground; Simple tent site* (Camping-; Lagerplatz*)
- 🛒 🏪 Shopping facility*; Kiosk* (Einkaufsmöglichkeit*; Kiosk*)
- 🪑 🏠 Picnic tables*; Covered stand* (Rastplatz*; Unterstand*)
- 🏊 🏊 Outdoor pool; Indoor pool (Freibad; Hallenbad)
- 🚰 🅿 Drinking fountain*; Parking lot* (Brunnen*; Parkplatz*)

Schönern Picturesque town (sehenswertes Ortsbild)
(ℹ🛏⛺) Facilities available (Einrichtung im Ort vorhanden)

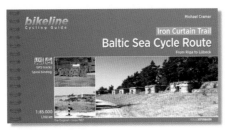

Iron Curtain Trail
Baltic Sea Cycle Route - From Rīga to Lübeck
1 : 85.000, 1.700 km
200 pages, ISBN 978-3-85000-730-6, € 16,90

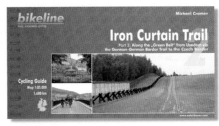

Iron Curtain Trail
Along the German-German Border to Hof
1 : 85.000, 1.600 km, 84 maps, acc.,
272 pages, ISBN 978-3-85000-278-3, € 13,90

Iron Curtain Trail
From Hof to Szeged
1 : 85.000, 1.730 km
172 pages, ISBN 978-3-85000-727-6, € 16,90

Iron Curtain Trail
Along the Green Belt to the Black Sea
1 : 300.000, 3.300 km, 56 maps, city maps,
180 pages, ISBN 978-3-85000-279-0, € 15,90

Content

Citymaps

Planning your tour

Along the Norwegian-Russian and Finnish-Russian border

Before you can start the tour along the "Iron Curtain Trail", you first have to get to Kirkenes in northern Norway. There are various options of getting there. You can either take the train from Helsinki to Rovaniemi and then take the bus or take a direct flight from Oslo to Kirkenes (it is no problem taking your bike with you).

There is a night train which leaves Helsinki at 7.27pm. This may be the best choice as this train is equipped with sleeping compartments. The train arrives at 11.10am the next morning. After your arrival, continue the journey by taking the Eskelisen Lapinlinjat bus to Inari. The bus leaves the station at 11.10am and arrives at Inari at 4.55pm, where you change to the bus to Kirkenes. It is possible to take your bike on these busses. The bus to Kirkenes only leaves once a day at 8.30am. This of course means that you have to spend one night in Inari. Accommodation is offered by the following hotels: Inari, Inarin Kultahovi and Uruniemi Camping. You can check www.vr.fi/heo/eng/index.html for potential timetable changes.

There is also a bus from Kirkenes to Grense Jakobselv on which you can take your bike.

Visa

You need a visa for the journey through the Russian part. It is best to ask for it at the travel agency (some months in advance), so that no extra costs arise.

Overnight stays

Camping is allowed everywhere in Norway and Finland, as long as tents are not put up in the middle of a private garden. The individual parts of the long-distance cycle path are designed in a way to allow overnight stays at a camping site or rent a wooden cabin. However, it is also easily possible to adapt the relevant parts and sleep in the forest.

Recommendations for travellers

Bicycle

We recommend wide tires for the forest tracks. However, good suspension at the front is not strictly necessary.

Communication

You can communicate relatively easily in English in Norway, Finland, Estonia and Latvia, especially with young people. In some regions, however, many older people will only be able to speak Russian.

Currencies

Norway: Norwegian Krone
Russia: Ruble,
Finland, Estonia, Latvia: Euro

The author

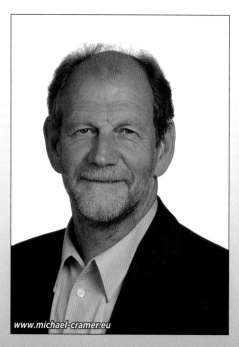

www.michael-cramer.eu

Michael Cramer was born on 16 June 1949 in Gevelsberg, Westphalia and attended the Reichenbach grammar school in Ennepetal. He studied music, sports and education in Mainz from 1969-74. From 1975-95 he taught at a grammar school in Berlin-Neukölln.

From 1989-2004 he served as transport spokesman for The Greens in the Berlin House of Representatives. Alongside his work as an MP he took several teaching positions relating to transport and urban policy at the Otto Suhr Institute of the Free University of Berlin. Michael Cramer has been a member of the European Parliament since 2004 and he served as the chairman of the Committee on Transport and Tourism from 2014-2017. He also continues to pursue several journalistic activities through publications in journals and books.

Three key events from his youth acted as the catalyst for his intensive study of the German-German history. The first was in 1961 when the Wall was built and he went on his first holiday without his parents to the North Sea resort of St. Peter Ording. There, he did not just marvel at the beach sailors but was also able to listen to the legendary 80-year-old Count Luckner (1881–1966), who was said to be able to tear telephone books apart as well as bend and flatten 5-Mark coins with his bare hands.

Whilst on holiday he read a newspaper with the headline: "Berlin Wall – is this the start of World War III?" At once he remembered the stories his parents and teachers had told him about the war period and grew increasingly anxious that he too, might live to experience such terrible times.

Two years later he journeyed with his football club TuS Ennepetal to West Berlin and played against BFC Südring. Whilst there he ate his first curried sausage - which did not yet exist in West-Germany - played for the first time Mini-Golf in the Hasenheide – which back then was not possible in Ennepetal - and drank his first Fassbrause lemonade – something that cannot be found today in West-Germany. His aunt gave him a camera for the trip and the first pictures he took were of the Wall at Bernauer Straße.

Every time he returned to Berlin thereafter, he went to Bernauer Straße and recorded how the Wall changed. Initially, only the windows were bricked up on the ground and the first floor. A short while later, however, the windows on the other floors were also bricked up. Eventually, the houses that stretched to the first floor were replaced by the "modern" Wall.

A year later he read his first book on politics: "Child of the revolution" by Wolfgang Leonhard (1921-2014), who in 1935, as a child of Communist parents, fled from Nazi Germany with his mother, Susanne Leonhard, to seek refuge in the Soviet Union. After a short time, however, his mother was arrested and exiled to a labour camp in Siberia. Her son Wolfgang was brought up as a "socialist" in children's homes and boarding schools. As a committed communist, he was part of the "Ulbricht Group", which after the war was sent from the Soviet Union to live in occupied Germany.

From July 1945 to September 1947 Wolfgang Leonhard worked for the Central Committee of the Communist Party (from 1946 known as the SED) and was active in the department of "agitation and propaganda" and also taught from 1947-49 history at the "Karl Marx SED school" in Kleinmachnow. In 1948, Wilhelm Pieck, the man who would later become GDR president, helped him retrieve his mother from Siberia and bring her to Germany. Susanne Leonhard (1895-1984) first lived in East Berlin and then in the spring of 1949, moved to

West-Germany. She was arrested by US intelligence CIC (Counter Intelligence Corps) and detained until April 1950. As a committed anti-Stalinist socialist, she declined to work for the US as a spy. In 1956 she published the book "Stolen Life. The fate of a political emigrant in the Soviet Union". In 1949, her son Wolfgang broke with Stalinism, fled via Prague to the "non-aligned" Yugoslavia and has been living in the Federal Republic of Germany since the 1950's.

After studying in Mainz and as an active "Germany politician", Michael Cramer moved to Berlin (West) in 1974 and confirmed the frequently quoted observation: "Either you pack your bags and leave Berlin after six months or you stay and live forever in Berlin." He stayed.

In the summer of 1989 he cycled for the first time along the 160 km long "patrol route" around West Berlin, which had been created by the Western Allies behind the Wall. It was impossible to get

Berlin at the time of the Wall

lost because you just stayed on the West Berlin side and followed the Wall. Then the Wall fell and he was able to repeat this tour around the Wall in the spring of 1990 on the patrol road between the front wall and the hinterland wall. It was during one of such cycling rides that the idea for cycling tours involving the Berlin Wall was born.

However, it took another ten years until it could take shape. After the fall of the Wall, the slogan in Berlin was: "The Wall must go". The responsibility for this task fell upon the shoulders of the GDR border guards who were in charge until 2 October 1990 and who carried this out with typical Prussian-Socialist thoroughness. It was only in those parts where district councils, organisations or individuals intervened that parts of the Wall were left standing.

On the 40th anniversary of the Wall, Michael Cramer returned to his original idea and in the summer of 2001, organised public "Wall-forays". The Senate and House of Representatives of Berlin decided to protect the remaining Wall by making it a listed monument, added signposting to the Berlin Wall, made it bike-friendly and put up a memorial stele for the last fugitive shot, Chris Gueffroy. These measures were completed in 2007.

The book "Berlin Wall Trail" was first published in 2001 by the Esterbauer publishing house, and detailed a route of 160 kilometres along the former border to West Berlin. It was presented by Volker Hassemer, who had served for many years as the Berlin Senator for Urban Development and Environmental Protection. This book has since been revised several times and was also printed in English in 2003.

The book "German-German Border Trail" first appeared in the summer of 2007 - in English in 2008 - and was presented at the European House in Berlin by Wolfgang Thierse, the then President of the German Bundestag (1998-2005). He quoted the former President of the European Commission, Jacques Delors (1985-1995), with his statement: "The European Union is like a bicycle. If you stop riding it, it will fall over."

The three volumes of the "Europa-Radweg Eiserner Vorhang" were published in 2009 and as the "Iron Curtain Trail" in English in 2010. They were also presented in the European House in Berlin by Hans-Gert Pöttering, the then President of the European Parliament (2007-2009). The revised version of the southern part from Hof to Szeged with a unified scale of 1:85,000 was published in 2014 - in English in 2017 - and presented by the EU Commissioner for Regional Development, Johannes Hahn, in the European House in Vienna. The updated version of the Northen section from Rīga to Lübeck was published in 2016 - in English in 2017 – also with a scale of 1:85,000.

Michael Cramer has been getting around Berlin without a car since 1979. He uses his bike as well as busses, trains and taxis and prefers soft tourism when on holiday. This is why he was able to experience many of the Velo Routes in the USA – in 2004 his "San Francisco Bay Trail" was published, a 750-kilometre-long bike trail around the bay of San Francisco – as well as Switzerland, Austria, France and Germany.

Berlin Wall Trail
212 p., 1 : 20,000, **ISBN:** 978-3-85000-458-9, **€ 13,90**

Iron Curtain Trail

The Iron Curtain divided the continent into East and West and extended from the Barents Sea through Europe to the Black Sea - a distance of 10,000 kilometres. Until the Peaceful Revolutions in Eastern Europe, it was the physical and ideological border between two mutually hostile blocs. It did not just divide many neighbouring states, but it also divided Germany into East and West. Few things remain of the former death strip today. The few relics that are still there remind us of our past but no longer separate us.

Therefore, it is imperative to make the memories visible! We know that there is no common interpretation of history between the West and the East, that the memories of Europeans east and west of the border differ, not least because their perspectives were often shaped completely differently depending on the of-

ficial policy in both parts of Europe. The Warsaw Pact countries had interpreted the border as a "protection against the class enemy". For the West, it represented the lack of freedom which existed in the socialist East.

Berlin Wall Trail

Visible memories already exist with the "Berlin Wall Trail", which has been signposted since 2001 by the Berlin Senate and made with cyclists in mind.

To compliment the various stops along the former Wall, the "Berlin Wall History Mile" was launched, a permanent exhibition with artistic designs of the crossings in four languages (German, English, French, Russian), with about 30 panels detailing the history of the division of Berlin, the Wall construction and when it came down. Photographs and short texts describe events that took place at each location. The

The Brandenburg Gate, 1961/1976

"Berlin Wall Trail" became part of Berlin's tourism program and is the first project that combines soft tourism and city tourism. In Berlin you can really experience history, politics, nature and culture.

German-German Border Trail

It was not just Berlin that was divided for decades, it was the rest of Germany, too. The memory of the present 1,400-kilometre inner-German border strip must be preserved. With this in mind, on 30 June 2004, the coalition parties of the SPD and Bündnis 90/Die Grünen brought forward the motion in the German Bundestag (DS 15/3454) to convert the former death strip into a habitat. They argued that it should be developed for sustainable tourism and for the "European Green Belt" along the "Iron Curtain". The German Bundestag voted unanimously in favour of these plans in December of 2004.

The "German-German Border Trail" along the "Green Belt" runs through 150 nature reserves and encompasses numerous flora-fauna habitat areas (FFH), including the three biosphere reserves of Schaalsee, Elbaue and Rhön as well as the Harz National Park. The route leads from the Baltic Sea

Signpost of EuroVeloroute 13

to the Czech border with numerous rivers and lakes along the way and covers not just the elevation of the Harz mountains but also the Thuringian Forest. There are many monuments and border museums to discover, as well as some remaining watch towers.

Iron Curtain Trail

Europe was also divided for decades. The Iron Curtain ran from the Barents Sea on the Norwegian-Russian border to the Black Sea on the Bulgarian-Turkish border. Today, it no longer separates us but is rather a symbol of a common European experience in the reunified Europe. This is another reason why the European Parliament in 2005 approved my resolution with a large majority from all the member states and all political groups. The resolution called on the Commission and the member states to implement the "Iron Curtain Trail initiative [...] to further the European identity".

The division of Europe

Europe's division does not begin at the end of the Second World War, but rather with Hitler seizing power on 30 January 1933 and the beginning of the Second World War on 1 September 1939, when German soldiers marched into Poland. Had it not been for Nazi Germany and the Second World War, Europe would never have been divided.

Despite their ideological differences, the anti-Hitler coalition was united in a common struggle against Nazi Germany. The respective own interests soon came to the fore, however, after the unconditional surrender of the German army. On 5 March 1946, British Prime Minister Winston Churchill who had been voted out of office after the war, stated in his famous speech in Fulton/Missouri that a division of Europe had occurred and that part of Europe now found itself behind an "Iron Curtain". The Cold War had begun.

The leaders of the Warsaw Pact countries were not willing to grant political freedom and proved unable to solve the economic problems which resulted in repeated uprisings. The first in the Soviet sphere of influence took place on 17 June 1953 in the GDR. This was followed in June 1956 in June by the Poznan demonstrations in Poland and in October of the same year by the Hungarian Revolution, then the Prague Spring followed in Czechoslovakia in 1968, the workers' uprising in 1970 in Poland, Charter 77 in Czechoslovakia in 1977 and in 1980 the emergence of the Solidarity movement in Poland, that with 10 million had more than four times as many members as the Communist state party. The activities of Solidarity movement, the successful orientation of Hungary towards the west, the "Singing Revolution" of independence movements in the Baltic states, the "Velvet Revolution" in Czechoslovakia, together with the increasingly strong opposition movement

in the GDR as well as the dismantling of the barbed wire on the Hungarian-Austrian border by the two Foreign Ministers Gyula Horn and Alois Mock on 27 June 1989 finally paved the way for the fall of the Berlin Wall on 9 November 1989 and the Iron Curtain in Europe.

Following the successful example of the Berlin Wall Trail and the German-German Border Trail, a hiking and biking trail is envisaged along the former Iron Curtain on the former death strip, to help us retrace the footsteps of this shared European history.

The Green Belt –
from death strip to natural habitat

The 10,000 kilometres of "Green Belt" from the Barents Sea to the Black Sea have been since 2002 under the patronage of Mikhail Gorbachev, the President of Green Cross International (GCI) since 1993. By the way he was in March 1985, with a majority of just a single vote, elected General Secretary of the Communist Party of the Soviet Union.

Since 2002, the 10,000-kilometre-long European "Green Belt" from the Barents Sea to the Black Sea has been under the patronage of Mikhail Gorbachev, who has been the president of Green Cross International (GCI) since 1993. By the way, he was

Alois Mock and Gyula Horn cutting through the Iron Curtain on 27 June 1989

elected secretary general of the Communist Party of the Soviet Union in March 1985 with a majority of just one vote.

The importance of the Green Belt for conservation and its value as a symbol of the union between East and West is internationally recognised today. Once Member States, in cooperation with the European Parliament and the European Commission, have fully developed the project, you will be able to learn even more about European history, politics, nature and culture.

Border at Görsdorf (Thuringia), 1984/2006

Twenty countries are participating in this project, including 15 EU Member States. Starting at the Barents Sea, the hiking and biking trail extends along the western border of the former Warsaw Pact countries to the Black Sea. You begin by cycling along the Norwegian-Russian and Finnish-Russian border until you reach the Baltic Sea and continue along the shoreline of Russia, Estonia, Latvia, Lithuania, Kaliningrad, Poland and the former GDR. The route from the Priwall peninsula at Travemünde to the Saxon-Bavarian-Czech border triangle follows the former inner-German border strip. It then leads over the elevations of the Bohemian Forest, past Moravia and the Slovak capital Bratislava, and here, one must cross the Danube. The route takes you along the southern border of Hungary, across Slovenia and Croatia. Between Romania and Serbia, it largely follows the course of the Danube, then continues through Bulgaria, Macedonia and Greece and ends on the northernmost tip of Turkey on the Bulgarian Black Sea coast.

The route passes through several national parks, each with a variety of interesting flora and fauna and combines a beautiful assortment of unique landscapes that have remained largely untouched due to its remote border location and the former exclusion zones. It also connects numerous memorials, museums and open-air facilities, which remind us of Europe's division and how it was overcome by the Peaceful Revolutions in East Central Europe.

As with the "Berlin Wall Trail" and the "German-German Border Trail" the "Iron Curtain Trail" partially makes use of paved former patrol roads along the old border. Many countries and regions in Europe are still working on the project and numerous sections have already been signposted and expanded.

The proposed route

There are, of course various ways in which you can move around in the Green Belt by bike. You can cycle on the western or the eastern side, closer to the border or further away, on paths with perforated plates or on asphalt. The proposed route was selected based on the following five criteria:

- as close as possible to the former border
- preferably as comfortable as possible
- avoid busy roads
- frequent crossings of the former border
- integrate as many historical testimonials as possible

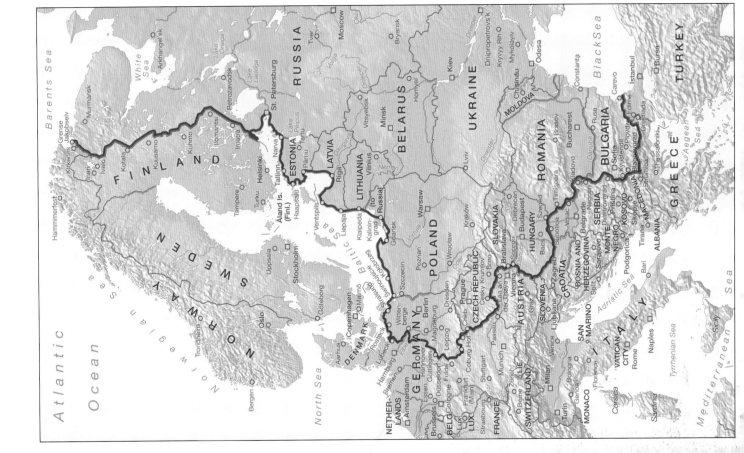

Václav Havel Marianne Birthler Lech Wałęsa

The suggested route is to be understood as a "work in progress". It should go without saying that the local people know more about their area, and there is always the possibility of construction works. And sometimes, of course, a detour is suggested to take in a nearby tourist attraction. This has been done sparingly, however, because otherwise the whole route would become very long. With this in mind, the author and the publisher hope the readership of this book will take this into account, but are nonetheless pleased to accept suggestions and improvements bearing in mind the criteria mentioned above.

Acknowledgements

This edition of the "Iron Curtain Trail" would not have been possible without the support of other individuals and institutions. I would like to thank Roland Esterbauer and his team, who has supported the project from the beginning and professionally implemented everything.

For the new edition of this book I cycled nearly the entire route myself. I was also able to use numerous tips provided by many cyclists. In particular I would like to thank Janis Humann, Niklas Prenzel and Roman Schulte-Sasse for their support. They not only cycled from the Barents Sea to St. Petersburg but also described the route from Virolahti at the Finnish-Russian border to St. Petersburg.

I would also like to extend my gratitude to Raija Ruusunen who went along the Finnish section with her students from Joensuu University and who was able to accompany me from Helsinki to Lappeenranta as well as from Ilomantsi to Kesälahti. From Käylä to Kuhmo I was accompanied by Morag Donaldson and Hannu Takkula, whom I would also like to thank very much. The same applies to Anne-Lise Alleaume, Eric Alleaume, Dara Chaboud, Audric Mitraros and Jens Müller, who cycled from St. Petersburg to Tallinn and were also able to provide me with valuable information about the route.

Additionally, I would like to thank Raltis Sijats, who accompanied me from Virolahti to Tallinn via St. Petersburg and from Ainaži to Rīga. He also found a route in Latvia that is largely located away from the busy coastal road. I would also like to extend my gratitude to Margo Märtsoo and Wouter de Peuter, who found good alternative routes along the Baltic Sea in Estonia.

For the coordination of the project as well as the editing of the books I was greatly supported by Philipp Cerny, Alexander Kaas Elias, Jens Müller,

Sara Ott, Anna Rittweger and Erdmute Safranski, whom I would also like to thank very much.

I would like to pay special thanks to the European initiative European Green Belt (www.greenbelt.eu), which together with conservationists from the Central and Eastern European countries brought the project "Green Belt" to life - now one of the most successful and at the same time one of the most symbolic European projects.

On 23 September 2014 a "Memorandum of Understanding" was signed in Slavonice by Gabriele Schwaderer for the European Green Belt Initiative, Daniel Mourek for the European Cyclists Federation and Michael Cramer for the European Parliament, with the aim to protect the Green Belt and enable cycling in it.

As part of both projects, the signing institutions undertook to support sustainable tourism, the protection and preservation of the special flora and fauna as well as the awareness of the history and culture. They are unified in their conviction that these goals can only be reached together with the population. Sustainable tourism in particular strengthens the local economy which is also supported by improving the existing infrastructure.

I would also like to thank Mikhail Gorbachev, who has been the President of Green Cross International since 1993 and who gave his full support as patron of the "Green Belt" project.

And last but not least, I would like to thank Marianne Birthler, Vaclav Havel (1936-2011) and Lech Wałęsa, who are serving as patrons of the "Iron Curtain Trail".

History workshop live

More than 25 years have passed since the fall of the Iron Curtain in Europe. In Wilhelm von Humboldt's words: We know that "only those who know their past have a future", which is why we have to first deal with the past. Therefore, we maintain with gratitude the memory of the Peaceful Revolutions in Eastern and Central Europe in order not to forget the decades of division on our continent.

With all this in mind, I wish you great pleasure along your journey of exploring European history, politics, nature and culture.

Michael Cramer

About this book

This cycling guide contains all the information required for a cycling tour along the Iron Curtain Trail: precise maps, detailed route descriptions, accommodation options and the most important practical information about tourist attractions and sights worth seeing.

And all that information comes with our **bikeline pledge**: The route described in this book has been tested and evaluated in person by the author! To assure that the book is as up-to-date as possible, we welcome corrections submitted by readers and local officials or businesses. We cannot, however, always check and confirm such changes before deadline.

The maps

The detailed maps are at scale of 1:400,000 (1 centimeter = 4 kilometers) and 1:120:000 (1 centimeter = 1,2 kilometers). Apart from the exact route, the maps also provide information on the nature of the surface (solid or unsurfaced), gradients (light or strong) and distances as well as cultural, touristic and gastronomic facilities along the route.

However, even the most accurate maps cannot replace a look at the description of the route. Please note that the recommended main route is always indicated in red and purple, with variants and detours in orange. The exact significance of the individual symbols is given in the legend on pages 6 and 7.

Route altitude profile

The route altitude profile in the introduction provides a graphic depiction of elevations along the route, the total length, and the location of larger towns and cities along the way. Additionally, a detailed altitude profile is provided at the beginning of each section which shows many of the smaller centers along the way. The latitude profiles do not show every individual small hill and dip, but only the major changes in elevation. On the detail maps smaller gradients are shown by arrows that point uphill.

The text

The maps are supplemented by a written text that describes the recommended main route. Key phrases about the route description are indicated with the   symbol.

The description of the main route is also interrupted by passages describing alternative and excursion routes. These are printed in orange colour.

Furthermore, the names of important **villages**, towns and cities are printed in bold type. If a location or community has important points of interest, addresses, telephone numbers and opening times are listed under the headline with the name of the place.

Descriptions of the larger towns and cities, as well as historic, cultural and natural landmarks help round out the travel experience. These paragraphs are printed in italics to distinguish them from the route description.

TIP Text printed in purple indicates that you must make a decision about how your tour shall continue. For instance, there may be an alternative route that is not included in the tour description, or a turn-off to another location.

EXCURSION These also indicate excursion suggestions, interesting sights or recreational facilities that are not directly on the main route.

List of overnight accommodation

The last pages of this cycling guide provide a list of convenient hotels and guest houses in virtually every village or town along the route. This list also includes youth hostels and campgrounds.

For overnight stays in sparsely populated Finland you can use so-called "homestays". This is overnight accommodation offered by private individuals in their homes. You can find a list of possible addresses at www.homestay.com.

From Grense Jakobselv to Virolahti 1.780 km

The first part of this book of the "Iron Curtain Trail" takes you along the Russian border through the impressive and vast landscapes of Norway and Finland all the way to the Baltic Sea coast. The bike path starts in Grense Jakobselv at the Barents Sea, which is part of the earth's cold chambers.

This part of the Arctic Ocean was named after the Dutch seafarer and explorer Willem Barents (1550-1597). He was one of the greatest Arctic seafarers of the 16th century and was in search of the north-east passage to India and China. On his journey, he faced adversities such as pack ice, polar bears and blizzards, and in the end, he lost his ships as well as his life.

The route to Vorilahti along the Finnish-Russian border does not just take you through many forests and past numerous lakes but you can also see various memorials commemorating the Finnish Winter War (1939-40) and the Continuation War (1941-44).

The border river into the Barents Sea at Grense Jakobselv between Norway and Finland

Grense Jakobselv

This village is very popular among tourists due to its location at the Arctic Ocean and its close proximity to Russia. If you like rough terrain and seeing the natural power of the ocean, then this will be the most spectacular part for you along the entire route. In the village, you can visit a chapel named after King Oscar II and a stone church dating back to 1869 which was intended to mark the border to Russia.

Fishing in the border river Jakobselv, one of Norway's famous waters containing salmon, is only permitted if you are a Norwegian citizen as the river marks the border to Russia.

There is no overnight accommodation in Grense Jakobselv but you can easily put up your tent at the beach of the Arctic Ocean and enjoy a wonderful sunset.

The history of Norway

Norway has a population of around five million and one of the longest Atlantic Ocean coastlines, stretching over 2,650 kilometres. "Yes, we love this country" is the first line of the Norwegian national anthem. It was also the home and birthplace of great artists such as dramatist and lyricist Henrik Ibsen (1828-1906). He created a stage version for his poem "Peer Gynt", for which Edvard Grieg (1843-1907), the most famous Norwegian composer, wrote the music. His suites of the same name belong to the most popular orchestra pieces of the romantic music era. Another famous Norwegian artist was Evard Munch (1863-1944). His painting "The Scream" is one of the most famous paintings in the world today.

After centuries of foreign rule by Sweden and Denmark between 1380 and 1905, only interrupted by a brief period of independence in 1814 when the country established a constitution that remains largely unchanged to this day, Norway finally gained independence in 1905. Prince Carl of the House of Glücksburg became the first king as Haakon VII.

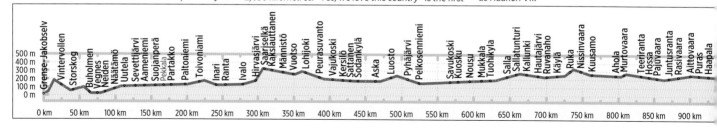

During the First World War, Norway declared neutrality alongside Denmark and Sweden and joint the League of Nations in 1920.

In the Second World War, however, neutral Norway was occupied by Nazi Germany in April 1940 as part of Operation "Weserübung", the main aim of which was to cut off British access to the Swedish iron ore supply lines. This was not only intended to help the economy of the German war, but also to promote the creation of a "great European economic area" under German rule.

The Norwegian resistance held for a mere six weeks as the German navy was too strong. Additionally, there were Norwegian Nazis who joint their German counterparts and thereby rose to power. From 1942 until 1945, Vidkun Quisling (1887-1945), who had founded the fascist party Nasjonal Samling in 1933, served as the prime minister of a puppet government set up by the Third Reich.

Around one third of the Norwegian Jews was deported to Auschwitz and killed there. After the end of the war he was sentenced to death and executed. The name "Quisling" has been adopted in some language as a synonym for collaboration and treason.

As the majority of the Norwegian population rejected the occupiers, numerous resistance groups were formed. When the German troops withdrew from Norway, they pursued their "scorched earth policy", leaving many towns and factories in northern Norway completely destroyed.

In 1949 Norway was one of the founding members of NATO. In 1960, the European Free Trade Association (EFTA) was formed, together with Denmark, Austria, Portugal, Sweden, Switzerland and the United Kingdom.

Since 1969, the country's history has been characterised by growth and prosperity from crude oil. However, referendums have repeatedly rejected membership of the European Union. In many respects, as a member of the European Economic Area (EEA), Norway is treated similarly to an EU Member State and is also, as part of the Nordic Passport Union, a member of the Schengen Agreement.

From Grense Jakobselv to Hesseng   50 km

The route from Grense Jakovselv to Kirkenes has beautiful scenery but is also challenging as it leads through the hilly fjord landscape. Take semi-paved road number 886 for 10 kilometres along the border river to Bjornstad, where you turn right and cycle through Finnmark.

Finnmark

Finnmark is located in the north-east of Norway. Once home to Finnish settlers, it has a population of 75,000 today, of which 60,000 belong to the indigenous Sámi tribe. By way of comparison, the province is the size of Denmark, which has a population of around six million.

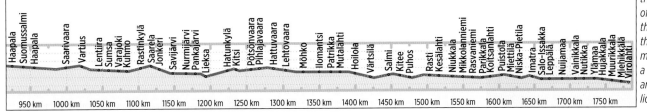

The Sámi also live in Sweden, Finland and Russia but nowhere else do they have as many rights as they do in Norway. There is a daily news broadcast in Sámi and an increasing number of books are translated into Sámi.

Continue on road **886** to **Storskog** via **Vintervollen** and **Tarnet** and past the 2-3 billion-year-old rocks. Once in Storskog, you will reach road **E 105**, into which you turn right. The road to the left leads to Norway's only official border control point with Russia. Directly opposite this Norwegian border station with its police and customs points you can see the Russian watch towers.

Border Museum in Kirkenes

A bit further down the road you will find Sollia Gjestegård, a restaurant by the lake which also offers accommodation in amongst the most beautiful scenery and only 300 metres away from the Russian border.

Shortly behind this, turn left onto the old country lane, which lead to the new **E 105**, into which you turn left onto the bike path. You can see the new bridge but stay on the old road which is now a great bike path. Then turn left onto the bike path of the new **E 105** and you will reach **Hesseng** where you can find shopping possibilities as well as overnight accommodation.

EXCURSION Once there, you can turn right and continue for five kilometres on a paved bike path along the railway tracks to Kirkenes. The main route continues towards Neiden.

Kirkenes

Kirkenes belongs to the parish of Sør-Varanger, which stretches over 4,000 square kilometres and is home to 10,000 people. The town itself has a population of around 6,000 but despite its relatively small size, it offers a good selection of accommodation and restaurants to travellers as well as some interesting sights. You can find a tourist information centre in the town centre (Presteveien 1). The nearest camping site Kirkenes Camping Maggadalen is located ca. seven kilometres outside the town towards Neiden. The proximity to Russia is reflected in the town.

The road signs are bilingual – Norwegian and Russian. While taking a break at the harbour you can admire the Russian fishing vessels.

The longest road routes in Europe start here. The E 105 runs from Kirkenes to Crimea and the E 6 runs all the way to Trelleborg. The border museum "Sør-Varanger" has changing exhibitions on display. You can also find the Savio Museum (Saviomuseet) with works of the famous Sámi artist John Andreas Savio (1902-1938) in the same building. A dedicated museum building is currently under construction. The Russian Red Army monument also bears witness to the turbulent and changing war history of this border region. The monument was erected to commemorate the liberation of Sør-Varanger in the autumn of 1944 after four years of German occupation.

Kirkenes was the most frequently bombarded town in Norway during the Second World War and was almost completely destroyed. This is why nearly all buildings here are relatively new. The former air raid bunker Andersgrotta is used today to show films about the war history of Kirkenes.

The Russian market in the town centre has a variety of Russian produce on offer and is a particular attraction.

ALTERNATIVE The route along the Norwegian-Russian border to Ivalo via Nellim takes you from Kirkenes along the border river Pasvik. This river is the second longest

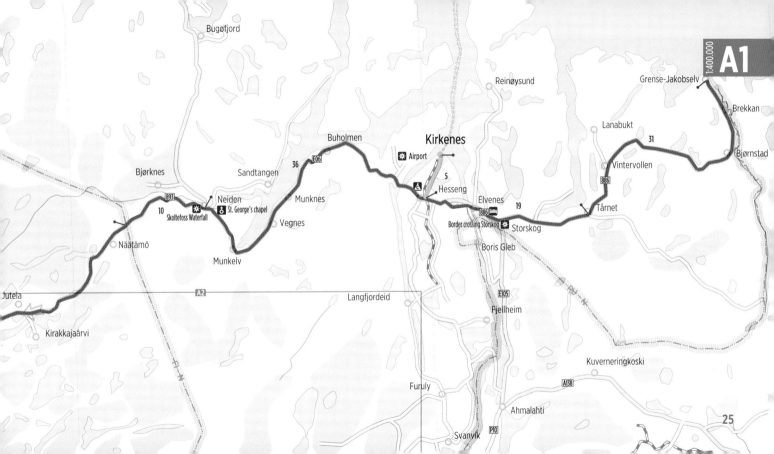

Orthodox Chapel of St. George in Neiden

river in Norway. You will also pass a Russian watchtower in Svanvik as well as a German radio station in Skogfoss, which was in operation between 1942 and 1944.

In Vaggatem you can visit a prisoner of war camp for Russian soldiers from the Second World War. The route also takes you through the border triangle of Norway, Finland and Russia.

You can find overnight accommodation and restaurants in Svanvik, Vaggatem and Nellim. The cafeteria in the

tower at Svanvik boasts beautiful views across the landscape while dining and with a bit of luck you will be able to see a few bears.

The route can currently only be travelled on the Norwegian side until you reach the border triangle. There are also plans from Finland to develop the route with signposts and suitable for bikes in a way that it can be used for cross-country skiing as well as the Iron Curtain Trail. In light of this, it is advisable to check the current state of this project before taking this route.

From Hesseng to Sevettijärvi   *78 km*

From the city centre, continue straight on **Storgata** and then turn right just before its end into **Pasvikveien**, which leads to **Solheimsveien**, into which you turn left. At the roundabout, the bike path continues on your left and along the eastern lake shore. Pass the borderland museum, cross under a road, pass the hospital and you will reach the bike path running parallel to road **E 6** as well as the railway tracks on the western lake shore. The bike path crosses underneath the railway tracks and then leads further and further away from the E 6. You will cross a river and then turn right into a residential street just before reaching the E 6 with the two petrol stations. At the end of the residential street, turn left

onto the non-paved path and you will reach the **E 6**, into which you turn right.

You will pass the camping site Maggadalen, continue at first along a military restricted area, then past the airport and then continue your journey on the E 6 and you will reach Neiden via **Buholmen** and **Munkelv**. Neiden is located around 43 kilometres from Kirkenes and ten kilometres from the Finnish border.

Neiden

This settlement by the river Neidenelva that powerfully plunges into the ocean is famous for its salmon waters and is seen as the centre of the Norwegian East Sámi people. It is also home to many people with Finnish roots. The orthodox chapel – the only one in Norway – was built in 1656. The Lutheran Protestant church dates back to the late 20th century. You can also find the Neidenelven Camping Motel as well as the Neidenelven Turisthotell here that both have restaurants.

The intersection at which you turn left towards Finland is located before the bridge across Skoltefossen waterfall. Stay on the **E 6** if you would like to pay a visit to the town.

From Neiden, continue on the **893** towards the Finnish border and then towards Näätämö.

The history of Finland

With its 5.5 million inhabitants and only slightly smaller than Germany, the "Land of a Thousand Lakes", is one of the most sparsely populated countries in Europe. Finland was the first country in Europe to give women the right to vote in 1906 - New Zealand was the first country in the world to do so in 1893. It also was the first country in Europe to elect a female president (Tarja Halonen 2000-2012), who was also a single parent. The progress of male emancipation was also demonstrated in 1998 when Paavo Lipponen was the first prime minister worldwide to take parental leave.

The "three S" are considered the most important features of the country: "Sisu, Sibelius, sauna". Sisu is the Finnish word for stubbornness, a trait that is said to be characteristic of Westphalians in Germany. Jean Sibelius is world-famous as a composer and state president Urho Kekkonen negotiated state treaties in saunas, among others with Leonid Brezhnev.

Up to the 20th century, Finland's history was largely dominated by foreign control: for 600 years, most of what is now Finland was under Swedish rule, and its southern part became a fixed part of Swedish territory in the 14th century. The population was Christianised and in the Middle Ages a society based on a class system was established.

In the 18th century, however, Sweden lost power in the region. After a constant battles, it was finally forced to cede the Finnish territory to Russia in 1809. The area was then merged into the Grand Duchy of Finland and became an integral part of the Russian Empire. In 1812 Helsinki was declared the capital and replaced Turku. The country was given an autonomous government and in 1863 a permanent parliament.

In the second half of the 19th century, Finnish politics experienced a lot of change, particularly due to the greater freedom of movement under Tsar Alexander II. After the removal of economic restrictions, industrialisation began to take off. A Finnish national feeling slowly began to develop when state-like structures were established in the autonomous Grand Duchy. However, as a result of increasing centralisation and growing pressure for Russianisation, tensions started growing.

Finland was not involved in the First World War. When the Russian tsardom collapsed as a result of the February Revolution, the Finnish Parliament declared Finland's independence on 6 December 1917. This was also recognised in January 1918 by Bolshevik Russia and numerous other states. The separation from Russia was accompanied by severe internal conflicts. On 27 January 1918, there was an attempted socialist coup by the "Reds", followed by a three-month-long civil war. In the end, it was won by the bourgeois "Whites" under the command of General Gustav Mannerheim (1867-1951), who had served as Finnish officer in the tsar's army for three decades.

In 1919, the young Finland established a republican constitution with a parliamentary democracy, both of which are still in existence today. The country achieved international recognition and, in 1920, an agreement with the Russian Soviet Republic regarding the former Grand Duchy's borders, also granting Finland the Petsamo area with its access to the Barents Sea.

However, as early as 1939, the existence of the state was again in danger: as Molotov and Ribbentropp had agreed in the Hitler-Stalin Pact, the Soviet attack on 30 November 1939 was the start of the three-and-a-half month-long "Winter War". Despite many successful defensive battles, Finland was on the verge of collapse and was forced to sign the "Treaty of Moscow" on 13 March 1940. Finland had to cede large parts of Karelia with the second largest Finnish city of Vyborg as well as other areas to the Soviet Union.

When Hitler invaded the Soviet Union on 22 June 1941 ("Operation Barbarossa"), Finland entered the war on the German side, which is known as the "Continuation

Oncoming traffic in Lapland

War". After the successes of the Red Army and the renewed threat from Soviet troops, Finland - under President Gustaf Mannerheim, who was elected on 4 August – agreed to a "separate Moscow peace treaty" with the Soviet Union on 19 September 1944, ending the "Continuation War". The losses of territory during the Winter War were confirmed and the Petsamo area was ceded to the Soviet Union.

In addition, the country undertook to expel the German troops. This led to the German-Finnish Lapland War, Finland's greatest military success. The Wehrmacht troops were expelled from Finland, leaving large parts of Lapland completely destroyed and Rovaniemi almost completely burnt down as a result of the "scorched earth policy" of the retreating German troops. The Lapland War

ended on 27 April 1945 with the withdrawal of the last German troops. The end of the state of war was finally decided by the peace treaty of Paris (1947). As a result, 420,000 people lost their homes, fled to the West and had to be integrated.

After the Second World War, Finland maintained its independence. It played a special part in the Cold War, as it maintained neutrality and sought good relations with the Soviet Union right up to the end of the conflict. To some, this policy appeared to give the impression of premature obedience and was criticised by many Western European partners as "Finlandisation".

The defining political figure was state president Urho Kekkonen (1900-1986), who was in office from 1956-1982 and made an important contribution to securing peace in the Cold War with the "Conference for Security and Cooperation in Europe" (CSCE), which ended in 1975 when 35 states signed the Final Act in Helsinki. This also strengthened Finland's position as a neutral state.

After the end of the Soviet Union, the Finnish economy, which was strongly oriented towards the east, plunged into a crisis. The country moved its policies towards the west and finally became a member of the EU in 1995.

Näätämö

Together with Neiden, which is today located in Norway, this town used to be the westernmost settlement of the Skolt Sámi people. However, it was officially divided in 1852.

You can visit the House of Cultural Heritage of the Skolt Sámi people and buy their arts and crafts in a shop. You can also find the small supermarket Näätämön Kvalinta, Kahvila Stoppari cafeteria as well as a motel with a restaurant in this town.

Road **971** leads from Näätämö to Sevettijärvi.

Sevettijärvi

This village with 350 inhabitants was founded in 1949 when 51 families were settled here after they had been displaced from the Petsamo area, which Finland had to cede to the Soviet Union. The biggest Skolt Sámi settlement is not a self-contained village but the houses are spread out along the road over a distance of not less than 60 km.

The Orthodox church is dedicated to St Tryphon of Pechenga and is open to visitors in July and August. Around three kilometres behind the Orthodox Church you will find the holiday camp Sevettijärven Nili-Tuvat on the right side of the road, where you can rent wooden cabins. There is also a restaurant, a sauna by the lake and a camping site.

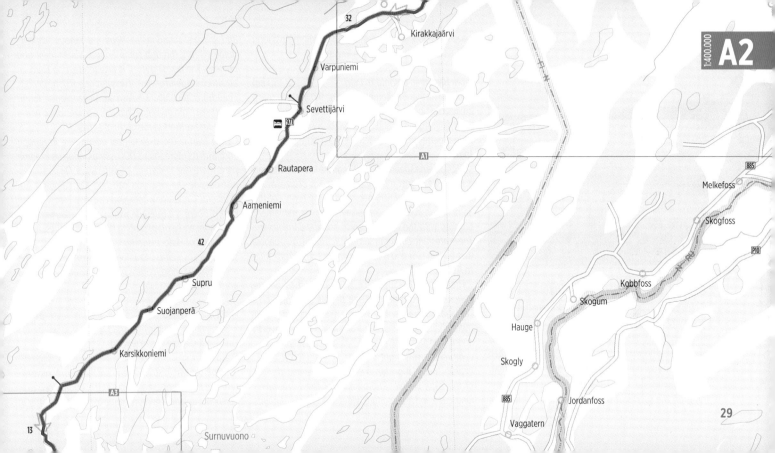

32

Kirakkajaärvi

Varpuniemi

Sevettijärvi

971

A1

885

Melkefoss

Rautapera

Skogfoss

Aameniemi

P10

42

Kobbfoss

Supru

Skogum

Suojanperä

Hauge

Karsikkoniemi

Skogly

A3

885

Jordanfoss

13

Vaggatern

Surnuvuono

Lake Inari at Sevettijärvi

From Sevettijärvi to Hietajoen Leirintä   55 km

Follow the relatively quiet quiet **971** towards Inari. It mainly takes you through forests and moorland. It is very likely that you won't see another person for the next fifty kilometres. This will only change once you see **Hietajoen Leirintä** on your right, where you can take a coffee break. The camping site is set in beautiful surroundings and right on the shores of Lake Inari with its crystal clear water. It is 50 kilometres wide and 80 kilometres long and is the third largest lake in Finland.

From Hietajoen Leirintä to Inari   60 km

After a further 32 kilometres on the **971** you will reach an intersection at which you turn left into road **4**. This road is slightly larger and there may be more traffic. After 24 kilometres you will reach the town centre of Inari.

Inari

With an area spanning 17,400 square kilometres, Inari is Finland's largest municipality in terms of size, but is only inhabited by 7,500 people. It is the centre of the Sámi region in Finland and also houses the parliament building with the cultural centre and the Sámi library. The Protestant-Lutheran Sámi church in the town centre was built in 1951 and is open to visitors daily from June to August.

The Sámi Museum, which is considered to be the national museum of the Sámi people and the North Lapland Nature Centre, where visitors can find out more about the region's flora and fauna, are well worth a visit. The Sámi Museum and its exhibitions provide a comprehensive insight into the annual life cycle and explain the relationship between nature and the life of the Sámi people. Photographs of the surrounding landscape and local culture, videos, diagrams of plants and animals, sound installations and various artefacts guide visitors through summer and winter, past and present. The building itself is also interesting from an architectural point of view. It was designed by the famous Finnish architect Juhani Pallasmaa. Archaeologists found 9,000-year-old evidence that this site was once home to the first settlers in the north of Lapland.

Lake Inari is the sixth largest inland lake in Europe and, with its more than 3,000 islands, appears in some parts more like a labyrinth of waterways. On its shores, just outside the city, you can find the camping site Uruniemi Camping, where you can also rent wooden cabins. There is a cafeteria with a kiosk, a sauna by the lake shore and a place renting boats and canoes. In the restaurant of Hotel Inarin Kultahovi you can enjoy local specialities as well as beautiful views across the lake. The restaurant has also made a name for itself as Finland's northernmost jazz club.

From Inari to Ivalo   38 km

Continue the journey on road **4** and you will reach Ivalo on a slightly less hilly road.

Ivalo

Ivalo is the administrative centre of the Inari municipality and at the same time an important economic centre in northern Lapland. There is a range of services on offer in the town centre. You can find hotels, restaurants as well as a shop. Additionally, the Protestant-Lutheran church built in 1966 and the Orthodox St.-Nicholas church from 1960 can be found there. Lapland's Orthodox community has further churches in Rovaniemi, Nellim and Sevettijärvi.

Ivalo also has an airfield with direct flights to Helsinki. It is also possible to take a bus to Rovaniemi via Sodankylä. Busses from the company http://www.eskelisen.fi/en/ also transport bikes.

Protected primeval forest

Northeast of Ivalo are the last eight large primeval forests of Finland. They can only be found in parts of Eastern Europe and were unprotected for many years. After long and hard negotiations, in 2009 almost 100,000 hectares were placed under nature protection for 20 years. A further 93,000 hectares are farmed as environmentally friendly as possible. The Finnish primeval forest consists, among others, of more than 600-year-old trees. Before 2009, the Metsähallitus State Forestry Administration had released them for felling by the semi-governmental Stora Enso group to produce paper.

You can also find hundreds of endangered plant, fungus and animal species here, especially beetles and birds. The Finnish primeval forests are also the basis for the traditional way of life of the Sámi people.

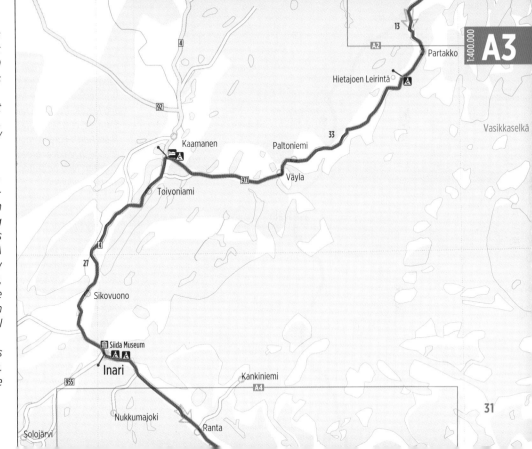

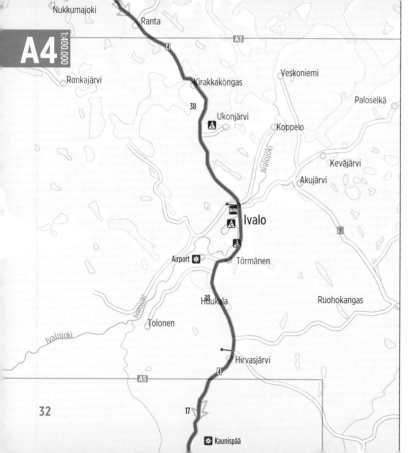

The Sámi people

The Sámi people are the last indigenous people in the EU. Their home territory Sápmi stretches across the whole Lapland region – also in Norway, Sweden and Russia. There are said to be 75,000 Sámi left, of which 9,000 live in Finland. These North-European native inhabitants engage in reindeer breeding. These animals can feed on cotton lichens during the harsh winters.

The Sámi people have had their own parliament in Inari since 1996. It has an advisory function and 21 members.

Kalevalski National Park

The area on the Finnish-Russian border, which is still strictly guarded as an external border of the EU, was placed under protection and named Kalevalski National Park on the Russian side in 2006, and has been protecting one of the last European primeval forests ever since. In addition to bears, it is also home to the wolverine, one of the shyest mammals in Northern Europe.

Kalevalski National Park is the third largest rainforest reserve in Karelia. Until 1996, the two largest Finnish paper companies had obtained raw wood from this forest, which was then processed into pulp and paper in Finland. After strong protests, they ended their logging practices and the Russian government of Karelia decided to establish the national park stretching across an area of 75,000 hectares, which is three times the size of the Bavarian Forest National Park.

Its untouched tree population is home to some endangered species in the north of Europe. These include large animals such as brown bears, wolves and lynxes, but also smaller animals such as flying squirrels, three-toed woodpeckers and eagle owls.

Next to Paanaiarvi National Park and Kostomuksha Reserve, this national park is third large primeval forest in Karelia, from which chainsaws have been banned forever.

From Ivalo to Vuotso   **72 km**

In Ivalo, follow road number 4 and you will reach **Hirvasjärvi**. In Törmänen, turn right to get to the airport.

EXCURSION "Kaunispään huippu", a café situated on the mountain Kaunispää, is well worth a visit. You can get to the top of the mountain by following a narrow, windy road for about two kilometres. You will see "Näköalaravintola" written on a road sign.

After this, you will reach the tourist town of Saariselkä.

Saariselkä

This village with a population of just 300 is frequented by wintersport tourists and is the biggest holiday centre in Finnish-Lapland. Apart from hotels and restaurants you can also find supermarkets in the village. Saariselkä is also the name of the mountainous area which belongs to Urho-Kekkonen National Park and stretches all the way to the Russian border. The biggest elevation is Fjell Sokosti with a height of 718 metres, located in the Sodankylä area.

Continue the journey on road number **4** through **Kakslauttanen** and after around 32 kilometres you will reach Tankavaara, which turned gold washing into a tourist attraction.

Tankavaara

You can visit the Gold Museum (Kultamuseo) here as well as the Golden World exhibition. While the latter takes an international view of the topic, the Gold Museum is dedicated to the Finnish tradition of gold washing. You can also try some gold washing yourself. The museum also hosts the inofficial gold washing world championship. In the village you will find Wanha Waskoolimies restaurant. Those wishing to spend the night can rent a wooden cabin at the Gold Museum.

From Tankavaara continue until you reach Vuotso.

Vuotso

Vuotso is a village with a population of 300, a small shop as well as a restaurant. It is part of the parish of Sodankylä and

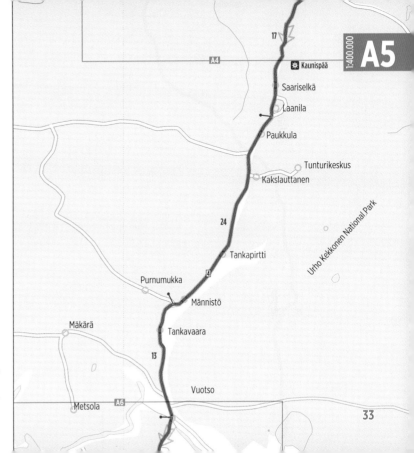

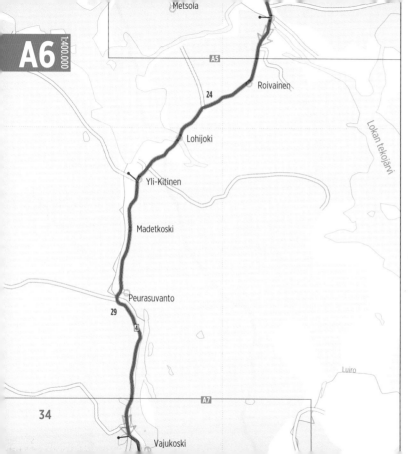

the southernmost point of the Sámi region where it is possible to stay overnight.

From Vuotso to Sodankylä   91 km

From Vuotso, the route continues comfortably towards the south. After 38 kilometres you will reach **Peurasuvanto**, where Peurasuvannon Siltamajat lets out wooden cabins as well as a restaurant with 50 spaces. Cycle past lake Bajunen and then turn left towards Vajukoski. However, just before you turn into this, it is recommended to continue for a further 200 metres, leave your bike on a car park at the side of the road and take a little walk across the moors on the Ilmakkiaapa nature path.

Ilmakkiaapa-swamp

The scenic Ilmakkiaapa swamp is part of the northern Finnish peat bog belt and stretches over an area of 6 square kilometres. It is part of a state programme to protect the moors.

Shortly after the turn, the power plant of Vajukoski as well as Vajusuvanto cam-ping site will come into view. This is located in the village of **Petkula** (population: 100) at the shore of the river Kitinen. You can find a snack bar, a sauna and various bathing spots there. It is also possible to go fishing there, collect berries or rent a boat.

Just before Sattanen, cross a river and then turn left into **Sattasentie** and continue between the road and the river. You will then reach road **4** again and shortly afterwards turn left again into **Pohjantie**. Cross over the 75 and continue parallel to it until you reach the centre of Sodankylä.

Sodankylä

Sodankylä has about 10,000 inhabitants and offers a wide range of services. There are several bars, restaurants and hotels. The town is well known in cultural circles thanks to its annual film festival held in June. The Midnight Sun Film Festival was first held in 1986 at the initiative of Finnish filmmakers Anssi Mänttäri, Aki Kaurismäki and Mika Kaurismäki. The atmosphere is worldwide unique. Internationally renowned directors, new talents and an international audience come together under the midnight sun. Movies are shown around the clock in three halls. Regardless of the time of day, visitors can expect bright daylight, whether they leave the building after a performance at four o'clock in the morning or at mid-day.

Sodankylä Museum consists of 13 historical buildings and presents the life of the rural population at the beginning of the 20th century. The main building, Kuukkeli, was built in 1906. Originally located in the town of Riesto, which disappeared in the water after the dam was built, it

Statue of a Lapp and reindeer in Sodankylä

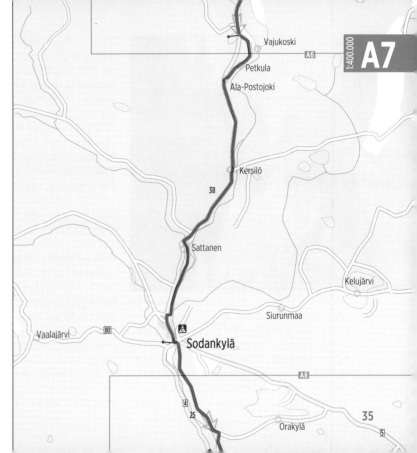

35

Pyhä Luosto National Park

was moved to the museum grounds in 1962. There are also other historic buildings, a smoke sauna and parts of a reindeer fence. The oldest piece of the exhibition on local history is a 700-year-old ski.

Church services are held in the more recent stone church dating from 1859 as well as the old wooden church from 1689. It is one of the best preserved churches in Finland and one of the oldest wooden churches in Lapland.

It was restored in 1980 under the supervision of the Antiquities Office. Both churches are open during the day. In Sodankylä you can see the works of local and nationally acclaimed naive painters, such as Andreas Alariesto (1900-1989). The Riikka Gallery and Risto Alariesto Lapinkuvat is located in the same building as the tourist information office and is open during the day.

Camping Sodankylä Nilimella is located directly behind the town centre, on the other bank of the river Kitinen. A few hundred metres further along the bank you will find a restaurant, a beach and sauna facilities.

You can take a bus from Sodankylä to Ivalo and Rovaniemi. Busses from the company http://www.eskelisen.fi/en/ also transport bikes.

From Sodankylä to Savukoski   128 km

Continue east on road **5** and cross the river Kitinen, then turn right into **Orajärventie** at the intersection and cycle along the eastern river shore. Then turn right into **Kurkiaskatie** and follow the road at the edge of the lake to the other side of the lake and then a bit further north towards road **63** again, into which you turn left.

Behind **Aska** you will cross a river and then turn left into **Sillankorvantie** which leads to **Alakitisentie**, into which you turn left. At its end, turn left into road number **962** and you will reach **Luosto**. The little village in the heart of the national park is one of the smaller skiing centres of Lapland. You can stop here for a bite to eat and also stay overnight.

Pyhä-Luosto National Park

The national park covers an area of 150 km² and consists of the fjells Pyhätunturi and Luosto. It was established in 2005, when Pyhätunturi National Park, founded in 1938, was joined together with the north-eastern area around the Luosto fjell.

The two fjells (mountains) form a 35 km-long mountain range, together with Mount Noitatunturi (540 m) and Mount Ukko-Luosto (514 m), which noticeably stands out from the otherwise flat landscape. Mount Ukko-Luosto can be climbed via a staircase with 670 steps and offers spectacular panoramic views of Lapland, the surrounding mountains and across vast forests.

The mountain range was formed two billion years ago. The mountains consist of hard quartzites, which were able to withstand erosion and were ground down to round fjells by the glaciers of the ice age. The melt water from the glaciers carved deep valleys between the mountain peaks. The largest of these is the 220-metre-deep Isokuru valley between the summits of Mount Kultakero and Mount Ukonhattu.

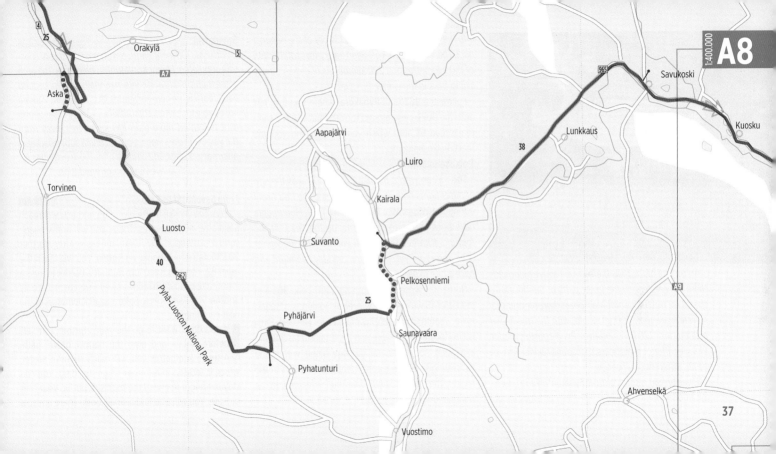

1:400.000

Orakylä

25

4

5

A7

Aska

Torvinen

Luosto

40

1962

Pyhä-Luoston National Park

Aapajärvi

Luiro

Kairala

Suvanto

Pelkosenniemi

25

Pyhäjärvi

Saunavaara

Pyhatunturi

Vuostimo

965

Savukoski

Kuosku

Lunkkaus

38

A9

Ahvenselkä

37

The reindeer as a constant companion

At the foot of the fjells there are extensive moorlands there are conifers on the lower parts of the slopes. To the south-west of the mountain peaks there are primeval forests more than 400 years old, with the tree line at an altitude of 320 to 400 metres. Pyhä-Luosto's wildlife includes otters, brown bears, moose and reindeer as well as 128 different bird species.

There are ski resorts, both at Pyhätunturi and Luosto. An information centre at Pyhätunturi provides insight into the surrounding nature and history of the national park. There is a network of hiking trails with a total length of 150 kilometres and 220 kilometres of cross-country skiing trails in the winter.

Follow the **962** until **Pyhäkora**, where you turn left onto the **9621**, cycle around the lake and you will then reach road **63**, into which you turn left and you will reach Pelkosenniemi.

Pelkosenniemi

This village with a population of 1,000 was the site of bitter fights between the Finnish and the Red Army during the Winter War in December 1939. Monuments have been put up to commemorate the dead. At the foot of 540m-fjell Pyjätunturi you will find the winter sport resort of Pyjä, where you can stay overnight and have a bite to eat.

North of Pelkosenniemi turn right into road **965** and just before Savukoski you will reach "Joulupukin Muorin maja" (Santa Claus' wife) camping site. The Geo-Pirtti is also located at this site and it contains a fascinating exhibition about general geology along with some interesting facts about some geological aspects of the region. The "wife of Santa Claus' hut" is located on the right hand side of the road.

Savukoski

With ist 1,000 inhabitants, Savukoski is also very sparsely populated. Mount Korvatunturi belongs to the area of the municipality and is internationally known. Legend has it that it is the home of Santa Claus. However, you will not be able to see Korvatunturi when you are in Savukoski as it is located more than 100 kilometres away from the village. In the village, you will find a supermarket, a pharmacy, a bank and a range of outdoor activities for tourists as well as overnight accommodation.

From Savukoski to Salla   79 km

From Savukoski, follow road **965** and you will reach **Saija** after 40 kilometres. There, you will find a village shop which is open every day of the week. After a further 20 kilometres and going via **Kotala**, you will reach the quiet **82**, into which you turn right. The border to Russia is only a few hundred metres away. From here it is only another 20 kilometres to **Salla** and 30 kilometres to the next camping site.

TIP If you don't want to go this much further, turn left before Kotala and onto the narrow gravel path. After 15 kilometres you will reach Naruska hostel, which is located in a former school building. You can stay overnight in one of the rooms or put up your tent outside. You will also find a small kiosk. There is also a camping site in Naruska but its amenities are quite basic. The only washing facilities are located in the sauna and at the nearby river shore.

Continue on road **82** along the railway tracks and you will reach Salla via Kolloselkä.

The „Battle of Salla"

At the entrance to the village there is a memorial site with a tank barrier and original trenches to commemorate the Winter War. On 30 November 1939, Salla was overrun by Soviet troops who were to advance via Rovaniemi all the way to Tornio at the Baltic Sea. In the "Battle of Salla", which lasted until 28 February 1940, Finland suffered heavy losses but managed to defend itself and stop the attackers. Despite this, Finland had to cede the eastern half of the Salla municipality to the Soviet Union in 1944 after the "Peace of Moscow". The War Museum provides some information on this.

Salla

Salla is a village with nearly 4,000 inhabitants. Its main source of income is tourism. There are a few shops, a library and some restaurants. Most of the hotels and wooden cabins are located outside the village, on Mount Salla, which is ten kilometres away. The tourist information centre is located in the Town Hall.

Behind the village the road runs along the mountain of the same name, which is the main tourist attraction of the municipality. At its foot there is a ski area. In the summer you can go to the summit, for example by all-terrain vehicle (ATV).

The presumably oldest ski was found in Salla in 1939. The 5,000-year-old piece is kept under lock and key in the National Museum in Helsinki.

Reindeer

Salla province, which is twice the size of Germany's Saarland but only has a population of 5,000 is home to 10,000 reindeer. Since the hairs of their fur have

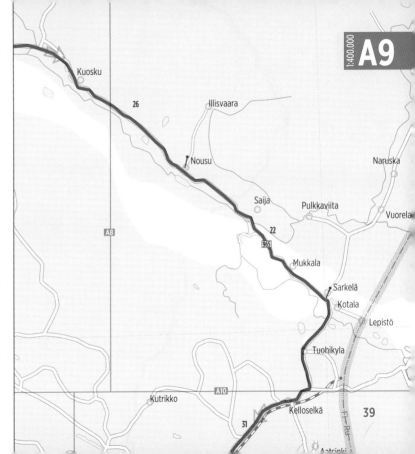

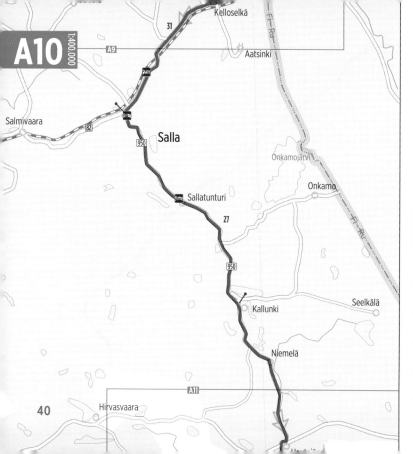

hollow chambers, they can survive even temperatures of 40 degrees below zero.

From Salla to Käylä　　　71 km

Coming from Salla, turn left into road 950 and after 10 kilometres you will reach Sallantunturi, where you can find numerous camping sites. After a further 34 kilometres you will reach Hautajärvi. You will reach Käylä via Ruvanaho and Ollila, where you can go shopping and have a bite to eat.

EXCURSION In Käylä you can turn left onto the relatively ide gravel road (8693), which will take you to Oulanka Nature Centre in Juuma.

Oulanka National Park

The nature centre is run by the State Forestry Office and is open from July to September. It provides information about the national park and other local tourist destinations. In the centre there is a cafeteria, a gift shop as well as the village shop Kaamosvalinta, which also offers overnight accommodation.

Extraordinary flora and fauna can be found in this area. Melt water from the ice age has formed the region's spectacular ravines, canyons, valleys and riverbeds. The park was founded in 1956 and expanded in 1982 and 1989. It is visited by more than 160,000 people every year.

Oulanka National Park camping site has a small shop selling fishing licences. The nature centre provides an introduction to the river habitat as well as the diverse flora and fauna. It also offers various travel and hiking services.

From Käylä to Kuusamo　　　50 km

In Käylä, continue straight on the **950** until you reach road 5, into which you turn left. Shortly before Ruka, turn left towards the winter sports centre.

Ruka winter sports resort

Ruka winter sports resort is a venue for international competitions and is located at an altitude of 500 metres at fjell Ruka, one of the southernmost mountains in Finland near Lapland. A fjell (tunturi) is a treeless mountain formed by a gla-

cier during the ice age several tens of thousands of years ago. In the summer, travellers can take a cable car up to the summit. There are several places offering overnight accommodation and restaurants in the vicinity as well as a supermarket. Kuusamo, although it likes to promote itself as a part of Lapland, is under the administration of the Northern Ostrobothnia region, which is the narrow stretch of land between the regions of Kainuu and Lapland.

Behind Ruka, turn left again into road **5**. Around 5 kilometres from Kuusamo town centre you will find two camping sites, Matkajoki Camping, which is less frequented by tourists, and Rantatropiikki a bit further away.

Just before **Huttulampi**, turn left into **Ukkoherrantie**, which leads to **Talvijärventie**, into which you turn left. At the end, turn left into **Rukajärventie (8692)**, which you follow until lake Rukajärvi and then continue to the **E 5**, into which you turn left.

At Nissinjärvi, continue left into **Nissinjärventie**, which you leave again just before road 5 and turn left into **Kitkantie**. The road on your right leads to the Holiday Club and golf course. Follow Kitkantie until you reach Kuusamo town centre.

This route offers many possibilities to leave the busy 81 and continue on the old country lane. However, unfortunately there is a lack of signposting.

Kuusamo

Kuusamo has a population of 16,000 and is the economic centre of northeastern Finland. In the town centre you can find many restaurants, overnight accommodation, a bicycle shop and a bowling

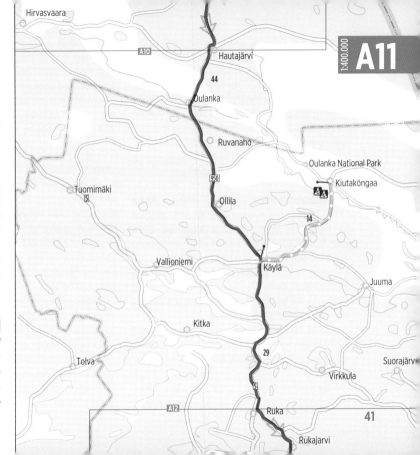

alley. Due to its proximity to Ruka winter sports resort, wintertime is the main season in Kuusamo.

At the beginning of the Winter War, Kuusamo was evacuated in December 1939 for fear of a Soviet invasion. During the Continuation War of 1941-44, German Wehrmacht troops were stationed here. When the German troops were pushed back during the Lapland War, they burnt down the church village. It was only rebuilt in 1952. In 2000, the municipality became the town of Kuusamo. There are direct flights to Helsinki from here.

From Kuusamo to Hossa   80 km

From the town centre, continue on **Kitkantie** and then turn right at the sports centre into **Ouluntaival**, which leads to the **E 63**, into which you turn left after having crossed underneath it on the bike path. You will notice that the traffic is much lighter after road 20 has branched off. Just before the road leading to **Poussu**, you will find the last possibility before reaching Hossa to go shopping, stay overnight or have a bite to eat.

In **Ahola**, turn left onto the quiet **843** and you will reach the village of Hossa via **Murtovaara** and **Teeriranta**, where you will find a camping site with a sauna.

Hossa

Hossa is one of the most popular nature travel destinations in Kainuu. You can find various places offering overnight stays as well as a small supermarket here. The area is said to be a fishing paradise. At Hossanlahti Bay there is Hossa-Lumo Camping, where you can put up your tent, go for a bite to eat or rent a wooden cabin. Near the nature centre you will find Karhunkainalo Camping, which offers a wide range of services, including caravan rental, camping sites as well as a sauna by the lake.

Hossa National Park

In order to mark the 100th anniversary of independence, Hossa was declared to be the 40th national park in the country. The reason this site was chosen is also due to its history. In April 1917, the citizens of the village gathered in a church here as they were dissatisfied with their life as servants of the Russians. They decided to send a delegation to Helsinki and demand Finland's independence. No one had dared to do that before.

The national park has about 90 kilometres of signposted nature trails of varying degrees of difficulty. The paths are lined with resting places and bonfire places as well as wooden cabins for rent and open shelters.

Near Hossa you can find the oldest rock paintings in Finland. The 60 figures were painted with red ochre 4,000 years ago. The early history of the region is documented in the Jalonniemi museum complex.

Ruka Winter Sports Resort

From Hossa to Soumussalmi   97 km

In Hossa, continue on road **843** to **Juntusranta**. 30 km behind Hossa you will find a small shop selling groceries. You will reach **Aittovaara** via **Rasivaara**, where you will find a monument commemorating the Second World War. Once there, turn left onto the semi-paved road towards Puras. Around 7 km after Aittovaara you will find holiday homes at the lake with sauna. Depending on the season it is sometimes possible to rent them spontaneously. Once in **Puras**, continue straight towards **Haapala**.

If you would like to go to Suomussalmi, which is 20 km away, turn right in Haapala into road **912**. At the end turn left onto the bike path of the **9151** and then right again behind the river onto the **912**. Then continue straight onto **Viitostie** and you will reach Suomussalmi.

Suomussalmi

The village of Suomussalmi has a population of 8,300 and it became famous for its resistance in the bloodiest battle of the Winter War, when Finnish associations succeeded in stopping the advance of the Red Army.

These events are documented in the Winter War Museum, the Border War Museum, the Winter War Memorial, the

Border Soldier Museum in Raate as well as along the Museum Road to Raate. The Flame Monument, which was designed by Alvar Aalto, also commemorates the Finnish victims of the Winter War.

In the city centre you can find numerous places offering overnight accommodation as wel as restaurants. You can also stay overnight at Kiantajärvi Camping by the lake of the same name between the town centre and the old village of Suomussalmen kk, where you can also rent wooden cabins. Other facilities on offer include boat hire, the beach, sauna facilities and a cafeteria with a kiosk. Passenger transport to and from Suomussalmi is provided by buses.

From Soumussalmi to Vartius   81 km

Coming from Suomussalmi, continue on the separate bike path along the lake until you reach the bridge, where you turn left and cross lake Kiantajärvi.

Behind the bridge, keep right onto road **912**, pass **Ala-Vuokki,** where you can go shopping and have a cup of coffee, and

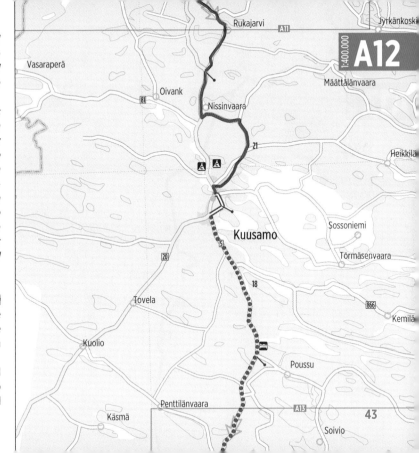

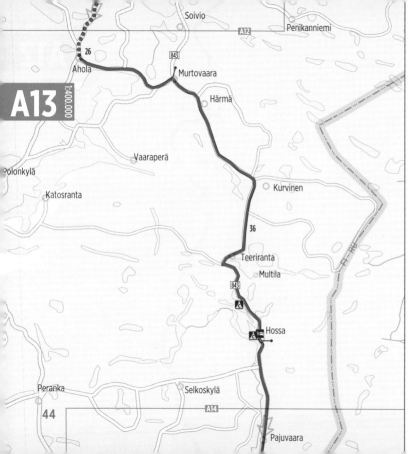

once in **Haapala** you will reach the main route again. At the next branch you will see the museum "Raatteen Portti" on your left with its "Winter War Memorial", which was inaugurated in 2003.

Winter War Memorial

Raatteen Portti Museum was inaugurated in 2003 and houses the permanent exhibition "The Winter War in Suomussalmi". It is a tribute to all the veterans of the Finnish-Soviet war (1939-1940) and to all those who suffered from this war. Its peaceful message is also underlined by the fact that the monument was created as a common memorial of both sides, which were previously opponents during the war.

It consists of a stone field and a central monument. The number of stone blocks spread over three hectares corresponds to the number of Suomussalmi inhabitants killed in the Winter War. The central monument "Open Lap" extends its protective wings over the still field of steles. The following words are carved into the stone: "Man dies, but memory lives on". The 105 copper bells - one for every day of the Winter War – were installed to play their quiet message of the madness of war in the wind.

With the help of modern technology, visitors are transported back to the time of the war on Raate Way. You can also find a café-restaurant there.

At the museum, turn left into the semi-paved "Museum Road" towards Raate.

Museum Road

The decisive battle of Suomussalmi lasted from 30 November 1939 until 10 January 1940, when the 44th division of the Soviet armed forces, who were much stronger in terms of numbers, was scattered into individual groups along Raate Way and finally dispersed. An estimated 20,000 Ukrainian Red Army soldiers lost their lives in this bloodbath. Some of the insufficiently equipped soldiers also died from hunger and the cold.

The Museum Road is 17 kilometres long and has several monuments commemo-

Central Monument „Open Lap" at the Winter War Memorial in Suomussalmi

Museum of Border Protection

The building was restored and returned to its original 1939 condition. It is Finland's only remaining border protection building from the time before the Second World War and illustrates life during this period. It is located directly on the border between Finland and Russia, which has not been changed since 1595 and is considered one of the oldest borders in Europe. The museum shows an exhibition about the "Continuation War" (1941-44) and is open from 12 June to 13 August from 11am to 5pm.

Retrace your steps from the museum at the border and then turn left at the next branch into the semi-paved **Honkajärventie**, at the end of which you turn left into road **912**.

If you would like to go shopping, turn right towards Ala-Vuokki, where you can also have a cup of coffee.

The **912** will take you to Mäkelä via **Sarivaara**, where you can also stay overnight.

rating the Second World War. At its end you will reach the "Museum of Border Protection" in **Raate**.

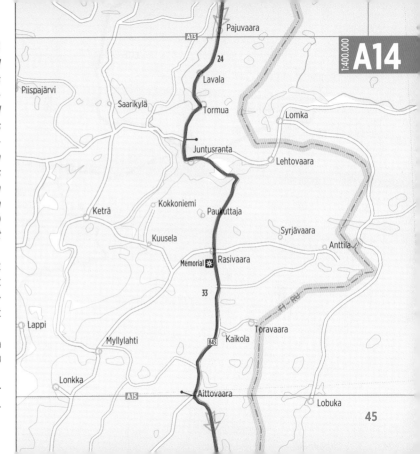

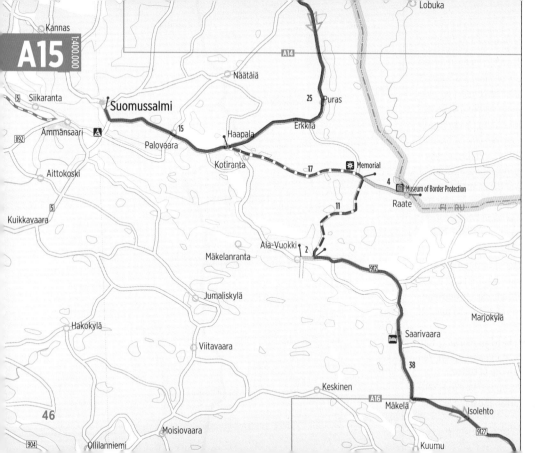

Once in **Mäkelä**, turn left into road **9127**, on which you will reach Vartius after 16 km.

Vartius

  There is a border crossing into Russia in this village as well as a café selling goods (Rajakontti) and a motel. You can also see a watchtower on the Finnish side. The Wild Brown Bear offers overnight accommodation and food.

From Vartius to Kuhmo   67 km

  Cross the railway tracks on road **9127** and you will reach road **89**, on which you continue straight south. After 6 kilometres, turn left into road **9123**. If you turn left at the first opportunity, you will find cabins for rent. After 18 kilometres you will reach road **912**, which will take you to Lentiira.

Lentiira

  The church of Lentiira was destroyed in an arson attack in 1989 and the new church, designed by Hannu Pyykkönen, was completed in 1991. Churches had also been set alight in Lentiira previously. Kirveskansa church of 1812 burnt down on the last day of the Winter War. A memorial was erected at the site here to commemorate this event.

  In the holiday village (Lentiiran Lomakylä) you can rent a wooden cabin or put up your tent. Canoes and boats are also available for hire. You can go swimming or fishing or relax in one of the smoke saunas. The restaurant serves traditional meals and local specialities.

Stay on the **912**, pass **Maaselkä**, **Sumsa** and **Varajoki** and then cross the Tönölänsalmi shortly before Kuhmo. Behind the bridge, keep left and you will reach Kalevala Camping.

Kalevala Camping

This camping site offers wooden cabins as well as places to pitch your tent. You can also find a cafeteria with a kiosk here. Additionally, you can rent a boat on the lake shore to explore Lammasjärvi. The camping site is located about three kilometres from Kuhmo town centre.

Kalevala village and the Winter War Museum are also close to the camping site. In the village, visitors can gain an insight into the local culture and tradition of singing from the Finnish national epic Kalevala. In the Winter War Museum, which belongs to the town of Kuhmo, the exhibitions on display give an impression of the Winter War in Kuhmo through artefacts, photographs, true-to-scale

models and sound installations. You can also familiarise yourself with the everyday life of displaced civilians and Finnish and Russian soldiers.

Stay on the bike path, cross underneath the 912 and you will reach the centre of Kuhmo on the **Koulukato**.

Kuhmo

The city of Kuhmo has a very lively cultural scene, which has a good reputation throughout Finland. There are restaurants, cafeterias and hotels. The Juminkeko Centre, dedicated to Karelia's culture and the Kalevala tradition - Kalevala is the Finnish national epic – is located in the town centre. It organises various events and exhibitions throughout the year. The building's architectural style, on the other hand, represents the modern culture of Finland. It is built in the style of the new Finnish wooden architecture of internationally acclaimed architects Mikko Heikkinen and Markku Komonen.

Kuhmo is best known as the venue of the chamber music festival taking place annualy in the summer. The success story

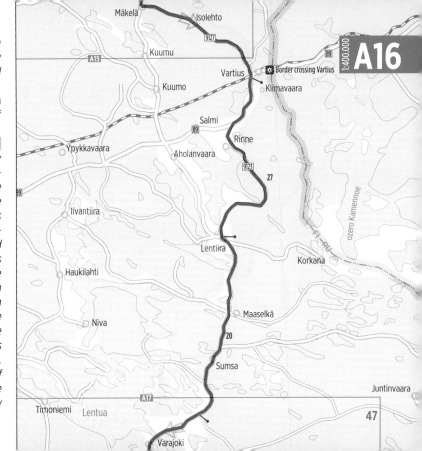

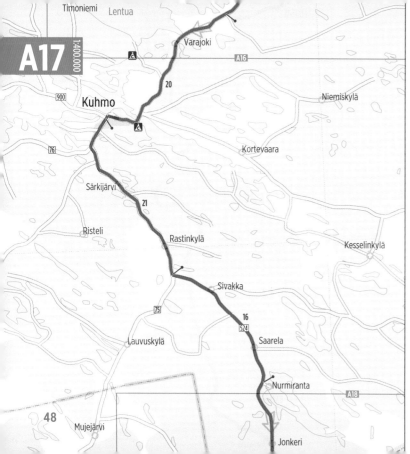

Tank Monument at Kuhmo

began when the melodies of Telemann's concerto for four violins in G major were heard in 1970. Every year, the festival attracts numerous chamber music fans from Finland and abroad and is the highlight of the summer for many classical music lovers and experts.

From Kuhmo to Nurmiranta   37 km

Leave Kuhmo on the bike path on **Kainuuntie**. This turns into road **76**, on which you will pass the war memorial Jyrkänkoski.

Turn left onto road **75**, then left again after **Rastinkylä** into road **524** and you will reach the village of **Nurmiranta** via **Saarela** and **Sivakka**. In Nurmiranta you will find a café as well as a possibility to stay overnight for free. However, this is only a basic cabin with a toilet and a fireplace. You therefore need a sleeping bag as well as a camping mattress. In order to get to the cabin, turn left into a field path shortly behind Nurmiranta. The path is signposted for walkers with a small sign.

From Nurmiranta to Lieksa   69 km

Continue on the **524** to **Savijärvi** via **Jonkeri** and **Teljo**, on a windy and very hilly road. This part of the route will lead you through a forest which was untouched for a long time. After around 15 kilometres you will pass the ruins of an old water mill and after a further 13 kilometres you will reach Nurmijärvi.

Nurmijärvi

Due to its location in the greater Helsinki region and therefore close to the Finnish capital, Nurmijärvi has grown rapidly in recent years. Today, it is Finland's largest rural community with a population of 40,000. The village has been an independent parish since 1605. The administrative community was formed in 1775 and was named after the former Lake Nurmijärvi. This was located in the middle of the municipality, but was drained to produce arable land between the 1920s and 1950s.

In Nurmijärvi there is a supermarket, "Aunes Café" and various places offering

overnight accommodation. It is also the birthplace of Aleksis Kivi.

Aleksis Kivi

The Finnish national poet is considered to be the father of modern literature in the Finnish language. Previously, the literary language was Swedish. The coat of arms of the municipality includes "The Seven Brothers". Einojuhani Rautavaara wrote the opera of the same name about Aleksis Kivi (1834-1872), which had its premiere in Savonlinna in 1997.

Stay on the **524**, pass **Pankajärvi** and after 24 kilometres turn left into road **73** towards the centre of Lieksa.

Lieksa

Lieksa is one of the most important touristic spots in Northern Karelia. Set against a beautiful backdrop in the midst of hills and a lake, this Northern town has 12,000 inhabitants and offers a wide range of accommodation and restaurants.

Timitraniemi camping site is located near the town centre Lake Pielinen, Finland's fifth largest lake. You can rent

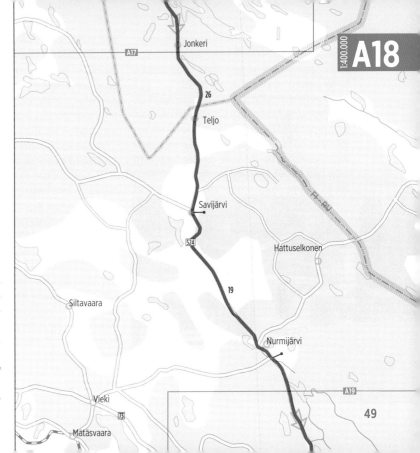

wooden cabins as well as spaces to put up your tent here. There is also a cafeteria and a supermarket. Visitors can use the sauna or swim in Lake Pielinen. It is also possible to hire a boat or canoe and explore the lake.

Pielinen Museum is the second largest open-air museum in Finland. Visitors can learn about the agricultural and forestry culture of Eastern Finland and the architecture associated with it. There are three building complexes in the museum grounds. The oldest building, Lukan pirtti, dates back to 1765 and there are also four raftsmen's houses. For the construction of the three older ones,

Pielisen Museum in Lieksa

tree trunks and an axe was used. The more recent cottage consists of squared timber. The most important exhibitions can be found in the main building and are dedicated to the early history of the Lieksa region, traditional ways of life, agricultural tools and implements, traditional remedies, local aristocratic families, toys and the Second World War.

For travellers interested in classical music, we recommend the annual brass music festival known as Lieksa Brass Week (Lieksan Vaskiviikot). It is one of Finland's popular summer festivals and takes place at the end of July/beginning of August.

In the summer, you can also take a ferry from Lieksa to the other side of the lake to the 347-metre-high Mount Koli. From there, you have perhaps the most magnificent views over the hilly landscape of Northern Karelia. At the same time, you can admire the Finnish lake scenery. By the way, the view from Mount Koli inspired many Finnish artists at the end of the 19th and beginning of the 20th century. If Karelia is considered to be the heart of Finland, Mount Koli is Karelia's soul. The mountain has thus become what is known as the unofficial Finnish national landscape.

From the station, there are direct trains to Nurmes and Joensuu, from where there are direct trains to Helsinki.

The history of Karelia

Karelia is a historical landscape that is today divided between Finland and Russia. It was originally inhabited by the Finno-Ugrian Karelia people. After the third "Swedish Crusade" (1293-1295), the territory was divided in the Treaty of Nöteborg (1323).

Wiburg became the capital of the Swedish province. In the peace treaty of Nystadt (1721) Russia received the largest part of Karelia again, which was called Old Finland. In 1809, the whole of Finland fell to Russia. As a sign of good will, Tsar Alexander I united Old Finland with the former Swedish territories in 1812 to make it the Grand Duchy of Finland.

After the October Revolution and the Finnish Declaration of Independence (1917), Karelia became the scene of some bloody battles. Finland's independence within the borders of the Grand Duchy was recognised by the Russian Soviet Republic in 1920.

After the defeat in the Winter War (1939-1940), a large part of Western Karelia fell to the Soviet Union, which is why 450,000 Finns fled or were displaced from the occupied territory. In the Continuation War (1941-1944), Finland reclaimed the territories that were ceded and occupied most of Eastern Karelia. When Finland was

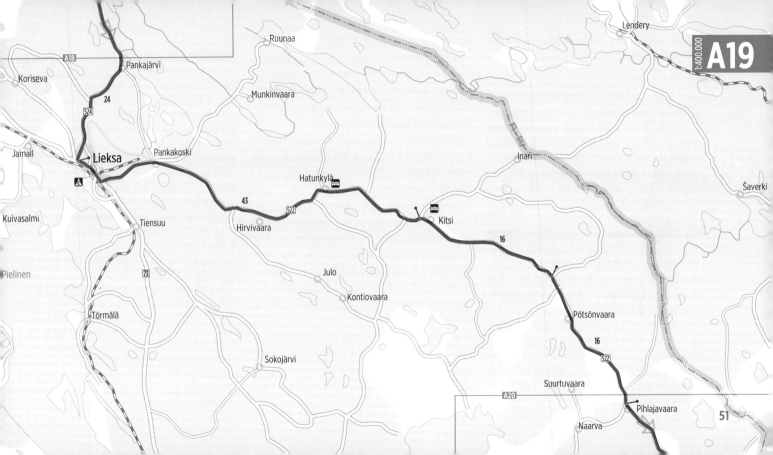

Lendery

Ruunaa

A18

Pankajärvi

Koriseva

524

24

Munkinvaara

Inari

Šaverki

Jamall

Lieksa

Pankakoski

Hatunkylä

Kuivasalmi

Tiensuu

43

522

Hirvivaara

Kitsi

16

Pielinen

73

Julo

Kontiovaara

Pötsönvaara

Törmälä

16

522

Sokojärvi

Suurtuvaara

A20

Pihlajavaara

Naarva

51

defeated again in 1947, the present border was established in the peace treaty of Paris.

Karelia Suite

Jean Sibelius was born in Vyborg in 1865, which belonged to Finland at the time, whose three-movement Karelia Suite is one of his earliest and most popular works. He had composed this collection of orchestral pieces in 1893 for a patriotic parade of the students in Vyborg. Karelia always played a special role in his life. The region's folke music inspired him and he also spent his honeymoon there.

From Lieksa to Hattuvaara   94 km

In Lieksa, cycle on **Siltakatu** across the river and then continue straight into **Mähköntie**, which turns into **Lamminkyläntie**. This will take you to road **522**, into which you turn left. Via **Pankakoski** you will reach **Hatunkylä**, where you can stay overnight.

Continue on the **522** and you will reach **Kitsi**, where you can go for a bite to eat and stay overnight. In **Pihlajavaara** the Ulvovan Suden Majatalo offers overnight accommodation but no breakfast. From there, the route continues to Hattuvaara on a comfortable road through the surrounding forests.

Hattuvaara

Hattuvaara is the easternmost continental European town in the EU (only Cyprus is located further east) and has been inhabited since the 17th century. The Makkola museum farm shows the traditional agriculture of Northern Karelia in the 17th and 18th century.

The "Tsasouna" was built in the 1790s and is the only Karelian Orthodox chapel on the Finnish side of the border. The annual church festival takes place on 29 June (Peter and Paul).

Several monuments were erected in and around Hattuvaara to commemorate the Second World War. The decisive battle of the Finnish-Soviet war took place in Ilomantsi towards the end of the Continuation War in the summer of 1944. In the eastern part of the municipality there were fierce battles in which two Soviet divisions were encircled and in the end almost completely wiped out.

The history of the war is also the topic of the Taistelijan Talo (House of Fighters). This was built in honour of Finnish veterans of the Second World War and houses a restaurant in addition to the exhibitions. There are also wooden cabins for rent.

From Hattuvaara to Ilomantsi   65 km

In Hattuvaara, follow the **522** and once in **Lehtovaara**, turn left into path which is not in a very good condition. After 8 kilometres and having gone through **Kuittila** again, keep left into an even more narrow road. After 14 kilometres turn right into road **5004** and you will reach Möhkö.

Möhkö

The houseboat Möhkön Manta has a summer café and in the holiday village of Möhkön Karhumajat (Jokivaarantie 4) you can rent a wooden cabin or put up your tent. The café there humorously refers to its "most eastern patio of the EU" and the proximity of the border to Russia. In Karhumajat you can also go to the sauna, rent a canoe or go fishing. Nearby are two waterfalls, Möhkönkoski and Lotinankoski.

The Ironworks Museum provides information on the extraction and refining of sea ore. From 1849 to 1907, raw iron was produced in the ironworks - the largest in Finland at that time. Several hundred people worked there. The sea ore was extracted from the bottom of the lake and transported on rafts. It was melted into iron in the smelting furnace and then transferred to the plant in Värtsilä or to the foundries in St. Petersburg for further processing.

The **5004** will take you past various war memorials. Behind **Kuuksenvaara**, turn right into road **500** and at its end right again into road **74**, which will take you to Ilomantsi.

Ilomantsi

Ilomantsi is the easternmost municipality in Finland. It has 5,600 inhabitants and is known for its tradition of songs from the popular epic Kalevala, the strong influence of Russian Orthodox culture and its war history. It has diverse flora and fauna, including large predators.

In the town centre there is a wide range of accommodation and restaurants, as well as a Protestant Lutheran and an Orthodox church. The latter is dedicated to the prophet Elijah and is the largest wooden Orthodox church.

The Flora and Fauna Museum, which was created from a private collection of about 350 stuffed animals, provides information on local hunting culture.

Ilomantsi is one of the most important places in the history of war between Finland and the Soviet Union. It was only

here, that battles took place at divisional level within the current Finnish borders during the Winter War (1939-1940) and the Continuation War (1941-1944). The most famous was the defence battle of 1944, which took place in a location typical of Mottisota tactics.

Mottisota means that the enemy army is encircled and dispersed into isolated groups (Finnish: motti) that are eventually wiped out. The stations of the defensive battle of Kaatiolampi were declared a military-historical arena of the highest rank.

From Ilomantsi to Värtsilä   66 km

It is advisable to replenish your supplies for this part of the route as you will not find any possibilities to go shopping or for a bite to eat until you reach Värtsilä. From the town centre, continue on the bike path of the **74**, cross the railway tracks, then turn left into road **500** and follow the road to the right. Via **Patrikka** you will reach **Mutalahti**, which is located very close to the border. You will find an

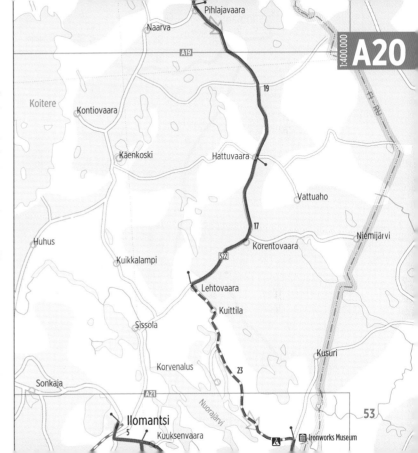

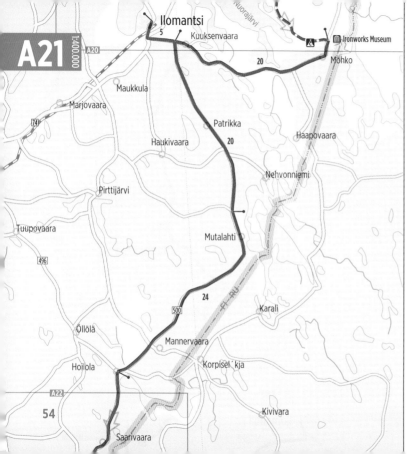

orthodox church dedicated to the Virgin Mary here and you can see a watchtower on the Russian side. There is a church fete every year in September. After a further 20 kilometres on comfortable paths you will reach Hoilola via **Mannervaara**.

Hoilola

After the Second World War, a Protestant Lutheran church was built with the help of donations from the American Lutheran churches. The second - Orthodox - church is dedicated to St. Nicholas and dates from 1959. Both churches contain artefacts from Kopriselkä church as well as other churches that are now on the other side of the border.

On the bank of the river Onnivirta rises the ancient Sacred Rock of Spuassa with the former hotel Korpiselkätalo, which is unfortunately not open to tourists. Just

Orthodox Church in Ilomantsi

54

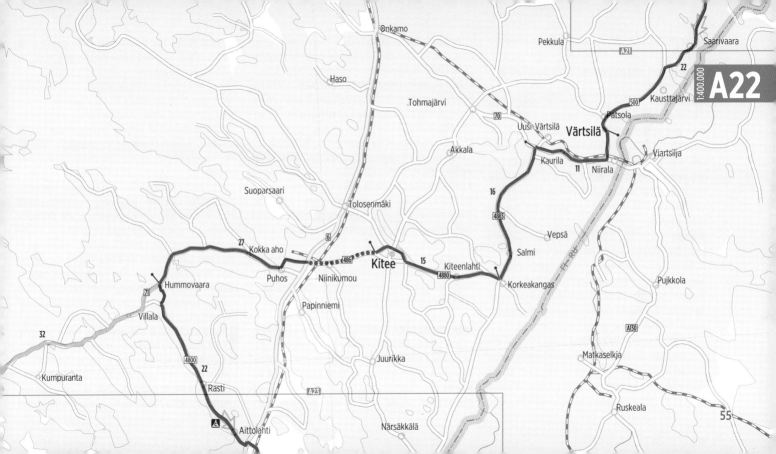

before the bridge, a wooden staircase leads down to a resting area.

Stay on road **500** and you will reach Saarivaara after nine kilometres.

Saarivaara

Saarivaara has a youth club housed in a 1920's log cabin and an Orthodox church (Tsasouna), which was completed in 1976. The "Praasniekka" church festival is celebrated here every year on 6 August. In the cemetery a crucifix procession is held in memory of the dead. The Russian watchtower can only be seen from the hill.

Follow the **500**, turn left in **Patsola** and you will reach Värtsilä.

Värtsilä

This town was divided due to the new border demarcation after the wars between Finland and the Soviet Union. The church built in 1950 is well worth a visit. Its chandeliers are remnants from the old church of the village, which remained on the other side of the border. You can also see photographs of the old church in the rooms.

The Mill Museum (Myllymuseo) is located in an old mill. The collection contains a large number of historical agricultural tools and implements. The heart of the exhibition are the instruments of the Värtsila Workers' Association Orchestra, which existed from 1910 to 1937.

The Niirala border inspection point which was set up here, is the easternmost land border inspection point in the EU and is located 280 kilometres from Petrozavodsk (Finish: Petroskoi), the capital of the Republic of Karelia, and 350 kilometres from St. Petersburg. It is the second busiest border crossing point for trade between Finland and Russia and, with 950,000 people, was the third busiest crossing point for passenger traffic in 2005.

In Värtsilä (Värtsiläntie 43) you will find Hotel Joki as well as Majatalo Sinilintu guesthouse, which offers bed & breakfast and camping facilities. You can also explore the countryside on numerous trails or rent a canoe. The guesthouse also runs a restaurant where popular dancing evenings take place. There is also a Finnish border guard tower nearby.

The railway tracks are only used for freight trains of the border traffic. However, busses are running to Joensuu from Tohmajärvi, which is 20 km away. There are direct trains from Tohmajärvi to Helsinki.

From Värtsilä to Kesälahti   91 km

Cycle southbound on the **500** until you reach road **70**, which leads into Russia. Turn right onto the 70, follow the railway tracks and you will reach **Uusi-Värtsilä** via **Kaurila**. Once there, turn left into road **4883** and just before **Salmi** you will reach a shop which also offers food and drinks. Turn right at road **4880**, pass a large lake, then bear right and follow the bike path until you reach the centre of Kitee.

Kitee

This rural town has nearly 11,000 inhabitants. In the town centre there are various places offering accommodation and restaurants, ranging from traditional cuisine to kebabs. Kitee is known for his "moonlight liqueur". The Museum of Local History also displays tools for its production.

In the town centre you will also find two churches, a one-hundred-year-old Protestant Lutheran stone church and the more recent brick building of the Orthodox church. Both can be visited daily in summer. From the station there are direct trains to Helsinki and Imatra.

In Kitee, turn left onto the **486** and cross the railway tracks as well as road 6 just after **Niinikumpu**. At the end bear left and once in **Puhos**, turn right into road **71**. You will pass **Kokka-aho** and then reach **Villala**, where you can have a bite to eat.

TIP If you would like to stay overnight, follow the busy 6 for around six kilometres in a southerly direction. You can stop at Pajarinhovi, a typical Finnish tourist town. In Pajarinhovi you can rent wooden cabins as well as spaces to put up your tent. There are various shops, a restaurant and a popular dance pavilion. In the animal

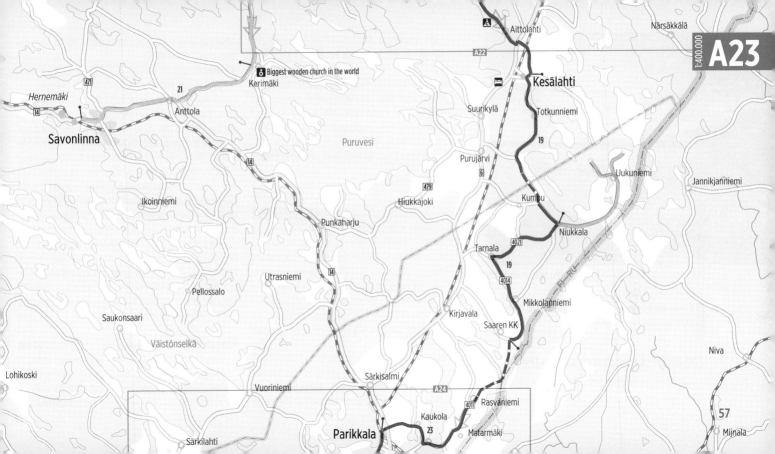

Närsäkkälä

Aittolahti

A22

Kesälahti

Kerimäki
Biggest wooden church in the world

Suurikylä
Totkunniemi

471
Hernemäki
21
Anttola
19
Uukuniemi

14
Savonlinna
Puruvesi
Jannikjanniemi

Purujärvi

Ikoinniemi
14
Kumpu

479
Hiukkajoki
Niukkala

Punkaharju
Tarnala
4021

6

Utrasniemi
14
4014
19

Pellossalo
Mikkolanniemi

Saukonsaari
Kirjavala

Väistönselkä
Saaren KK

Niva

Lohikoski
Särkisalmi
A24

Vuoriniemi
Rasvaniemi
4011

Kaukola
Matarmäki

Särkilahti
Parikkala
23
Mijnala

At the beach of Lake Puruvesi before Kesälahti

park you can see animals found in the wild in Finland, such as bears, skunk bears and lynxes

EXCURSION If you would like to visit Savonlinna, stay on the 71 until you reach Kerimäki.

The biggest wooden church in the world

Die Kirche in Kerimäki mit einer Grundfläche von 40 mal 40 Metern und einer ebenfalls 40 Meter hohen Kuppel wurde nach dreijähriger Bauzeit 1847 fertiggestellt. Die Gesamtlänge der Kirchenbänke erreicht 1,5 Kilometer und bietet Platz für 5.000 Menschen. Die riesigen Ausmaße werden oft damit erklärt, dass die Baumeister die im englischen Fuß-Maß (30 cm) angegebenen Längen in Meter umgesetzt hätten. Das wird allerdings durch die noch vorhandenen Originaldokumente widerlegt. Vielmehr sollte in der Kirche ein Großteil der Bevölkerung Platz finden, weshalb beim Bau sämtliche Bürger geholfen haben.

After 22 kilometres you will reach Savonlinna via **Anttola**.

Savonlinna

Savonlinna is the largest city in the Saimaa lake region, a lake district in the east of the country that looks like a green and blue mosaic on the map with its 7,000 lakes and 13,000 islands. The city's landmark is Olavinlinna Castle, which is considered the best preserved medieval fortress in Northern Europe. Inaugurated in 1848 and with a 37-metre-high tower, the castle was designed to protect the then Swedish empire on its eastern border from Russia.

The main route continues to the left in Villala and along road **4800**. This will take you along the lake to **Aittolahti**, via **Särkänpää** and **Rasti**. There is plenty of overnight accommodation along this part of the route.

After crossing road 6 and the railway tracks, you will then reach Kesälahti.

Kesälahti

In this village with its 2,500 inhabitants there are two sights worth seeing, the church from the 1950s and the local history museum, which is open in summer. In the centre there is the usual range of services of a small town, including a cafeteria and a restaurant. From the station there are direct trains to Helsinki and Joensuu.

To the west of the centre, on the shores of Lake Puruvesi, you will find the guesthouse Karjalan Kievari (Lappeenrannantie 18), where you can rent rooms, a wooden cabin or a space to put up your tent. The guesthouse also has a restaurant serving traditional Karelian specialties. Lake Puruvesi is best known for its whitefish. It belongs to the salmonids and is the most important commercial fish of professional fishermen in Finnish inland waters. It is an oily fish and has a pleasantly mild taste. It is normally used for the traditional Karelian fish dish Kalakukko, which is fish baked in bread.

From Kesälahti to Parikkala   61 km

Leave the town via the small **Taipaleentie** towards Niukkala. Pass the church and the churchyard with the graves of people who died in the war and then continue along the Pyhäjärvi. Follow the signs to **Uukuniemi** until you reach **Niukkala** via **Totkunniemi**, where you can find a small supermarket and where you turn right.

A 10-kilometre detour to visit the village of Uukuniemi as well as Papinniemi camping site is recommended.

Uukuniemi

The biggest attraction of this village, which is about 30 kilometres from Kesälahti, is the wooden church from 1797 with a cross-shaped floor plan. Despite its simplicity, another interesting site to visit is an abandoned place off the road leading to Papinniemi camping site. This site is large and interesting in many respects. Together with a small cemetery this used to be the site of the most important Orthodox church of Uukuniemi, surrounded by a settlement. This may have been an Orthodox village abandoned by its inhabitants in the 17th century. It is possible to explore the area on foot.

Papinniemi camping site is only four kilometres from the church of Uukuniemi: a beautiful place on the shores of Lake Pyhäjärvi, an excellent lake for fishing. The camping site also has wooden cabins for rent. Additionally, you will find places for swimming, sauna facilities directly by the lake as well as a rowing boat rental. It is worth visiting the fishing port of Kalasatama, from where you can see Russia.

To get there, follow the road to Kalalahti. The camping site has been redecorated and is characterised by its beautiful location on a spit of land as well as its nice atmosphere. Since the season usually only lasts until the end of August, it is better to phone ahead to make sure that the camping site is open.

The main route turns right in Niukkala into road **4021** until you reach **Tarnala** and you will reach **Mikkolanniemi**. Once there, continue straight on and then left into road **4014**, on which you will reach Saaren kk.

Saaren kk

In Saaren kk (Saaren kk means "Saari village") there is a beautiful brick church from 1934, designed by Ilmari Launis. Nearby is also the small but very interesting museum of horse-drawn carts and agricultural equipment (Hevosvetoisten ajoneuvojen ja työkoneiden museo), which was founded in 1986. In the summer, the shop Neulansilmä sells arts and crafts.

Once in Saaren kk, turn left into road **4011** and then continue south along the border, passing through **Rasvaniemi**. Just past lake Sokkiiselkä at **Kannas**, turn right and you will reach lake Siikalahti, the most interesting bird lake in Finland, which has been a site of natural protection since 1982. You will find numerous breeding birds. There are also many migratory birds passing this area and searching for food. After crossing the railway tracks and road 6 you will reach the centre of Parikkala on road **4017**.

Parikkala

Travellers will find various restaurants and places offering accommodation in this community with 5,000 inhabitants. The wooden church in the town centre with a double crucifix was built in 1817 and is well worth a visit. The village also has the (quite unique) East Finnish Dairy Museum, located in the courtyard of the Arts and Crafts Centre. The exhibitions illustrate the work in an early 20th century dairy plant. There is also a small museum of local cultural history where the rural artefacts are displayed. The opening hours correspond to those of the Dairy Museum.

From the station there are direct trains to Helsinki, Savonlinna and Joensuu.

From Parikkala to Imatra   **68 km**

Coming from the centre, continue on road **4015** until you reach the busy **6**. Around three kilometres behind the intersection you will find Veijo Rönkkönen's sculpture park on the left side of the road. In the park you can see the result of the works he produced over the course of forty years. There is also a café nearby.

59

Sculpture park

Veijo Rönkkönen (1944-2010) was awarded the State Award in 2007 and is regarded as a master of Finnish outsider art. He completed his first sculpture in 1961 and more than 500 works of art can be found in this enchanting garden today. 200 are self-portraits in different yoga positions. The concrete sculptures have false and real teeth and are equipped with hidden speakers.

Veijo Rönkkönen stands for a special kind of folklore art which is very popular in Finland and is often found next to farms in the form of sculpture parks full of cheerful and engaging fantasy figures. You can see this kind of do-it-yourself art all over Finland. Art historical research has also become aware of this phenomenon in recent years.

Continue on road **6** until you reach **Koitsanlahti**, where you turn left into **Koitsantie**. Cross road 6 and you continue on road **4051**, on which you will reach the centre of Simpele.

Simpele

This village has a population of 4,000 and offers visitors places to eat, spend the night and fish salmon. There is a stone church from 1933, designed by Elsa Arokallio and Elsi Borg. The altarpiece was painted by Finnish painter Alvar Cawen. Wanha Pappila Gallery displays high-quality art.

Once in the centre, turn left at the lake and into **Tehtaantie**, cross the railway tracks as well as the river and then turn right into **Änkiläntie**. Cross the railway tracks again and then continue up a steep hill. Afterwards, turn left into **Mäkiänkiläntie**, which leads to road **6**, into which you turn right. You will find a restaurant and a café at the petrol station there.

Continue on road **6** towards the old power plants of Ritakoski and Lahnasenkoski, that are signposted "Voimalat".

Voimalat

Lahnakoski hydroelectric power plant is the older one. It was completed in 1911 and is still largely in its original condition. Only the dams were renewed and extended. An exposed 5,000-volt cable transferred the power of the waterfalls to the wood grinders of Rautjärvi, which has the second oldest electric-powered grinding mill in Finland.

Ritakoski power plant was built in 1920 on the site of an old mill. In 1967 it was largely destroyed in a fire. The building has now been restored and put back into its original condition.

Once back on road **6**, turn left in **Puistola** and into road **3991**. This will take you to **Laikko**, where you will find a particularly beautiful bathing spot. There is also a small lake with crystal clear water on the right side of the road.

Sculpture Park of Veilo Rönkkönen in Parikkala

Cross the railway line and you will reach Miettilä, where you can find a shop and a bank as well as the former quarters of a garrison.

Miettilä

The army reserve barracks were built in the 1880s and are worth seeing as a historic place of interest. Among the remaining buildings are a summer house and the residence of the military commander, in which the town's municipal office was located until 1972. Kollaa Museum is located in the former military hospital building and is open only upon request. There is also an exhibition about the local cultural history. The garrison buildings are today used as private apartments.

Turn left behind Miettilä into road **3981** and then continue on **museum street** to **Niska-Pietilä** via **Pumujärvi**.

Museum Road

A 20-kilometer section has been a museum road since 1989. It runs along a border strip which at times belonged to Sweden and to Russia. The hilly road used to have a military function, for example during the civil war in the 1740s, when Russian troops advanced on it and destroyed the villages along its way. At that time, there were also guesthouses in the villages of Miettilä and Niska-Pietilä, where travellers could find accommodation and food. The owner of the guesthouse charged the guests a fixed amount and enjoyed certain privileges as a result of his occupation. For example, he had the sole right to serve and liquor in the district. He was also exempt from military recruitment measures. The road has remained almost unchanged for about two hundred years.

Continue on the bike path that starts at the end of museum street and you will pass the **Border Museum** (Rajamuseo) at Kivikatu in **Immola**.

Border Museum

The Border Museum at the garrison site of Immola was originally created on the initiative and as a pastime for local border guards. The permanent exhibition focuses

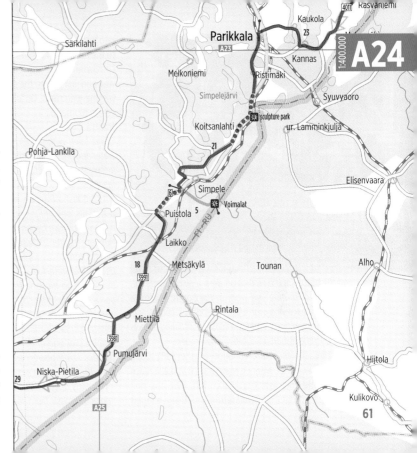

Niklas Prenzel, Roman Schulte-Sasse and Janis Humann on the bridge across the waterfall in Imatra

on the history of the Finnish borders. It also provides an overview of the life and work of the border guards in times of peace and war after Finland's independence. The exhibition has several showcases containing objects and documentation on guarding the borders.

Behind the museum, continue on the **3981** along the railway tracks. After crossing road 6 you will reach **Karjalantie**, into which you turn left. Pass the golf course, turn right into **Lakasentie** and at the end left

into **Vuoksenniskantie**. Continue along the river Vuoksi to the railway bridge, on which you cross the river. The comfortable bike path crosses underneath the motorway and just before the next bridge you will be able to see the waterfalls. Once there, turn right towards the centre of Imatra.

Imatra

This town with 28,000 inhabitants is surrounded by water and only 12 km from Russia. It has an art museum, interesting architecture and the most important public facilities.

Its biggest attraction, however, are the Imatrankoski waterfalls, one of Finland's most popular tourist destinations. Tourism began here as early as 1772, when the Russian Tsarina Catherine II and her entourage came here to admire the rapids of Lake Saimaa in the narrow bed of the waterfalls. In 1872 a cable car was built to transport the most daring of the travellers across the gorge in a gondola. This place was also of particular attraction to those who were tired of life. The sculpture "Imatran Impi" (Virgin of Imatra) by Taisto Martiskainen at the lower end of the waterfalls commemorates the suicides. Hydropower has been used to generate energy since 1929. For the pleasure of the spectators, the dam is regularly opened. The nightly illumination is accompanied by music from Jean Sibelius.

The waterfalls are surrounded by Kruunupuisto Park (Imatran Kruunupuisto), the oldest nature reserve in Finland. It was established in 1842 at the behest of Tsar Nicholas I of Russia.

The "Grand Hotel Cascade", founded in 1903, is also located on the shore. It is a cross between a knight's castle and Art Nouveau style, designed by the architect Usko Nyström. The waterfalls and the park are a living reminder of the Russian tsarist empire, to which Finland belonged from 1809 to 1917.

Finnish modern architectural style can be seen at the Church of the Three Crucifixes (Kolmen ristin kirkko). It was built in 1957 according to plans of architect Alvar Aalto. It has 103 windows, of which only two are the same. The altar is made of Italian marble, the pews of red pine wood from Eastern Karelia and the fabric used is linen. The steeple is 34 metres high. It has three bells, one of which originates from a cemetery chapel in the former Enso (today Svetogorsk), which is located directly opposite Imatra on the Russian side of the border.

You can also stop at Imatra Camping in Ukonniemi, near the Imatran kylpylä spa hotel. It is located five kilometres from the town centre on Lake Saimaa, where you can also swim and rent wooden cabins. You can also stay overnight at the camping site at Vuoksi Fishing Park (Vuoksen Kalastuspuisto), which is located near the town centre on Varpasaari Island on the river Vuoksi. The fishing park was founded in 1875 by British gentlemen from St. Petersburg, who gave it the name "The Vuoksi Fishing Club". At the camping site you can go fishing or take part in an organised tour. Apart from spaces for tents, the camping site also has wooden cabins for rent.

From the station there are direct trains to Helsinki and Joensuu.

From Imatra to Nuijamaa   41 km

Continue on the bike path of road **3952** to **Meltola**. Once there, turn left into road **3953**, which you will later follow along the border to Salo-Issakka. In **Salo-Issakka**, turn left onto the **3952** to **Leppälä**. In Leppälä, turn left to get to **Marttila**, where you turn left again towards **Kontu**. This road is easy to travel on and will take you along a large lake to road **3921**, into which you turn left and you will reach Nuijamaa.

Nuijamaa

This village belongs to the city of Lappeenranta and is an important hub for border traffic to Russia. The church, which was inaugurated in 1948, was built in place of an old one in the same place, which had been burnt down in 1941 during the Finnish-Russian Continuation War (1941-1944). It is the first of the so-called "reconstruction

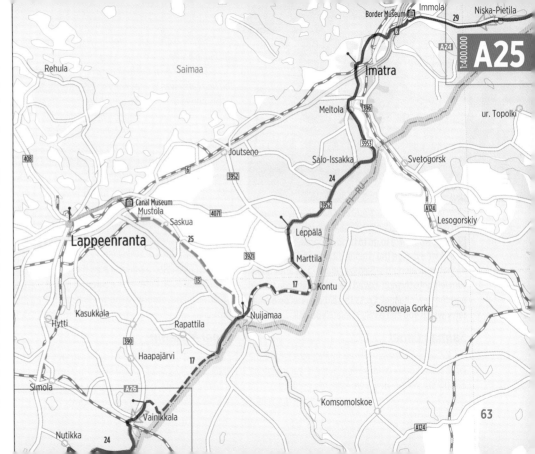

Self-service ferry at the Saimaa Canal

churches". You will also find a restaurant, a supermarket and a currency exchange office in the village.

EXCURSION If you would like to go to Lappeenranta, turn left into Suikintie before the channel bridge and continue on that road along the Saima channel. Just after Suikki turn left onto the non-paved bike path between the old and the new channel. Cross the old channel on a small ferry which you can easily operate yourself.

Saimaa Canal

The Saimaa Canal stretches 43 kilometres from the large Lake Saimaa to the Gulf of Finland. It is important for border traffic between Finland and Russia. The difference in height of the water is 76 metres and is regulated by eight locks, three of which are located on the Finnish side.

The Saimaa Canal can look back on a long history, as the first canal was built as early as 1856. Reconstruction works began in 1920, with only 40 percent of the canal remaining completely intact. The construction of the current canal began in 1963 and lasted until 1968. It was made possible by a treaty between Finland and the Soviet Union, under which the Soviet side of the canal was leased to Finland for 50 years. Already in the 19th century, the canal was a tourist attraction and it has remained so until today - even though the traffic with cargo and passenger ships as well as leisure boats has decreased. The lease agreement with Russia was extended by a further 50 years on 27 May 2010.

Stay on the western side and pass the lock at Soskua. At **Mustola**, turn right into **Itäinen Kanavatie**, cross underneath the motorway and you will reach the canal museum.

Canal Museum

The museum is located in the former cash desk building on the eastern side of the old Mälkiä lock. You can visit a photo exhibition, old ship models and the area of the Mustola lock from the early 20th century.

You will reach road **4071**, into which you turn left. Cross the channel and then turn right into **Läntinen Kanavatie**. Continue along the channel and follow the road which turns into **Luukkaankatu** until you reach road **4081**, where you turn left and continue on the bike path.

Cross underneath road **3821** and the railway tracks. Then bear right and you will reach **Reunakatu**, into which you turn right. Follow the road along the railway tracks, then turn left into **Ratakatu** after crossing the railway tracks and you will reach Lappeenranta station, from where you can take direct trains to Helsinki and Joensuu.

Lappeenranta

Lappeenranta is the capital of South Karelia and with its 72,000 inhabitants the eleventh largest city in Finland. It was founded in 1649 by the Swedish Queen Christina I. and became the capital of the province in 1721. For a long time, there were fierce battles about this border town. Sweden, Finland and Russia all claimed ownership at various times until the town finally became Finnish in 1741.

There are numerous sights worth seeing, including the wooden town hall (1829) of Carl Ludwig Engel, the oldest Greek Orthodox church (1785) in Finland and the harbour. The water tower gives visitors good views over the city, but is unfortunately closed to the public. The most important sight is the fortress on the northern edge of the city.

In Lappeenranta, the Saimaa Canal, built in 1845/1856, flows into the Finnish Lake District, connecting Lake Saimaa with the Baltic Sea near Vyborg. At the beginning of 2009, the neighbouring municipality of Joutseno and in 2010 the municipality of Ylämaa were combined with Lappeenranta. In 2015 it was declared the cycling city of Finland.

Lappeenranta has an airport and a train station. The bicycle shop Pyöra-Expert (✆ +358 5 4118 710) is located at Valtakatu 64.

Water fountain in Lappeenranta

From the station, continue on **Ratakatu** and then turn right at the second intersection into **Hietalankatu**, which turns into **Harapisentie**. Continue straight along that road, cross underneath the motorway and the railway tracks and in Pelkola you will get to road 13. Once there, turn left and then immediately right into **Soskuan sulkutie**, on which you cross the channel at Soskua lock and then immediately turn right onto the bike path between the new and the old channel, which you cross on a small ferry that is easy to operate yourself. Cross underneath the bridge, continue left into **Suikintie** and cycle up the hill. Then cross the channel and you will reach **Nuijamaa**, where you can go shopping and for a bite to eat.

From Nuijamaa to Virolahti   93 km

On the main route turn right onto the separate bike path of **Rajatie**, cross road 13 on your right and then continue along the border on road **3902** until you reach road **390**. Once there, turn left and you will reach Vainikkala.

Vainikkala

This village with about 400 inhabitants is an important border crossing point for rail traffic to Russia. It is of sad historical importance to Finland as this was the starting point for trains filled with industrial goods as reparation payments to the

Church of St. Mary (Marien kirkko) in Lappeenranta

Soviet Union. Today, Vainikkala has a shop, a bank and a restaurant.

Due to its cargo terminal, Vainikkala is an important hob for trade between Russia and the EU. From the train station there are direct trains to Helsinki and St. Petersburg.

In Vainikkala, keep left, cross the railway tracks and then continue on the comfortable road along the border to **Nutikka**, where you turn left. You will reach road **387** via **Villala**, into which you turn left.

65

Follow the road to **Ylämaa**, which has been part of Lappeenranta since 2010. In Ylämaa you can go shopping, have a bite to eat and visit the gemstone museum.

Ylämaa Gemstone Museum

The main attraction of this municipality with 1.500 inhabitants is the Gemstone Museum, which is open daily in summer from 10 am to 5 pm. The place is known for its spectrolite deposits, which were discovered by

Bunker of the Salpa Line at Miehikkälä

chance during controlled blasts in connection with the construction of the Salpa line. Since then, spectrolite has become a popular gemstone in Finland and throughout the world. It is used today for numerous decorative and practical purposes, such as table tops. However, the museum does not focus solely on spectrolite. Established in 1982, the exhibitions show more than four thousand gemstones, minerals and fossils from all over the world. Ylämaa also offers various courses and events, including gemstone tours in the area.

Continue on road **387** until you reach **Lahtela**, where you can have something to eat and stay overnight.

In **Hujakkala** turn left into a road which is easy to travel on and which is signposted as **bike path 7**. Shortly afterwards you will reach Rajamaja B&B, which is located very close to lake Väkevänjärvi. You can also put up your tent in the garden there. You can take a guided tour here and there is a viewing tower for bird enthusiasts. At the border near **Väkevä** you can see the yellow signs in five different languages, all prohibiting the entering of the border strip.

You will reach road **387** again, into which you turn left. Continue until you reach **Muurikkala**, where you can find a shop, a bank and a restaurant. As a visit to Salpalinjamuseo is "mandatory", turn right into **Muurikkalantie**, on which you will reach Miehikkälä.

Miehikkälä

In this village with 2,000 inhabitants there is an architecturally interesting brick church built in 1881 as well as the museum of local cultural history.

Museum about the Salpa Line

The main attraction is the "Salpalinjamuseo", which shows defence equipment from the time of the Second World War. It is located 2.5 kilometres from Miehikkälä. The museum building with its cafeteria and gift shop was originally a bunker complex, built to defend a regiment. The main exhibition, which also shows a multimedia presentation, is dedicated to the construction of the Salpa Line from a local and national point of view.

During the Second World War, the Salpa Line served as a defence structure along the eastern border of Finland. Although it never had to prove itself in combat, its deterrent effect was said to have had a decisive influence on the end of the Soviet offensive in 1944. The line was built in 1940/1941 and 1944 and stretches continuously from Virolahti to Salla and from there to the Arctic Ocean. It includes extraordinarily strong fortifications in 30 Finnish municipalities. As a military fortification it is, for example, comparable to the French Maginot Line.

Once in Miehikkälä, follow the quiet **384** to Virolahti, where two EuroVelo Routes meet.

Anti-tank obstacles of the Salpa Line

Virolahti

The village of Virolahti is one of the oldest in the region. It dates back to 1336 and has 3,500 inhabitants. The village first belonged to Sweden, and then in 1721 half came and in 1743 completely came under Russian rule. Since 1917, Virolahti has been part of the independent Finland and, following the demarcation of the borders after the Second World War, is once again a border town.

The town's attractions include an 18th century church with a vestry from the first half of the 16th century, a bunker museum showing defence structures from the Second World War, and a local history museum in the village of Pyterlahti. The archipelago off the coast belongs to the Eastern Gulf of Finland National Park.

From Virolahti there is also a bus connection to Helsinki, which allows you to take your bike with you. It is another 3 km to the Russian border, as well as to Valimaa camping site (Hämeenkyläntie 153).

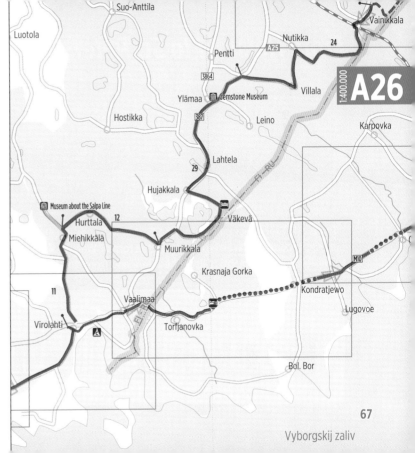

Vyborgskij zaliv

From Helsinki to St. Petersburg

The Baltic Sea Coast bike path - the EuroVelo Route 10 (EV 10) - starts in Helsinki and is identical with the Iron Curtain Trail (EV 13) up to Lübeck, because the western border of the former Warsaw Pact states also ran along the Baltic Sea coast. This is why the 180-km-long section from Helsinki to Virolahti is described here and from there the route to St. Petersburg.

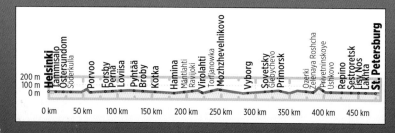

Helsinki

Originally founded in 1550 when it was part of Sweden, Helsinki is today the capital and by far the largest city in Finland with 630,000 inhabitants. Together with the neighbouring cities of Espoo, Vantaa and Kauniainen, it forms the so-called capital region, a metropolitan area with 1.4 million inhabitants, and therefore home to nearly one-fifth of Finland's total population. It is the political, economic, scientific and cultural centre of the country.

On 2 March 1808 the city was conquered by Russian troops during the Russian-Swedish War and almost completely destroyed in a fire. Subsequently, in 1809 Sweden had to cede all of Finland to Russia.

The capital of the newly established Grand Duchy of Finland was initially Turku, the country's largest and most important city until then. However, for Tsar Alexander I, Turku was too far away from St. Petersburg, which is why he decreed Helsinki as the new capital on 8 April 1812. German architect Carl Ludwig Engel was commissioned to rebuild Helsinki as a representative capital after its destruction by the fire. This is how the classicist centre around Senate Square was built. From 1819 onwards, Helsinki was the seat of the Finnish Senate and thus the capital of the Grand Duchy.

When Finland gained sovereignty on 6 December 1917, Helsinki became the capital of the new state. In the ensuing Finnish civil war, the Red Guards brought the city under their control on 28 January 1918, making the bourgeois government flee to Vaasa. In April, German troops intervened in their support and re-conquered Helsinki after two days of fighting on 13 April 1918. After the war had been decided in favour of the bourgeois "Whites", some 10,000 Red Guard supporters were imprisoned on Suomenlinna Island. Around 1,500 of them died of starvation or disease.

During the Second World War, Helsinki was subjected to several large-scale bombardments from the Soviet air force. Compared to other European cities, however, the damage was not too great, not least thanks to Finland's efficient air defence systems. The city was supposed to host the Summer Olympic Games in 1940, but due to the war they were postponed to 1952.

In 1975, the first Conference on Security and Co-operation in Europe (CSCE) was held at Finlandia Hall in Helsinki, which led to a rapprochement between the Eastern bloc and the West.

82 percent of Helsinki's population speak Finnish and 6 percent Swedish as their mother tongue. Officially, Helsinki is a bilingual city, with Finnish as the main language and Swedish as the second language. This is why the roads have Finnish as well as Swedish names and why all announcements on public transport are bilingual.

Helsinki Cathedral

From Helsinki to Porvoo 61 km

Continue east of the main station on **Rautatientori**. At the end turn right into **Vilhonkatu** and then left into **Itäinen Teatterikuja**, which will take you into a park. At the end of the lake turn right into **Kaisaniemen puisto** until you reach the roundabout, where you continue straight into **Liisankatu**. At the end, turn left before the bridge into **Pohjoisranta** and continue along the water. Then turn right and continue across the bridge. Behind the bridge, immediately turn right again and continue on the bike path along the water to Sörnäisten rantatie, into which you turn right. After crossing the metro tracks turn right into **Bradgårdsgatan** and then continue straight on and parallel to the tracks, past Kalasatama metro station and across **Kulosaaren bridge**. Behind the bridge, turn left onto the bike path of the quiet **Kulosaaren puistotie**. Pass Kulosaari metro station and then continue across the next bridge.

Behind this bridge, keep right, cross underneath the railway tracks and the motorway and then turn left into **Hitsaajankatu**. Then immediately turn right into **Suolaki-venkatu** on the unpaved but solid path along the shore.

Continue past a small harbour for sailing boats, always along the water and on a paved path. Cross underneath the motorway and then cycle along the water. At the end of the bike path, turn right into **Kivalontie**, which turns into the quiet and paved road **Marjalahdentie**. Continue along the beach and you will pass a harbour. You will then get to a wide bike path which is set a bit apart from the main street **Meripellontie**.

The route does not continue across the bridge but underneath it. Stay on the shore and the unpaved but solid bike path between the quiet street and the water will take you to **Varjakanvalkama**. At the end turn right into **Melatie**, which turns into **Tankovainiontie**. Follow this until you reach **Kallvikintie**, into which you turn left. This leads to road **170**, into which you turn right and then continue on the bike path which is paved and set a good distance away from the road. Cross the railway tracks and the motorway – just before this you will see Kaidas Café Leipomo – and you will then reach the village of **Söderkulla**, which is located around 35 km away from Porvoo.

The separate bike path stops shortly before **Boxby** and only the small strip on the side of the road remains. Bear right just before the railway crossing to get to the Cycle Service. After crossing underneath the motorway, turn right behind the river and into road **1541** to **Tolkkinen**. Then immediately turn right again into **Mustijoentie**, which turns into **Haikkoontie** after crossing the main road number 1543. Follow this quiet road on a comfortable bike path along the water to **Haikoo Kartano**. Later, the path is not paved anymore but still easy to travel on. At the river, turn left into **Kokonniementie**, where the path is paved again. Then, turn right and continue across the bridge of road **170** and you will reach Porvoo town centre.

The colourful, medieval-looking wooden houses and narrow lanes of the picturesque old town were mostly built after the great fire of 1760. Today, the former town hall of 1764 contains a museum. The rusty-red salt storage houses (18th century) on the banks of the river Porvoonjoki are also charming. The cathedral with its red brick gable is the city's landmark. It was completed in the middle of the 15th century but parts of it date back to around 1410. The cathedral was badly damaged by a devastating fire in 2006.

Located on the old King's Road, Porvoo was granted city rights by King Magnus Erikkson of Sweden in 1346, making it the second oldest city in Finland after Turku. In 1708, the city was destroyed by the Russians and in 1809 it became part of Russia along with the rest of Finland. From 28 March 1809, Tsar Alexander I held the first Finnish parliamentary meeting of the newly founded Russian Grand Duchy of Finland in Porvoo. In the 19th century the city became the residence of numerous Finnish poets and artists.

Since 1923 it has been the bishop seat of the diocese of Porvoo, which includes the Swedish-speaking congregations of Finland as well as the German Protestant Lutheran congregation in Helsinki. The Porvoo Community, a non-institutional association of twelve European

Helsinki

400 m

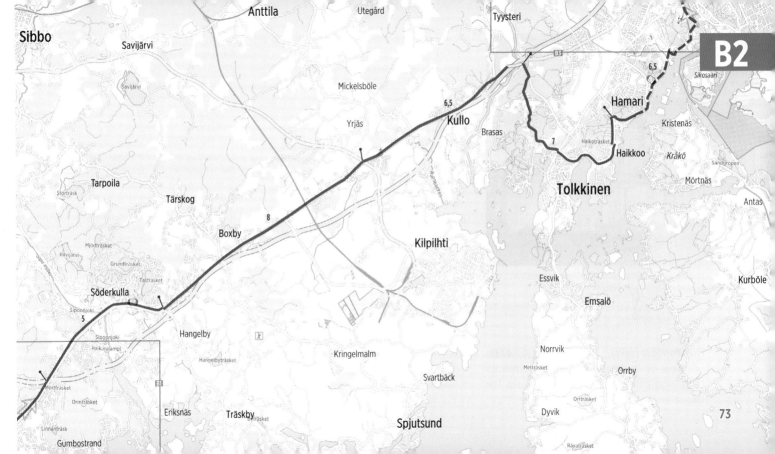

Sibbo

Anttila

Utegård

Tyysteri

B3

B2

Savijärvi

Savijärvi

Mickelsböle

6,5

Sikosaari

Hamari

Kristenäs

6,5

Yrjäs

Kullo

Brasas

Haikoträsket

Haikkoo

Kråkö

Tarpoila

Storträsk

Tärskog

7

Tolkkinen

Mörtnäs

Antas

Sandgropen

Mjödträsket

8

Boxby

Kilpilhti

Pilvijärvi

Sibbo träsk

Grundträsket

Essvik

Kurböle

Tastrasket

Söderkulla

Emsalö

Sipoonjoki

5

Hangelby

Sipoonjoki

Haikaralampi

Norrvik

Mettträsket

Orrby

Hangelbyträsket

Kringelmalm

B1

Svartbäck

Orrträsket

Eriksnäs

Träskby

Dyvik

Träsket

Spjutsund

Mortträsket

Ormträsket

73

Linnanträsk

Rävaträsket

Gumbostrand

Old town hall in Porvoo

churches of the Anglican and Lutheran confessions, was founded in the city in 1992.

Porvoo has 50,000 inhabitants and is bilingual, 64 percent speak Finnish, 33 percent Swedish.

From Porvoo to Loviisa   44 km

Continue on the bike path of **Mannerheiminkatu (170)**, away from the river and towards Kotka. The bike path in the road ends behind the last intersection,

i.e. before the motorway, but a small side strip with red markings.

Stay on the **170**, cross underneath the motorway and you will reach the town of **Forsby** via **Galmmelby** and **Illby**, where you cross the river Illbyån. In Forsby you can have a look at two destroyed bridges from the bridge across the river of the same name. Follow the **170**, cross over the motorway on a bike path, then turn right and continue on **Kuninkaantie** (the old King's road), on which you will reach the church village of **Pernå**. Turn left at the church dating back to ca. 1440, then right at the 170 and continue on the nice bike path until you reach Loviisa.

Loviisa (Swedish Lovisa)

The old King's Road, one of Scandinavia's oldest traffic routes, once led through this area. It originally ran from Bergen at the Atlantic Ocean all the way to Turku via Oslo and Stockholm. In Finland it ran from Turku to Vyborg and then on to St. Petersburg.

After Sweden had lost the city of Hamina to Russia in 1743 as a result of the peace treaty of Åbo, southeastern Finland needed a new port city. In light of this, the city of Loviisa was founded in 1745. It was named after the Swedish Queen Luise Ulrike (Lovisa Ulrika). In the 1760s, the sea fortress of Svartholm was built in order to protect the eastern border.

During the Third Russian-Swedish War, Svartholm Fortress surrendered to the besieging Russian army in 1808. As a result of the war, Loviisa fell to Russia, like the rest of Finland, and became part of the newly founded Grand Duchy of Finland.

The core centre of Loviisa, which is located at Loviisanlathi bay, received its present appearance after the city fire of 1855. The city's centrepiece is the Esplanadi, a wide promenade lined with lime trees. The western end is dominated by the neo-Gothic red brick church, which was built in 1862-67. On both sides of the promenade there are representative stone buildings, such as the town hall, built in 1862 in neo-Renaissance style.

The southern part of the city centre, the so-called lower town (Alakaupunki), was spared by the fire, leaving the old quarter with low wooden houses dating back to the 18th and 19th century intact.

The island fortress of Svartholm is located in front of Loviisa. Built in the 18th century, the fortress was destroyed in the Crimean War in 1855 and then restored from the 1960s onwards. Today, Svartholm is a popular destination and can be reached by boat. Another fortress was built at the same time as Svartholm but further inland. However, only very little of this still remains today: In the north of the

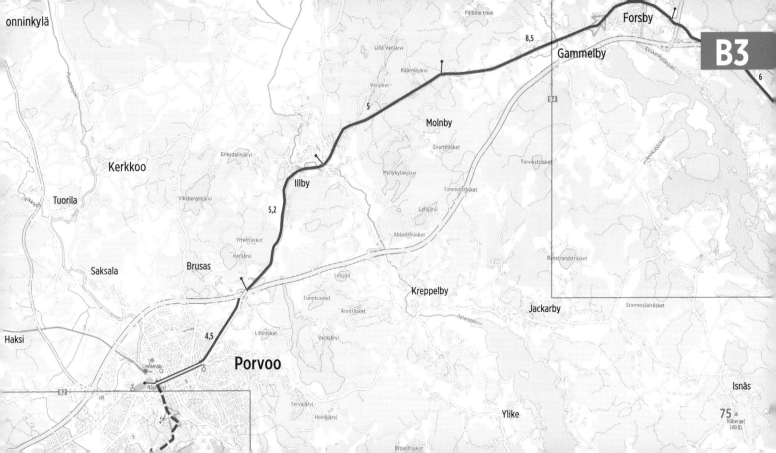

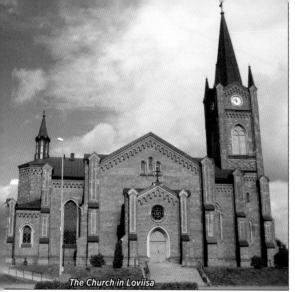
The Church in Loviisa

city you can still see the ruins of two bastions and the commander's house with two stone barracks from the 1750s.

Next to Loviisa church there are three other churches. The oldest is Pernå church, a medieval stone church from the 15th century. In Ruotsinpyhtää there is a wooden church from 1771 with an unusual octagonal floor plan. The wooden church of Liljendal dates from 1886.

In Ruotsinpyhtää you will also find the former Strömfors ironworks, which were founded in 1698. Numerous historical industrial buildings from the 18th and 19th century belong to the former factory grounds. The ironworks was in operation until the 1950s; today, it is a museum.

Shortly after Finland declared independence from Russia in 1917, the Finnish civil war broke out. Loviisa was initially held by the protection corps of the bourgeois "Whites", but then came under the control of the socialist "Reds" like the rest of southern Finland. After Germany had decided to intervene in support of the "Whites", a German unit with 2,500 soldiers arrived on 7 April 1918 as part of the so-called Finnish intervention and conquered the city without resistance. A statue commemorates this event.

There is also a nuclear power plant in Loviisay. The city has 15,000 inhabitants and is officially bilingual, with Finnish (54%) as the majority language and Swedish (43%) as the minority language.

From Loviisa to Kotka   49 km

EXCURSION Those wishing to cycle to the Baltic Sea coast, have to turn right before the bridge and continue along the unpaved but beautiful bike path. This will take you to the beach and its many cafés.

The main route continues on a nice bike path away from the road via **Vähä-Ahvenkorski** to **Pyhtää**, where you can stop for a drink and go shopping. Then, bear left and follow the old King's road for a short unpaved section without much traffic, which is easy to travel on. Continue through rocky woodland scenery.

Cross the motorway and then continue on a bike path which is set aside from the road. Where you can see the turning towards Kiviniemi on your right, continue straight on the eastern side of the lake.

Past **Broby** you will reach the bike path of road 170 again, into which you turn right. Continue parallel to the main road, which you then cross underneath and then cross over the motorway on a separate bike path. Turn right before the river Kymijoki onto the separate bike path of **Mussalontie**. Cross underneath the motorway and continue on numerous bridges connecting the islands. At the end, turn left and continue parallel to the railway – you should already be able to see the yellow lighthouse. Turn right behind the large bridge into **Haukkavuorenkatu**. Then, turn left into **Korkeavuorenkatu** and at the end left again into **Kotkankatu** and you will reach Kotka station.

Kotka

Kotka was granted city rights in 1878 and today has 55,000 inhabitants as well as the largest export port in

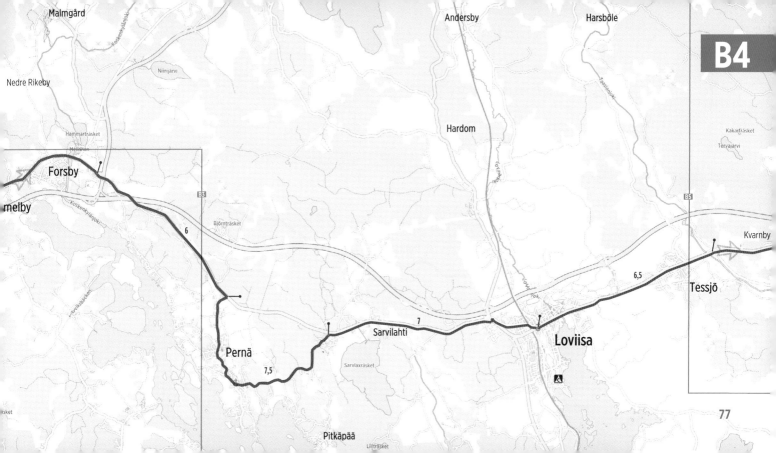

Malmgård

Andersby

Harsböle

Nedre Rikeby

Nilinjärvi

Kakarträsket

Tervajärvi

Hardom

Hammarträsket

Mellonön

Forsby

melby

Koskenkylänjok

B3

Björnträsket

6

Kvarnby

B5

6,5

Tessjö

7

Sarvilahti

Loviisa

Pernä

7,5

Sarvilaxträsket

Pitkäpää

Lillträsket

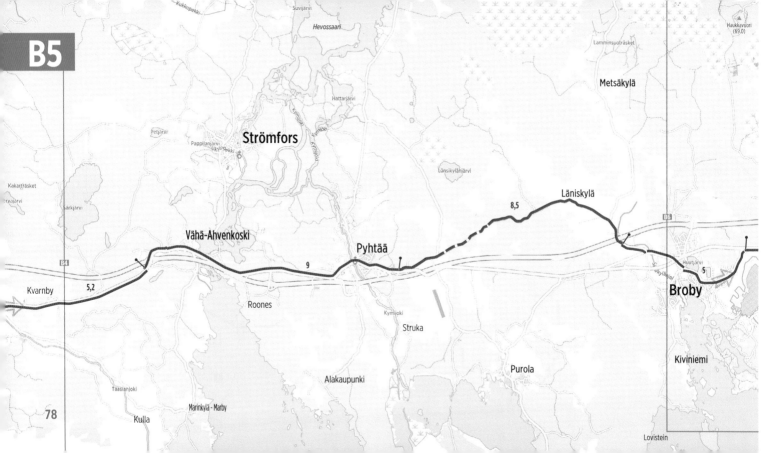

B5

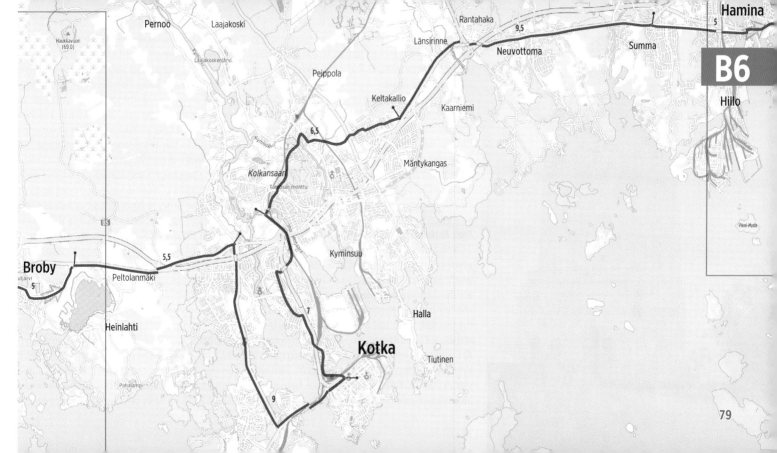

Kotka Lighthouse

Finland. Its history begins as a Russian fortress, which was destroyed by the British in the Crimean War in 1855. During the Second World War, large parts of the city were destroyed again.

Among the sights worth seeing are the lighthouse, the new town hall from 1934, the Orthodox church from 1795, the imperial fishing hut built in 1889 in Langinkoski Park for Tsar Alexander III as well as the Maretarium. Kotka port is also home to Tarmo, the world's oldest preserved icebreaking ship. The Arto Tolsa Areena was opened in 1952 and hosted four football matches during the 1952 Olympics.

From Kotka to Hamina   28 km

Coming from the station, turn left into **Kotkantie**, on which you cross the river Kivisalmi. Follow this road, which turns into **Huumantie** after crossing road 15 twice and then later into **Kymintie**. Just before the river Kymijoki, turn right into **Kantinkuja**, on which you cross the river Kymijoki. Then, turn right, cross the railway tracks and you will get to **Kaurankatu**, into which you turn left. At the end, turn left into **Kalevantie** and then right into **Kymintie** and cross the river Kymijoki again. Then turn sharply right into **Karhulantie**. Afterwards, turn left into **Virsumäentie** and cross the railway tracks. After crossing road 357, follow **Lautakatontie**. At the end, turn right into **Hüdenkirnuntie** and then left into road **170**.

The road to Hamina has very little traffic as it runs parallel to the motorway. Continue on a nice bike path far away from road 170. The route takes you closer to road 170 again, crosses over the motorway and then continues on a separate bike path. After crossing the railway tracks, turn left behind the second bridge into **Maariankatu** and you will get to Hamina town centre.

Hamina (Swedish Fredrikshamn)

The port town of Hamina has 20,000 inhabitants. Its location used to be the site of the town of Vehkalahden. Vehkalahden was built in the Renaissance style on the old King's Road in 1653. The fan-shaped road network started from an octagonal square, where the town hall dating from 1797 still stands today. After the fire of 1840 it was redesigned in the Neoclassical style and a tower was built.

When Vyborg fell to Russia in 1721 during the Great Nordic War, Sweden began to transform the town into a fortress. It was renamed Fredrikshamn by King Fredrik I, which the inhabitants of the region abbreviated to Hamina. Sweden also had to cede this town to Russia in 1742, following which Loviisa became the new border town. In 1809, the Treaty of Hamina reunited the eastern

territories conquered by Russia, including Hamina, with the rest of Finland.

Hamina is one of the most beautiful cities in southern Finland. The 15th century stone Church of St. Mary is the oldest building in the region. It received a Neoclassical facade during renovation works in 1820. Today, the building has a church museum attached to it. The Orthodox church Peter and Paul was built between 1832 and 1837 as a garrison church for Russian soldiers. It has a striking dome and was designed after a round temple. St. John's Church opposite the town hall was built in 1843 and has the shape of a Greek temple. Before the church was built, this was the site of the fortress commander's house, in which Treaty of Hamina was signed in 1809. There is a memorial stone next to the church commemorating this event.

Hamina Bastion was built from 1801 to 1811, with 58 bulletproof rooms. Today, the bastion is an event location and is used for tourist purposes.

From Hamina to Vaalimaa   44 km

Continue from the town centre southbound on **Maari-ankatu** and then turn left into **Merikatu**. The route does not continue on King's road but turns right into **Siltakatu**. At the end, turn right and then left into **Ristiniementie**,

which turns into **Kartanontie**. This is easy to travel on, with only a few exceptions.

Then, turn right into **Vilniementie** and then right again into road **3513**, which takes you to **Ravijoki** via **Mäntylahti** and **Klamila**.

TIP You can turn left here into Hovintie and you will reach Harjun Hovi, where you can go for a bite to eat and stay overnight. You can also visit the bunker complex of the Salpa Line here. This is descried in Miehikkälä on page 66.

The road on the lakeside continues on King's road to Virolahti, where the two EuroVelo Routes EV 10 and EV 13 meet. They are identical along the Baltic Sea coast.

Virolahti

From Virolahti, continue for three kilometres on road **7** and you will reach Vaalimaa.

Vaalimaa border crossing

With over two million border crossings per year, this is Finland's most frequently used and also the largest and most important direct border crossing point between an EU country and Russia. Near the checkpoint you will find Rajahovi Shopping Centre, where you can stop for refreshments and buy travel equipment.

From Vaalimaa to Vyborg   61 km

Once you have crossed the border, follow road E 18 for 19 kilometres until you reach Kondratyevo (Кондратьево). The further you get away from the border, the more the traffic increases. Alternatively, you can continue the journey on a 1.5-metre-wide gravel side strip.

The history of Russia

With 17 million km^2, the Russian Federation as the successor state of the Soviet Union is the largest country in the world in terms of area. Geographically, approximately 4 million km^2 are located west of the Ural mountain range in Europe and 13 million km^2 east of it in Asia. Today, Russia has 143 million inhabitants, has nuclear weapons, is a permanent member of the UN Security Council and is one of the G8 states.

The first East Slavonic state, the Kiev Rus, was founded at the end of the 9th century and was Christianised shortly before the end of the first millennium. After its disintegration in the 12th century and foreign – mainly Mongolian – rule, Ivan IV was crowned as the first "tsar of the entire Rus" in 1574. Furthermore, Siberia was conquered and the empire was subsequently extended to the Pacific Ocean.

Under Peter the Great (1672-1725) and Catherine the Great (1729-1796) Russia opened itself towards Western Europe. It continued pursuing a policy of expansion and extended its sphere of influence to the Black Sea coast. Napoleon's troops invaded the country in 1812 and managed to reach Moscow. However, after the French troops had suffered a devastating defeat, Russia was subsequently able to maintain its position as a major power.

Industrialisation was advanced in the cities, but in the countryside the feudal structures remained, which led to riots and unrest in the middle of the 19th century. However, despite this, Tsar Nicholas II was not prepared to carry out democratic reforms at the beginning of the 20th century.

After the defeat in the Russian-Japanese war (1904-1905), the mass demonstration on Bloody Sunday in 1905, during which hundreds of demonstrators were killed and thousands injured, Tsar Nicholas II had to approve Duma parliament, yet did not give it many powers. Shortly afterwards, he dissolved it again.

After initial successes in the First World War (1914-1918), especially against Austria-Hungary and the Ottoman Empire, the Russian front collapsed in 1917 after a gruelling position war with Germany. The discontent of the population and the desolate supply situation led to demonstrations from workers and farmers. After the

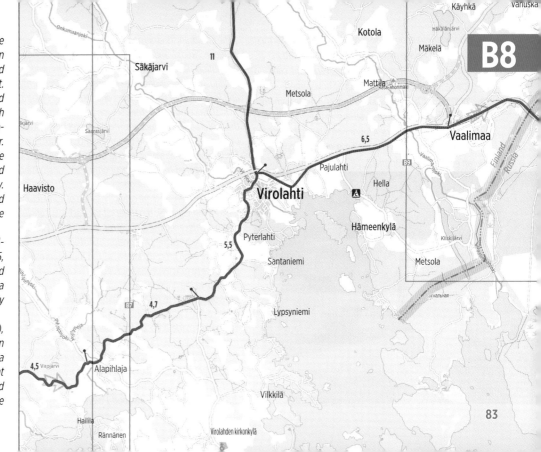

bloody suppression of the demonstrators, they stormed the Winter Palace and forced the tsar's abdication.

In February 1917 a provisional government came to power, which consisted of a dual government of the "provisional" bourgeois government (with the participation of the Mensheviks as well as social revolutionaries) and the Soviet workers. A few months later, the October Revolution led by Lenin, Trotsky and the Bolsheviks put an end to this government.

War Memorial at Sestoresk

The Communists emerged as victors from the civil war between "Reds" and "Whites" following the October Revolution. Estonia, Latvia and Lithuania, as well as Finland, won their independence against the Red Army and Russia lost parts of Belarus and Ukraine to Poland.

On 30 December 1922, the decision was made to merge the Soviet Socialist Republics into the Soviet Union. After Lenin's death in 1924 and the ensuing power struggle, Stalin emerged as victor, taking out his opponents by way of targeted terror. The economy was transformed through wide-spread nationalisation, the introduction of five-year plans and the collectivisation of agriculture.

On 23 August 1939, the Hitler-Stalin Pact was concluded, which is called the Ribbentrop-Molotov Pact in Eastern Europe after the two foreign ministers who signed it. In the treaty, officially known as the "non-aggression pact", the two dictators had agreed in a secret additional protocol to the division of Eastern Europe. This enabled the Soviet Union to re-annex Eastern Poland, the Baltic States as well as Bessarabia.

The Pact made it easier for Hitler to invade Poland a mere week later, on 1 September 1939. On 28 April 1939, he had unilaterally terminated the non-aggression pact concluded with Poland in 1934. On 17 September 1939, despite the non-aggression pact concluded with Poland in 1932, the Red Army invaded Poland from the east.

They met the German Wehrmacht in the middle of the country at the agreed demarcation line and both held a joint victory parade.

On 22 June 1941, Nazi Germany broke the "non-aggression pact" and invaded the Soviet Union, which lost about 10 million soldiers and as many civilians during the Second World War, which it called the "Great Patriotic War". A large part of the areas conquered by the Germans were devastated. It was not until the German troops had nearly reached Moscow that it was possible to stop their advance. They were finally defeated in the winter of 1942/43 at Stalingrad and in the summer of 1943 at Kursk.

Despite their differences in ideology, the USA, Great Britain and the USSR agreed on an anti-Hitler coalition as well as a joint alliance against Nazi Germany. Already during the war, they had decided that after its defeat, Germany should be divided into different zones of occupation and administered by the three victorious powers. The fourth occupying power, France, only joined the alliance after the Yalta Conference in February 1945.

In May 1945, Soviet troops conquered Berlin. After the end of the war, Japanese territories in the Far East and the northern part of East Prussia (Kaliningrad) also fell to the Soviet Union. Shortly after the end of the war, tensions started growing between the Western Allies and the Soviet Union. These tensions culminated in the Cold War between NATO on the one hand and the Warsaw Pact countries on the other.

Due to the fact that the governments of the Warsaw Pact countries were unwilling to grant political liberties and proved incapable of solving the economic problems, repeated revolts arose. The demonstrations in the GDR on 17 June 1953 were the first popular uprising in the Soviet sphere of influence after the Second World War. This was followed in 1956 by the Poznan demonstrations in Poland in June and in October of the same year by the Hungarian revolution, in 1968 by the Prague Spring in Czechoslovakia, in 1970 by the workers' uprising in Poland, Charter 77 in Czechoslovakia and in 1980 by the Solidarność movement in Poland with 10 million members, four times as many as the Polish Communist Party.

The reform of the Soviet Union based on the principles of Glasnost (openness) and Perestroika (reconstruction) started in 1985 after Mikhail Gorbachev had come to power. However, the reforms were too late. The activities of the Solidarność trade union, the successful orientation of the Hungarians towards the West, the independence movements in the Baltic States known as the "Singing Revolution", the "Velvet Revolution" in Czechoslovakia, the growing opposition movement in the GDR and the dismantling of the barbed wire at the Hungarian-Austrian

border by the two foreign ministers Guyla Horn and Alois Mock on 27 June 1989, were all factors that contributed fall of the Berlin Wall on 9 November 1989 and with it the end of the Iron Curtain in Europe.

A coup in Moscow in August 1991 was directed against the impending disintegration of the Soviet Union and the Warsaw Pact. After it was clear that it had failed, the President of the Russian Soviet Republic, Boris Yeltsin, announced the dissolution of the Soviet Union on 31 December 1991 and accepted, among other things, the independence of Estonia, Latvia and Lithuania. The Russian Federation became the successor state of the Soviet Union, with Boris Yeltsin as its president.

In 1993, Yeltsin cleared the way for neo-liberal reforms as well as a new constitution with a two-chamber parliamentary system, free elections and a strong president. Despite this, the Russian economy collapsed and only improved in 2000 after Vladimir Putin took office, although he curtailed many democratic achievements through his policy of "controlled democracy".

After his second term in office – Putin was not allowed to run for office again – Dmitri Medvedev became the new president and Putin took over as head of government. At the presidential elections in 2012, Putin was allowed to run again and was re-elected as president.

Monument of the 60th anniversary of the end of the war in St. Petersburg

The Hitler-Stalin Pact

In the document referred to as the "Secret Additional Protocol" to the Hitler-Stalin Pact, the German Reich and the USSR discussed "the issue of the demarcation of both spheres of interest in Eastern Europe". In it, the two totalitarian dictatorships, which until then had been absolute enemies and, indirectly, war opponents in the Spanish Civil War, agreed on the demarcation of their interests. Among other things, they agreed on the following:

"In the event of a territorial-political re-design of the areas belonging to the Baltic States (Finland, Estonia, Latvia, Lithuania), the northern border of Lithuania will also serve as the border of the spheres of interest of Germany and the USSR. In doing so, Lithuania's interest in the Vilnius region is recognised on both sides."

For neighbouring Poland, which had only been re-established as a state in 1918, a further division was agreed upon:*"In the event of a territorial-political re-design of the area belonging to the Polish state, the spheres of interest of Germany and the USSR end at the line created by the rivers Pissa, Narev, Vistula and San."*. According to Bertolt Brecht, this was the *"fourth division"* of Poland.

For decades, the Pact and its consequences could not be publicly mentioned, and the Soviet Union denied the existence of a secret additional protocol for decades. It was only when Mikhail Gorbachev was in power that its existence was admitted to.

In April 2009, the European Parliament decided to set up a pan-European memorial day to commemorate the Hitler-Stalin Pact. In 2009, on the occasion of its 70th anniversary, Marianne Birthler, Rainer Eppelmann, Joachim Gauck and many others published the following declaration in Germany, which was also very well received in Eastern Central Europe:*"Celebrating the year of 1989 means remembering the year of 1939".*

Declaration on the occasion of the 70th anniversary of the Hitler-Stalin Pact

"In these weeks and months, people throughout Europe remember Communist dictatorships being overcome in Central and Eastern Europe 20 years ago. Celebratory events and conferences, exhibitions and films recall the spirit of the many citizens who, with their peaceful protests, not only overcame the dictatorships but also created the conditions for establishing democracy and for overcoming the division of Europe and Germany. At the beginning of this division and the communist rule in Central and Eastern Europe, which lasted for over four decades, was the Second World War. And so we remember with shame and sorrow the 1st of September 70 years ago, when Nazi Germany invaded Poland. Eight days earlier, Germany and the Soviet Union had concluded the unfortunate "Hitler-Stalin Pact", with which the two totalitarian dictatorships had agreed on a division of the Baltic states and Poland, Finland and Romania among themselves. The invasion of Poland by Germany and the Soviet Union in September 1939 was the start of an unprecedented war of conquest and annihilation. With this war, Germany brought immense suffering to its neighbours throughout Europe, namely in Poland and finally also in the Soviet Union.

After the liberation of Europe and Germany from National Socialism, the people of all European countries were hoping for a future of freedom and democracy. However, this hope was soon shattered for many. In the Eastern Central European states weakened by war and Nazi rule as well as in parts of Germany, the Soviet Union imposed new dictatorial regimes: with devastating consequences for society, for the economy and culture and for countless people who were persecuted as political opponents or lost their lives because they stood in the way of those in power. And so the Germans not only bear a heavy burden of responsibility for the extermination of the European Jews, the persecution and murder of the Sinti and Roma, homosexuals, the disabled, those declared to be anti-social as well as political dissidents and the millions of people who fell victim to the war. We are painfully aware that without the Second World War, which was started by Germany, there would have been neither the communist dictatorships in Central and Eastern Europe nor the division of the continent and Germany.

Today, in 2009, when we look back on the history of Europe and Germany in the 20th century, we do so in the light of the calamity that was the Nazi rule, and we are glad that Germany is today an equal and respected member of the European family of nations.

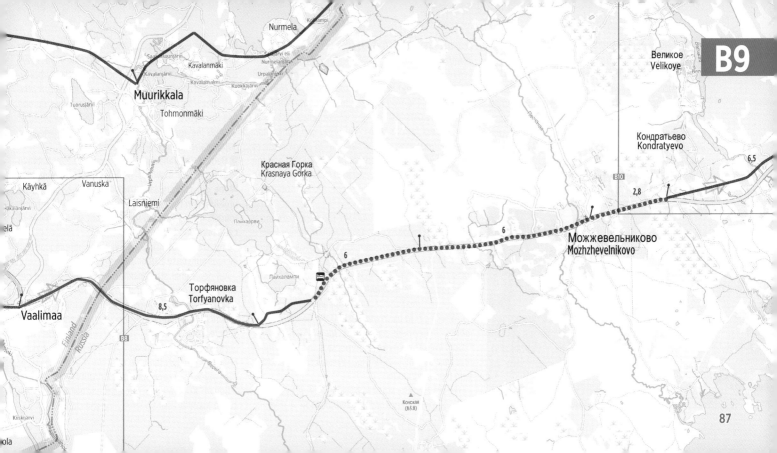

Nurmela

Великое
Velikoye

Kavalanmäki

Muurikkala

Tohmonmäki

Кондратьево
Kondratyevo

6,5

Красная Горка
Krasnaya Gorka

Käyhkä

Vanuska

2,8

Laisniemi

6

6

Можжевельниково
Mozhzhevelnikovo

Торфяновка
Torfyanovka

6

8,5

Vaalimaa

Конская
(65.8)

At the same time, we remember with gratitude and respect the people who, in the four decades after 1945, at great risk for themselves, had the courage to repeatedly challenge the communist dictators and to stand up for freedom and democracy. Quite a few paid for their courage with their lives. The revolts and freedom movements in the GDR, in Hungary, in Czechoslovakia and repeatedly in Poland, maintained people's hope for freedom and democracy over decades.

We will not forget that it was above all Polish people who first started to demolish parts of the communist

Old country lane parallel to the E 18

system of power for their as well as our freedom. We also thank the supporters of Charter 77, who encouraged us to live knowing the truth. We also remember all those who cleared the way for democracy in Hungary and opened the Iron Curtain in the summer of 1989. Long before Glasnost and Perestroika, Soviet dissidents campaigned for the protection of human rights. And last – but not least - we would like to thank those in the West who never accepted the Iron Curtain and the Communist dictatorships, and who insisted that human rights be respected and who supported the opposition to the regimes.

With their Peaceful Revolutions, the people of Central and Eastern Europe regained the freedom, independence and self-determination they had lost five decades before. These revolutions were the decisive factor in overcoming the division of Europe and Germany. When we went towards German unity after overcoming the SED dictatorship, the trust of our European neighbours was a precious gift to us. In the wake of the Peaceful Revolutions, all Germans can now for the first time in their history live in freedom and democracy, in prosperity, in recognised borders and in mutual respect and friendship with their neighbours.

Like 1939, 1989 - albeit in a somewhat different way - has become a year of European destiny. A free and

democratic Europe must be aware of its history. We need to remember the Communist era and how it was overcome. A first step has been made: in April, the European Parliament committed itself to this responsibility for the first time. This path now needs to be continued: Europe needs an active, responsible culture of remembrance that ensures the next generations are sensitive to emerging authoritarian and dictatorial developments."

TIP Behind Torfyanovka (Торфяновка) and Kondratyevo (Кондратьево) it would be possible to continue on the old country lane. However, this is said to be prohibited in this "border region". On the other hand, tourists have also been told that they were allowed to cycle here but not stop.

You will reach Kondratyevo by continuing on the increasingly busy **E 18** or on the old country lane.

Auf der immer stärker befahrenen **E 18** oder auf der alten Landstraße erreicht man Kondratjewo.

Kondratyevo (Кондратьево)

Until 1940, a church designed by the Finnish-German architect Johann Engel (who studied together with Schinkel) stood here, which fell victim to bombing in February 1940. Today, the only thing that remains of the church is an overgrown pile of rubble.

Behind Kondratyevo it is also unclear whether the seven-kilometres-long stretch on the old country lane

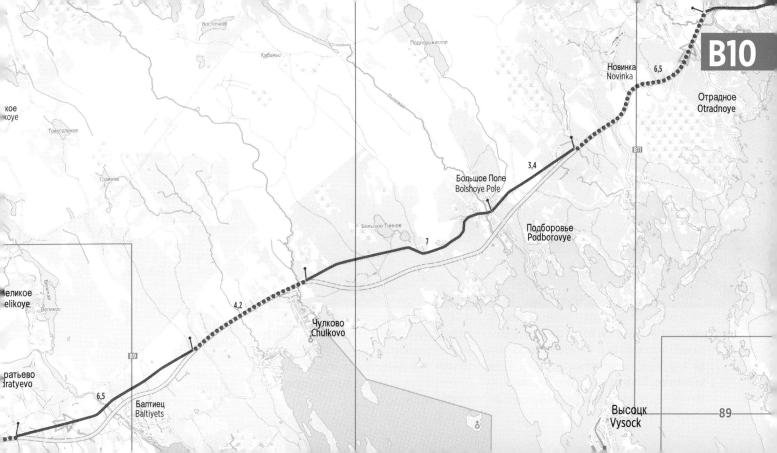

Восточнов

Кабанье

Подпорожистое

Подборжистое

Новинка
Novinka

6,5

Отрадное
Otradnoye

Треугольное

Травное

B11

Большое Поле
Bolshoye Pole

3,4

Большое Тинное

7

Подборовье
Podborovye

кое
коое

Ееликое
elikoye

Ееликос

4,2

Чулково
Chulkovo

ратьево
ratyevo

89

6,5

Балтиец
Baltiyets

Высоцк
Vysock

Castle in Vyborg

can be used. For the four kilometres after this, there is no alternative to the busy **E 18**. Behind **Chulkovo (Чулково)**, turn left after crossing the river onto the paved path with hardly any traffic. This will take you back to the E 18 after 10 kilometres. Turn right in **Seleznyovo (Селезнёво)**, cross the river Seleznevka (Селезнёвка) as well as the side arm of the Baltic Sea – note that the bridge has a bike path but the access has been blocked off – and turning left and continuing along the water you will reach the station, from where you can take direct trains to St. Petersburg. Continue straight on to reach the town centre and the beautiful old town of Vyborg.

Vyborg (Выборг)

The city of Vyborg with its 80,000 inhabitants is located in the historical Karelia region between St. Petersburg and the Finnish border. Founded in the Middle Ages by the Swedes, it was an important trading town with close ties to the Hanseatic League, which changed hands several times throughout the ages. In 1710, Tsar Peter I conquered the city, but 100 years later, his successors had to hand it over again to the newly established Grand Duchy of Finland, to serve as its capital. Until the Russian Revolution (1917), Vyborg, which at that time already had 50,000 inhabitants, was home to Finns, Swedes and Russians, many of whom were highly educated. It was the second largest city in the newly independent Finland until the Second World War.

After the Winter War (1939-1940) and the Continuation War (1941-1944), Vyborg fell to the Soviet Union. The German minority living in Vyborg since the time of the Hanseatic League had to leave the city in 1940, together with the Finnish and Swedish inhabitants or faced being expelled after 1944.

Today, visitors can see evidence of the city's changing history in its beautiful buildings and variety in architectural styles. Vyborg castle is located on a small island and was built in 1293 by Sweden as a stronghold. It is the only one of its kind in Russia. In its interior, you will find a museum of the history of the region and the castle tower offers great views over the city.

The street scene appears very "un-Russian", especially in the old town. Most of the buildings date back to the 16th and 17th century, why is why the dominant architectural style is Swedish-Finnish. A stroll through the small streets of the medieval European old town is well worth it. In addition to baroque and classicist buildings, there are also buildings of the "Nordic Art Nouveau" style, such as Pionerskaya Street (Пионерская ул.), which starts from the square of the same name.

Vyborg is also the location of Friedrich Murnau's silent film classic "Nosferatu", a genre pioneer of the vampire/horror film (1922). In order to avoid copyright problems with the original "Dracula", Murnau changed the setting. Therefore, the film is not about Vyborg, but about "Visborg" and the terror and plague that Nosferatu brought to the city.

Another interesting site are the defence facilities, that received their latest extensions in 1547-1550. The complex also includes the round tower "Fat Katharina", which is located at the market square and which today has a restaurant. The city library was built in 1927-1935 by Alvar Aalto.

In 1937, the Finnish diplomat Martti Ahtisaari was born in Vyborg (Viipuri). He served as the President of Finland from 1994-2000. Ahtisaari was awarded the Nobel Peace Prize in 2008 for his long-standing efforts to resolve international conflicts.

This very attractive harbour town is situated on a peninsula with several bays. It is also the starting point of the 1224-kilometre-long Baltic Sea pipeline, which was completed in 2011 and supported by former German Chancellor Gerhard Schröder. According to Vladimir Putin, it is "our window to Europe" and transports Russian gas directly to Greifswald in Germany.

From the railway station there are direct trains to Helsinki and Kouvola – with connections to St. Petersburg.

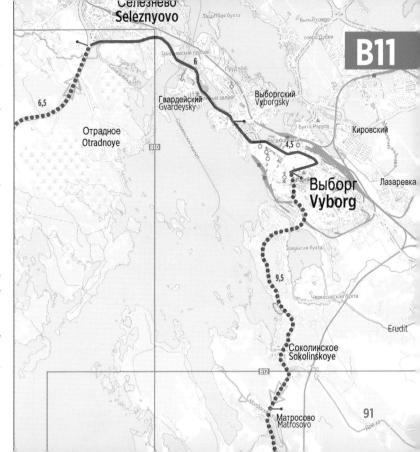

Jean Sibelius

Jean Sibelius (1865-1957) was born Vyborg, which was part of Finland at the time. He studied in Berlin and Vienna and is considered Finland's most important composer. His music style was shaped by the transition from late Romanticism to Modernity. Sibelius is one of the few who also became famous beyond the borders of his home country. He mainly became famous for his violin concerto in D minor and his symphonic poems, in which he included themes from old Finnish tales and mythology. His "Valse triste" became world famous.

With his musical poem Finlandia, which he composed in 1899 and which is considered to be the "secret national anthem" of Finland, he made a musical contribution to the identity of a Finland striving towards independence - from the Russian supremacy and the Swedish cultural hegemony. Along with the historical developments, the pieces turned from a battle song for the liberation movement into a victory anthem. Sibelius' Karelia Suite is also played very often.

Of great importance are also his seven symphonies, which are characterised by a high degree of transparency in spite of their high musical density, an abrupt nature, unconventional rhythm and melodic pathos.

From Vyborg to Primorsk   47 km

Coming from the station, continue on **Leningradskiy Prospect** (Ленинградский пр.) and then turn left into **Krepostnaya** (Крепостная ул.), which turns into **Gagarina** (Гагарина). After a left bend you will reach **Primorskaya** (Приморская), into which you turn right. Cross the railway tracks and then the river and you will find yourself on the busy **A 123**, which only has a small gravelled strip on the side.

Behind **Sokolinskoye** (Соколинское) in **Matrosovo** (Матросово), cross the waterway (Matrosovka).

After crossing the railway tracks at the station in Matrosovo, the traffic significantly decreases thanks to the new road.

Soldiers' cemetery at Primorsk

In **Sovetsky (Советский)**, turn right onto the well-developed bike path, cross underneath the railway tracks and then continue on a great bike path, that is a good distance away from the road, towards the town centre. You can go for a bite to eat at Johannes bar.

From the centre, continue towards Primorsk, then turn right onto the main road and then right again at a heliport and follow the signs towards Primorsk (Приморск). Continue parallel to the railway tracks on a quiet road and you will reach Primorsk, where you can go shopping, stay overnight and have a bite to eat.

Primorsk (Приморск)

The town of Primorsk with its 6,000 inhabitants is a Russian coastal town with the largest oil loading port in the Baltic Sea. Since 2001, it has been the western endpoint of the Baltic pipeline system, where four oil tankers can be loaded simultaneously.

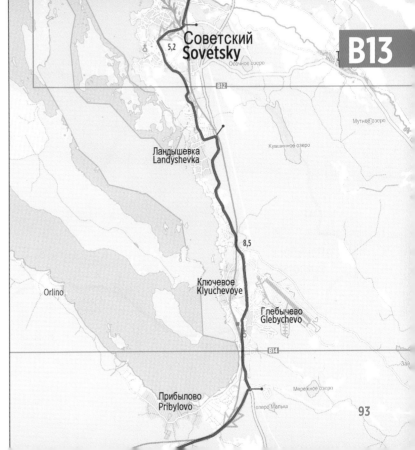

Манола
Manola

СТ Ручеек
ST Rucheyek

Прибылово
Pribylovo

4,7

6,5

Приморск
Primorsk

7

Карасевка
Karasevka

4

Ермилово
Yermilovo

5,2

Малышево
Malyshevo

Балтийское
Baltiyskoye

The town was first mentioned in 1268 in a Russian chronicle under the name of Beryozovskoye. Until the Second World War, the town was known as Koivisto and belonged to the independent Finland.

Opposite the harbour are the Birch Islands ("Beryosovsiye ostrova"), a bird sanctuary which falls under the Ramsar Convention. The church built in 1902-1904 by the architect Josef Stenbäck is also worth seeing.

From Primorsk to Zelenogorsk 78 km

Follow the quiet **A 123**, which runs parallel to the railway line. Along this stretch, you can frequently see the Baltic Sea through the trees. There are some beautiful spots for breaks along here. You will pass some monuments commemorating the Winter War and the dead. After crossing the river Gumalelninachti, turn right and continue on the A 123, which is busier along this stretch. Just before **Ozerki (Озерки)** you can have a bite to eat and stay overnight at the Baltic Sea beach. In the village, where you can also go shopping, there is a church and a war memorial.

The administrative district of St Petersburg starts 16 kilometres before Zelenogorsk. Traffic increases here but the former capital built a paved bike path here. This takes you along the road through the forest and is very comfortable to travel on. You will pass a big memorial side commemorating the Leningrad blockade and you will reach Zelenogorsk town centre.

Zelenogorsk (Зеленогорск)

Following the expansion of the railway line between St. Petersburg and Vyborg, Zelenogorsk, with its 12,000 inhabitants, has become a spa resort for wealthy people

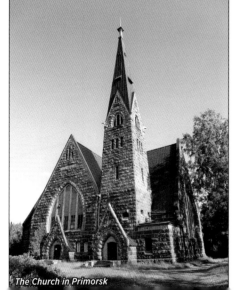

The Church in Primorsk

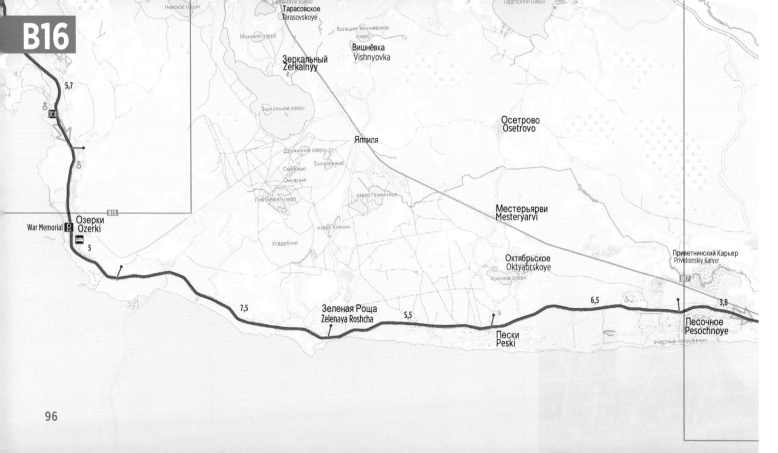

5,7

Тарасовское
Tarasovskoye

Большое Вишнёвое озеро

Вишнёвка
Vishnyovka

Зеркальный
Zerkalnyy

Осетрово
Osetrovo

Яппиля

Местерьярви
Mesteryarvi

Приветнинский Карьер
Privetninskiy Karyer

B15

Озерки
Ozerki

War Memorial

5

Октябрьское
Oktyabrskoye

B17

7,5

Зеленая Роща
Zelenaya Roshcha

5,5

6,5

3,8

Пески
Peski

Песочное
Pesochnoye

очистные сооружения

Ильичёво

Рощино
Roshchino

Красавица

Решетниково
Reshetnikovo

Сопки
Sopki

СТ Сосновая Поляна
ST Sosnovaya Polyana

Серово
Serovo

Ушково
Ushkovo

Зеленогорск
Zelenogorsk

Комарово
Komarovo

Молодежное
Molodyozhnoye

8,5

8

Смолячково
Smolyachkovo

8

B18

3,8

Песочное
Pesochnoye

Приветнинское
Privetninskoye

B16

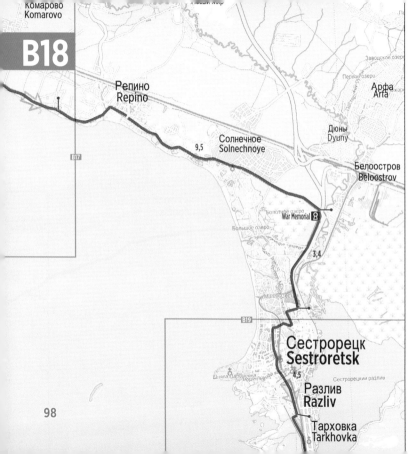

Комарово
Komarovo

Новый Мир

Репино
Repino

Заводское озеро

Перине озеро

Арфа
Arfa

B17

9,5

Солнечное
Solnechnoye

Дюны
Dyuny

Белоостров
Beloostrov

Болотное озеро

War Memorial 🎑

Большое озеро

3,4

Миллеевка

B19

Сестрорецк
Sestroretsk

Шляпа Наполеона

4,5

Сестрорецкий разлив

Разлив
Razliv

Тарховка
Tarkhovka

Warrior memorial at Sestoresk

living in the Gulf of Finland. The "Green City", which is the meaning of the name in English, is growing steadily and profits in terms of its economy and above all in terms of tourism from neighbouring Finland, to which it once belonged - like the whole region.

The famous beach is highly recommended for a swim in the summer and offers various hotels as well as the most natural and cheapest form of accommodation, as camping is allowed on the beach.

From Zelenogorsk to St. Petersburg 56 km

Follow the **A 123** and you will reach **Repino (Репино)**, where you can have something to eat and stay overnight. You will come across a monument in honour of the Russian painter Ilya Repin (1844 – 1930). The route takes you past numerous parks and through **Solnechno-ye (Солнечное)**. After crossing the former Finnish-Soviet border you will reach the **E 18**, into which you turn right and

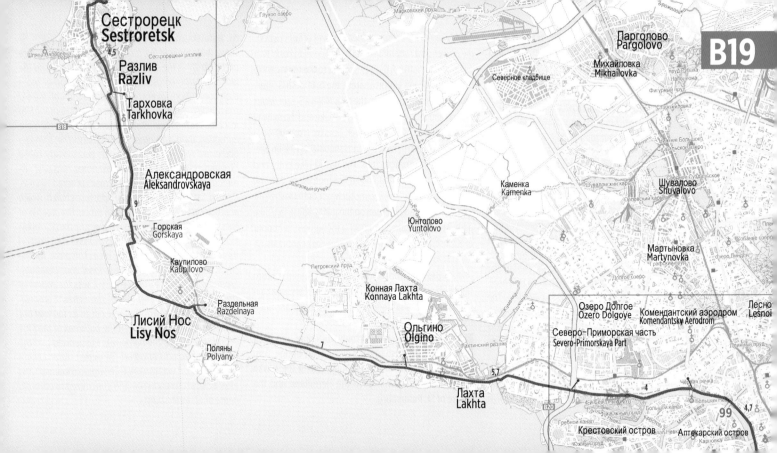

Сестрорецк
Sestroretsk

4,5

Разлив
Razliv

Тарховка
Tarkhovka

B18

Александровская
Aleksandrovskaya

9

Горская
Gorskaya

Каупилово
Kaupilovo

Раздельная
Razdelnaya

Лисий Нос
Lisy Nos

Поляны
Polyany

7

Парголово
Pargolovo

Михайловка
Mikhailovka

Северное кладбище

Каменка
Kamenka

Шувалово
Shuvalovo

Юнтолово
Yuntolovo

Мартыновка
Martynovka

Конная Лахта
Konnaya Lakhta

Ольгино
Olgino

Озеро Долгое
Ozero Dolgoye

Комендантский аэродром
Komendantsky Aerodrom

Лесно
Lesnoi

Северо-Приморская часть
Severo-Primorskaya Part

5,7

Лахта
Lakhta

4

B20

99

4,7

Крестовский остров

Аптекарский остров

B19

continue on the bike path. Behind the war memorial and the cemetery, turn right onto the side street and you will reach Sestroretsk.

Sestroretsk (Сестроретск)

Tsar Peter the Great founded a new settlement in 1714, which was later given the name of Sestroretsk ("town on the river Sestra") after the river Sestra. In 1724, a weapons factory was built there, which was one of the leading arms manufacturers in the Russian Empire in the 19th century.

In the middle of the 19th century, Sestroretsk served as a military base during the Crimean War (1853-1856). From the late 19th century onwards, the surrounding area developed into a popular summer residence and recreation area due to its attractive location between the Gulf of Finland and extensive coniferous forests.

In 1925, Sestroretsk received city rights. During the Soviet era, sanatoriums and spa facilities were built here, which were also very popular among celebrities. The former arms factory has been known as the "Sestroretsk device factory" since 1918. Today, the city has 37,000 inhabitants and from the station there are direct trains to St. Petersburg and Vyborg.

The most famous sights of the city include Dubki Landscape Park, where Peter the Great built a summer residence at the beginning of the 18th century, as well as

the city cemetery with a number of graves of famous people as well as a funeral site from the Second World War

It is 35 kilometres from Sestroretsk to the town centre of St. Petersburg. Unfortunately, the bike path is interrupted in some areas. Cross the river Malaya Sestra (**Малая Сестра**) and then continue along the lake and the railway tracks. After crossing the river Gorskiy (**Горский**) on a narrow bike path behind the hard shoulder on the bridge, immediately turn right from the paved bike path, and before the slip road leading to the motorway. You will then cross underneath the motorway, continue straight into the side road and then on the joint pedestrian/bike path. The route takes you past a monument in honour of Kronstadt and in **Lisiy Nos (Лисий Нос)** continues on the paved bike path of the E 18.

Cross the river Yuntolovka (**Юнтоловка**) and then turn right behind the bridge into **Savushkina (Савушкина)**, on which you cross underneath the motorway and then reach the Nevka shores.

CENTRE In order to get to the old town, turn right into Neva after the Nevka estuary and over Liteiny bridge. Turn right behind the bridge, continue along the Nevka shoreline and you will reach the Hermitage and the centre of St. Petersburg.

St. Petersburg (Санкт-Петербург)

As a metropolis of five million inhabitants, the "Venice of the North" is the second-largest Russian city and the world's northernmost city with a population of more than one million. Rivers and canals run through the old town, which was declared a Unesco World Heritage Site in 1990. With its numerous nationalities, it feels more European than any other Russian city. The splendid boulevard Nevski Prospect, which was already called "Tolerance Prospect" during tsarist times, runs past numerous churches, including a German Lutheran, Finnish, Roman Catholic and Armenian Apostolic church, which are all located very close to each other. The steeple of Isaac Cathedral is still the tallest building in the city today.

St. Petersburg was built in 1703 by Peter the Great on 44 islands in the marshy Neva area. The plans for the city were drawn up based on rational considerations. From the 18th to the 20th century it was the capital of the Russian Empire and one of the richest European cities. However, it owes its name not to its founder but to the apostle Simon Peter. At the outbreak of the First World War (1914), the name was Russianised and the town was named Petrograd (Петроград). After Lenin's death (1924), it was renamed Leningrad (Ленинград) and after a close referendum in 1991, the city regained its old name of St. Petersburg.

Hermitage in St. Petersburg

The area was originally inhabited by Finno-Ugrian people. At the beginning of the 14th century, there were clashes between Sweden and Novgorod over the territory. Three centuries later, Nyenschanz Fortress and the settlement of Nyen were built by the ruling Swedes. After both were destroyed by Russian troops in 1656, the city's actual history began in 1703 with the construction of the Peter and Paul Fortress. Contrary to the commonly told founding myth that St. Petersburg had been built as a "capital from nothing", the city initially only had the function of keeping the Neva estuary under control.

Despite the swampy landscape and recurrent floods, Peter the Great chose the city as his new capital, as it was very well suited for the construction of a seaport and closer to Western Europe. Tens of thousands of serfs lost their lives in the construction of the city. The Russian aristocracy was obliged to move to St. Petersburg. In 1712, it became the capital city and remained so until 1918, with the exception of a five-year period (1727-1732). In the 18th century, the city

was expanded under the empresses Anna, Elisabeth and Catherine the Great and in 1861, serfdom was abolished. St. Petersburg was flourishing at the end of the 18th and during the first half of the 19th century, when the city grew rapidly.

The historical part of the city has hardly changed and in large parts still looks like it did during the tsarist era. The city centre with its 2,300 palaces, stately buildings and castles, became a UNESCO World Cultural Heritage Site.

St. Petersburg is also the city of "three revolutions": Bloody Sunday in 1905 as well as the February and October Revolutions of 1917. Those 10 days in October 1917 that began with the occupation of the Winter Palace made world history. As a result of the ensuing civil war the number of inhabitants dropped considerably, also due to the relocation of the capital to Moscow. In 1935, the transformation of Leningrad, as it was then known, began. However, this was interrupted by the Second World War. For 871 days, from 8 September 1941 to 27 January 1944, it was besieged by Hitler's henchmen by way of a hunger blockade – the longest any city in the world ever had to endure. More than a million civilians and as many soldiers died in the battles to liberate the city, not least due to temperatures of up to 30 degrees below Celsius in this unusually harsh winter.

After the war, reconstructions began in the city and in 1999 the urban area was significantly enlarged. In 2003, for the occasion of the city's 300th anniversary, most of the grand buildings and large parts of the old town were restored - including the Winter Palace, the main residence of the tsar's family, as well as the Hermitage, which houses one of the world's largest art collections. On 31 May 2003, German Chancellor Gerhard Schröder and Russian President Vladimir Putin formally opened the reconstructed Amber Room at Catherine's Palace to the public.

The Erarta, the largest non-governmental museum of contemporary art in Russia, opened its doors in 2010 with over 2,000 exhibits by more than 150 Russian artists. The Museum of the Great Socialist October Revolution was renamed the Museum of Political History.

St. Petersburg's Bloody Sunday

In the first few days of January 1905, a general strike struck the shipyards, factories and weaving mills. On 22 January, tens of thousands of workers from the suburbs of St. Petersburg gathered at the Winter Palace, the tsar's residence. They wanted to demonstrate peacefully for more humane working conditions, agricultural reforms, the abolition of censorship and religious tolerance and called for the creation of a people's representation.

Bike path along the Neva in St. Petersburg

However, in front of the Narva Gate they were stopped by soldiers shooting at the crowd, leaving hundreds dead and thousands injured.

Dimitri Shostakovich

Dimitri Shostakovich (1906-1975) was born in St. Petersburg and is the most important Russian composer, alongside Sergei Prokofiev and Igor Stravinsky. Having idealised the October Revolution in his youth, he soon became a victim of the arbitrary regime. The party praised him and threatened him, awarded prizes to his works and made them disappear from the fixtures, charged him with offices and took them away from him again. Cellist Mstislav Rostropovich saw a "secret history of Russia" in his works.

St. Petersburg

400 m

- Leningrad Zoo
- Cathedral of Saints Peter and Paul
- Peter and Paul Fortress
- The Kunstkammer
- Eremitage
- Admirality Building
- Saint Michael's Castle
- Church of Resurrection
- Russian Museum
- Fabergé Museum

Narva Arc de Triomphe in St. Petersburg

Shostakovich was on the black list ever since Stalin had personally visited his opera "Lady Mcbeth of Mzensk" in 1936 and had subsequently described this work as "chaos instead of music".

He wrote the "Leningrad Symphony", a masterpiece against war, terror and violence, in 1941 during the German siege of his city. This established him as the most important Russian symphony composer in the world. The conductor Karl Eliasberg performed this 7th symphony for the first time on 9 August 1942, while the city was under siege. He played it with 15 survivors of the radio orchestra and other musicians from military and other bands.

In his memoirs, Dimitri Shostakovich write:"I feel insatiable pain for all those Hitler has killed. But the thought of those murdered on Stalin's order does not cause me any less pain. I grieve for all those who were tortured, tormented, shot and starved. There were already millions of them in our country before the war against Hitler began [...] I have no objection to the Seventh being called the 'Leningrad' Symphony. But it's not about the blockade. It's about the Leningrad that Stalin ruined. Hitler only finished it off."

After Stalin's death in 1953, Shostakovich's 10th Symphony was used to settle a score with the dictator. According to the testimony of his son Maxim, in the second movement he describes "the terrible face of Stalin", but

Church of Christ's Resurrection in St. Petersburg

ends the symphony triumphantly with the personal letter motif of D-E major-C-H, analogous to the well-known B-A-C-H motif. In 1957, he gave his 11th Symphony in G minor the subtitle "The Year of 1905", commemorating St. Petersburg's Bloody Sunday.

From St. Petersburg to Tallinn

598 km

This part of the route first takes you along the Baltic Sea Coast to Peterhof, where you can really experience the history of Russia.

Bor nuclear power plant is located in a military restricted zone on the coastal strip east of Lomonosov. Locals are also only allowed to enter the area with a special permit. Further west you will only find the busy coastal road which cannot be recommended for cycling.

This is why the route is described from Peterhof towards Dubki (Дубки) via Krasnoye Selo (Красное Село) and away from the coast. From Dubki, the route continues along the Baltic Sea coast again and takes you to Narva, via Ust-Luga (Усть-Луга) and Kurgolovo (Курголово).

From Narva, EuroVelo Routes EV 10 and EV 13 take you to Tallinn. They always follow the coast and do not use shortcuts to avoid the individual "fingers" of the Estonian Baltic Sea coast.

From St. Petersburg to Peterhof — 43 km

Continue from the city centre along the river shore and across Liteiny bridge to the other side of the river. The river Neva flows from Lake Ladoga, the biggest fresh water lake in Europe that also has the most amount of water in it, through St. Petersburg and into the Gulf of Finland. Its surface is bigger than the land mass of Thuringia.

Peterhof Palace

Behind the bridge turn right onto the main route and you will pass **Finland station** (Финляндский вокзал) with the statue of Lenin. Continue along the Neva shore on a nice bike path – if only the road and bridge crossings were more suitable for bicycles and pedestrians. At times there are not even traffic signals. The state of the route is quite annoying as it leads across stairs or makes significant detours.

You will see **Smolny cathedral** (Смольный собор) at the other side of the river and then cross the river Neva just before the **Holy Trinity cathedral** (Троице-Исмайловский собор) on **Alexander-Newsky bridge** (мост Александра Невского). Behind the bridge, continue straight in the park of **Alexander chapel**, cross the river and then keep right. Continue past the long queues of visitors, cross the river again on a small bridge and then continue straight on. At the next traffic light, turn left, cross the canal and then turn right.

Continue on the bike path along the canal. The bike path is interrupted in some parts and you have to change sides. Cross underneath the railway bridges of **Moscow station** (Московский вокзал) and **Vitebsk station** (Витебский вокзал) and then continue past the **Church of Christ's Resurrection** (Храм Воскресения Христова) and **Warsaw station**. Behind **Baltic station** (Балтийский вокзал), follow the tram tracks to the left into **Staro-Petergofsky-**

Prospect (Старо-Петергофский пр.). Then, turn right behind the cloister courtyard and you will get to the **Narva Arc de Triomphe** (Нарвские Триумфальные ворота), which commemorates Russia's victory over Napoleon in 1812..

Cross underneath the motorway, stay on the road and just before the next bridge you will come across a monument in honour of Alexander Marinesko.

Alexander Marinesko

Alexander Ivanovich Marinesko (1913-1963) sunk the German passenger ships Gustloff and Steuben as a submarine commander shortly before the end of the Second World War. Their demise is considered to be the biggest shipping catastrophe, as more than than 12,000 people lost their lives, most of whom were refugees.

He wanted to be seen as a hero of the Soviet Union for sinking these ships. However, he did not succeed. Instead, he was dishonorably dismissed from the navy after the war, and later spent two years in prison for theft.

In 1990, Mikhail Gorbachev rehabilitated Marinesko and posthumously appointed him to be a hero of the Soviet Union. In Kaliningrad he was honoured by having a part of the Pregel shore named after him as well as with a memorial at the palace pond. Marinesko plays an important role in Günter Grass's novel "Im Krebsgang".

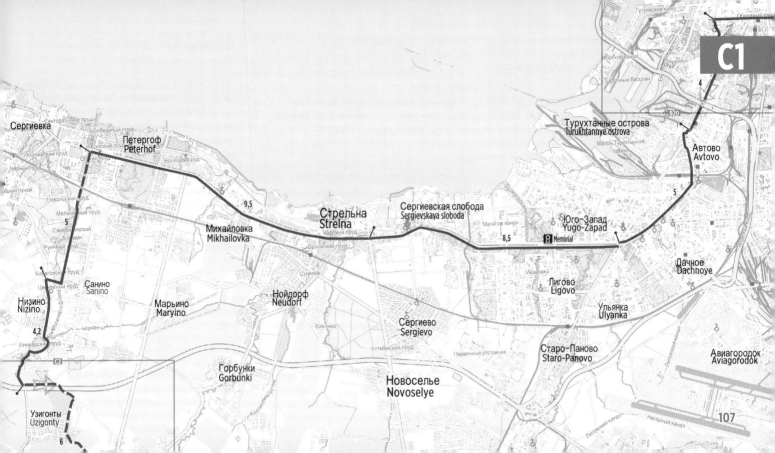

C1

Гутуевский ковш
Ольховый кан
Морской канал
В20
Барочный бассейн
Турухтанные острова
Turukhtannye ostrova
Малая Турухтанная
гавань
4
Автово
Avtovo
5
Юго-Запад
Yugo-Zapad
Дачное
Dachnoye
Сергиевская слобода
Sergievskaya sloboda
Матисов канал
8,5 Memorial
Лигово
Ligovo
Ульянка
Ulyanka
Стрельна
Strelna
9,5
Михайловка
Mikhailovka
Сергиево
Sergievo
Старо-Паново
Staro-Panovo
Авиагородок
Aviagorodok
Сергиевка
Петергоф
Peterhof
5
Санино
Sanino
Нойдорф
Neudorf
Новоселье
Novoselye
Низино
Nizino
Марьино
Maryino
Горбунки
Gorbunki
4,2
C2
Узигонты
Uzigonty
6

107

Pass **Kirovsky Zavod metro station** (Кировский завод), which looks more like a palace thanks to the columns lining the entrance. Afterwards, follow **Stachek Prospect** (пр. Стачек) until you get to the roundabout. Take the first exit on the right and then immediately turn left again into **Kronstadtskaya Ulitsa** (Кронштадтская ул.). Follow the tram tracks past the station and behind the bridge you will reach **Stachek Prospect** (пр. Стачек) again. You will see a monument on your left that has been built from an old tank of the Red Army.

Stay on the bike path of Stachek Prospect, which turns into **Petergofskoye Chaussee** (Петергофское шоссе), where there is a bike path is some distance away from the road. Continue past the lake, a war memorial and the park of Constantine's Palace and you will reach Strelna, where you will see a 24-hour supermarket on your left.

Strelna (Стрельна)

The first mention of this village dates back to 1500. The first palace was built in 1707 at the behest of Peter the Great and then extended by a magnificent park. Constantine Palace was built in 1720 by Italian architect Nicola Michetti. Strelna was one of the tsar's residences until the October Revolution of 1917.

During the Second World War, parts of the palace complex was destroyed by the German siege and many buildings were damaged. After the end of the war, *these damages were repaired and in 1990 the whole ensemble, together with Peterhof Castle and the old town of St. Petersburg, was recognised as a UNESCO World Heritage Site.*

Today, the palace serves as the residence of the Russian President in the region of St. Petersburg. In July 2008, Russia used the palace for a G8 summit. Eighteen luxurious villas were built next to the palace for the delegations of the participating countries. Today, a collection of Russian paintings from the 18th, 19th and 20th century is exhibited in the complex, including the famous collections of Rostropovich and Vishnevskaya.

At the start of the Peterhof area, the bike path ends and you have to continue on the dangerous **St. Peterburgskoye Chaussee** (Санкт-Петербургское ш.). Later, it is possible to use the bike path on the left side of the road and by continuing on the country lane you will reach the old **Tsar residency of Peterhof**, which is very popular among tourists from all over the world. Continue through the town on the main street and after 600 metres you will reach the famous grounds, that stretch from the area right of the main road all the way up to the coast. If you want to visit the grounds, turn right after you have passed the neo-byzantine church with the onion towers on your left.

The palace complex of the "Russian Versailles"

At the beginning of the 18th century, Tsar Peter I had a small country house built on the southern coast of the Gulf of Finland and after the victory over the Swedish army in 1709, it was converted into a residence. The construction began in 1714 and he engaged architects and artists from all over Europe, such as Andreas Schlüter, the Prussian architect of Berlin's city palace. The baroque-style palace was inaugurated in 1723. In particular, the Golden Cascade and a canal leading to the nearby Baltic Sea attracted a great deal of attention alongside the palaces of "Marly" and "Monplaisir". The tsar used the complex as a summer residence. After his death, they stood empty for five years before the palace was gradually extended by various tsaresses.

During the Second World War, German troops occupied Peterhof and destroyed the palace and the adjacent parks. In the post-war period, the complex was gradually restored, but it did not regain its full splendour until extensive restoration works were carried out on the occasion of the 300th anniversary of St. Petersburg (2003).

In Peterhof there is also a bicycle repair shop with good service, which is located in a monastery-like building made of red brick. Sanatori Petrodvorets (Санаторий Петродворец), ulitsa Avrova (ул. Аврова).

EXCURSION If you want to visit Lomonosov (Ломоно́сов), which is 10 kilometres away, follow St. Peterburgski Prospect (Санкт-Петербургское проспект) through Peterhof and past the right bend. You will pass a small lake en route. At the next intersection you will see a monument in a cage. It is in honour of those who died during the Second World War. You will also see some old Russian cannons there.

Stay on the country road and just before entering the town you will see a cemetery for those who fell during the Second World War. After a green and white church, you will reach the palace grounds.

Lomonosov (Ломоносов)

The UNESCO World Heritage Site of Lomonosov is located on a site donated by Peter the Great to his close advisor Aleksandr Danilovich Menshikov in 1707. Menshikov commissioned the architects Giovanni Maria Fontana and Gottfried Schädel to build a palace. The focus is on two spacious galleries. Over the course of time, several smaller buildings were built on the estate, including an imposing slide house and a Chinese-style pavilion. Unlike Peterhof, the estate was not taken over by German troops during the Second World War and was therefore considerably less severely damaged.

Bor nuclear power plant is located along a coastal strip in a military restricted zone. This is why the route continues to Narva via Krasnoye Selo, Dubki and Ust-Luga.

From Peterhof to Gostilitsi — 37 km

In Peterhof, turn left and and continue on the unpaved bike path on the western side along the canal. The path along the canal continues for around 8 kilometres along the supply canals of the palace grounds of Peterhof and through the forests. It is nearly entirely paved and is one of the highlights on the Russian part of **EuroVelo 10** and **EuroVelo 13**.

Cross the railway tracks, which is not too easy with your bike, and stay on the western side. Afterwards, continue on the paved bike path on the eastern side. Cross a road with a church on your right and then cycle through a few narrow barriers to cross a road with not many cars. Continue on the right side around the lake and you will reach the motorway. Due to the narrow pavement in this part you have to push your bike on the narrow pedestrian path along the canal underneath the motorway bridge. It is also possible to cross the motorway on the bridge left of the path.

Cross the canal on a small bridge with concrete slabs and then continue on the western side through beautiful river and forest scenery.

Canal path south of Peterhof

Cross a clearing in the forest with power lines and then cross through some private grounds next to a small lake.

Continue on a stony field path which is slightly tricky to travel on. You need to cycle uphill in order to reach the start of **Orzhitsy** (Оржицы). At an intersection with a red phone booth you will get to a country road, into which you turn right. After cycling uphill again, you will reach the town centre. You will find some smaller shops on your left. They are open until 10pm.

The route continues on the country road, which slightly bends left. After leaving the village you need to climb a short but steep hill. The country road continues through the village of **Vilpovitsy** (Вильповицы) and you will then

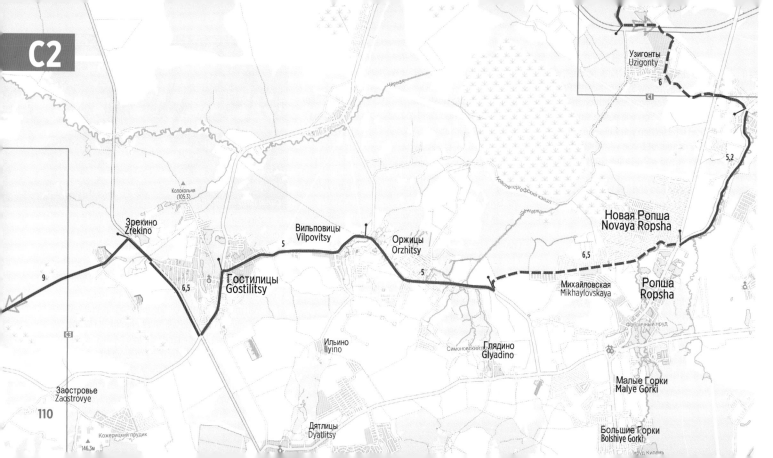

C2

Узигонты
Uzigonty

Новая Ропша
Novaya Ropsha

Зрекино
Zrekino

Вильповицы
Vilpovitsy

Оржицы
Orzhitsy

Михайловская
Mikhaylovskaya

Ропша
Ropsha

Гостилицы
Gostilitsy

Ильино
Ilyino

Глядино
Glyadino

Заостровье
Zaostrovye

Малые Горки
Malye Gorki

Дятлицы
Dyatlitsy

Большие Горки
Bolshiye Gorki

9

6,5

5

5

5,2

6,5

Колокольня
(105.3)

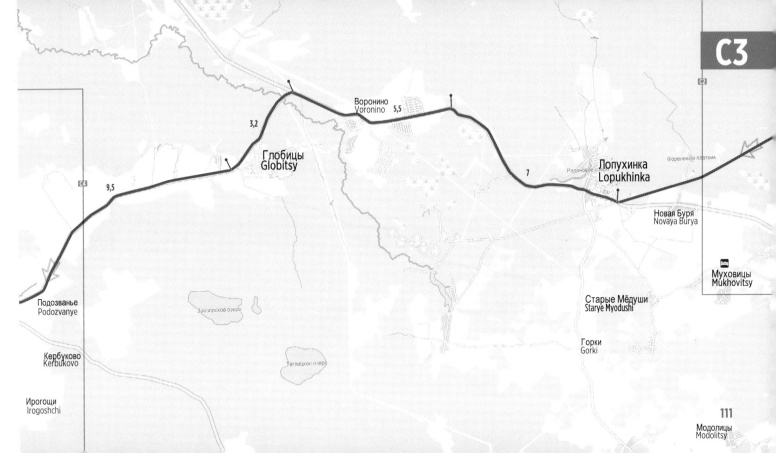

C2

C4

Воронино
Voronino 5,5

3,2

Глобицы
Globitsy

9,5

Подозванье
Podozvanye

Кербуково
Kerbukovo

Ирогощи
Irogoshchi

Заозерское озеро

Теглицкое озеро

7

Радоновое озеро

Форелевый плотник

Лопухинка
Lopukhinka

Новая Буря
Novaya Burya

Старые Мёдуши
Starye Myodushi

Горки
Gorki

Муховицы
Mukhovitsy

Модолицы
Modolitsy

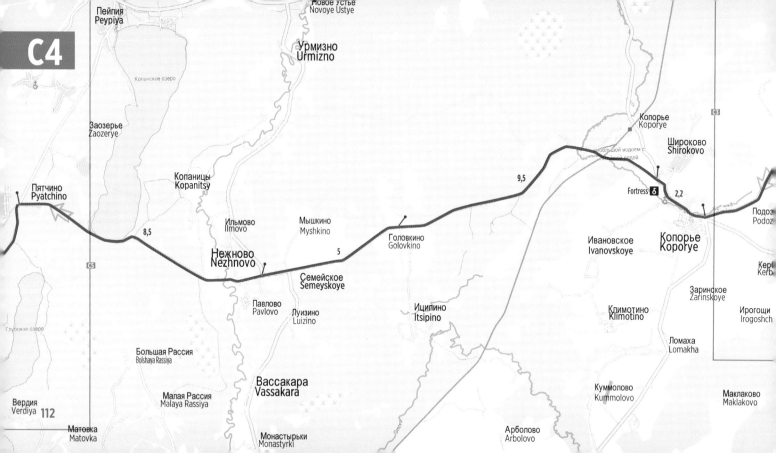

C4

Пейпия
Peypiya

Новое Устье
Novoye Ustye

Урмизно
Urmizno

Копорье
Koporye

Заозерье
Zaozerye

Широково
Shirokovo

наибольший водоём с
питьевой водой

Копаницы
Kopanitsy

Пятчино
Pyatchino

Fortress ♿ 2,2

9,5

Подоз
Podoz

Ильмово
Ilmovo

Мышкино
Myshkino

8,5

Головкино
Golovkino

Копорье
Koporye

Нежново
Nezhnovo

5

Ивановское
Ivanovskoye

Керб
Kerb

Семейское
Semeyskoye

Заринское
Zarinskoye

Павлово
Pavlovo

Луизино
Luizino

Иципино
Itsipino

Климотино
Klimotino

Ирогощи
Irogoshch

Большая Россия
Bolshaya Rassiya

Ломаха
Lomakha

Вассакара
Vassakara

Вердия
Verdiya 112

Малая Россия
Malaya Rassiya

Куммолово
Kummolovo

Маклаково
Maklakovo

Матовка
Matovka

Монастырьки
Monastyrki

Арболово
Arbolovo

reach **Gostilitsy (Гостилицы)**. Once there, you will get to road **P 35**, where you will find shops, a pharmacy and a monument in honour of those who died during the Second World War.

Gostilitsy (Гостилицы)

From Gostilitsy to Koporye   *41 km*

In Gostilitsy (Гостилицы) continue straight on, past the petrol station and then turn right at the traffic light into road **A 120**. After around 6 kilometres, turn left onto the paved path and then cycle past a military site. Then, continue on a paved bike path. After 10 km, turn right in **Lopukhinka (Лопухинка)**. There are shopping possibilities in **Laromiy Lapochkika**. Just before a branch in the road you can see Bor nuclear power plant at the coast and you will then reach Koporye (**Копорье**), where you can find a pharmacy as well as a few smaller shops.

Koporye (Копорье)

Koporye is famous for its fortress. Originally, the Teutonic Order had built a wooden fortress on the same site, which was first mentioned in 1240. It was destroyed by the Russians and subsequently rebuilt in stone. Over the centuries, the castle played an important role in the wars between Russia and Sweden.

You will reach the fortress by continuing straight on from the country road and into the village. Turn right

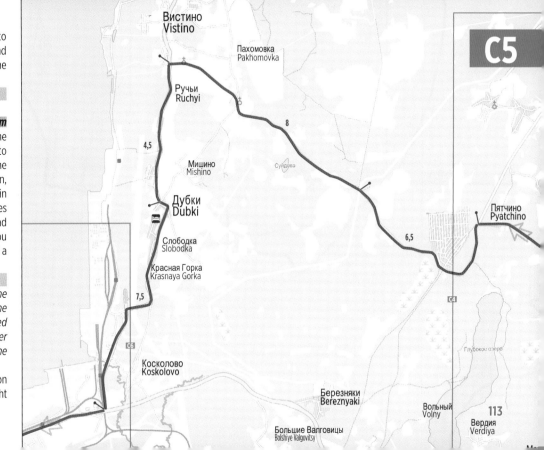

C5

113

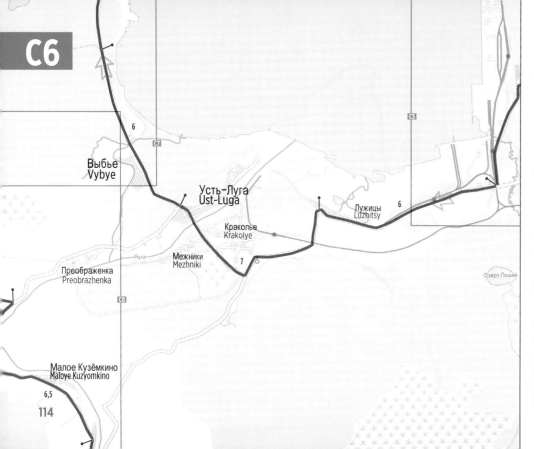

6

СZ

Выбье
Vybye

Усть-Луга
Ust-Luga

Лужицы
Luzhitsy

6

Краколье
Krakolye

Луга

Межники
Mezhniki

7

Озеро Лешин

Преображенка
Preobrazhenka

С5

С8

Малое Кузёмкино
Maloye Kuzyomkino

6,5

at the monument and then follow the road for another 500 metres.

From Koporye to Dubki 44 km

Continue downhill behind the fortress and then straight on in the next right bend and onto the semi-paved road, on which you cross the railway tracks. The route continues via **Golovkino (Головкино)** and **Semeyskoye (Семейское)**, then crosses a river and continues past a lake frequented by locals for swimming and barbecuing. After passing the monument commemorating the Second World War the traffic increases. The paved part of the road starts at the town sign, behind which you will see a cemetery. Turn left at the intersection and you will reach the town centre of Dubki.

Dubki (Дубки)

From Dubki to Ivangorod 99 km

Follow the road along the Baltic Sea coast, that you only rarely see, until you reach the **A 109**, where you turn right. Cycle along the railway tracks, on which there are very long freight trains. Pass a hotel, cross the railway tracks and behind **Luzhitsy (Лужицы)**, follow the **A 109** in a sharp left bend. At the next intersection, turn right and you will reach Ust-Luga.

Ust-Luga (Усть-Луга)

This village with 3,000 inhabitants was first mentioned in 1676 and is situated at the mouth of the river Luga, where it flows into Luga Bay in the Baltic Sea. The name is derived from the Russian word ustje for mouth.

The village is home to the largest and deepest Baltic Sea port, which is only iced up for a short time in winter. There is a ferry connection for rail, car and passenger traffic between the Russian mainland and the Kaliningrad oblast. In addition, boats also regularly call at the German ports of Kiel and Sassnitz on the island of Rügen.

Cross the river Luga on a bridge, where you can also find a shop and a café. The road then makes a bend but the main route continues straight on and then leads into the national park.

Cross a river on a bumpy, paved cobblestone street and then continue diagonally right into a better path, on which you will reach **Kurgolovo (Курголово)**.

You will get back to the A 109 via **Kaybolovo (Кайболово)** and **Konnovo (Конново)**. Turn right onto the **A 109**. Continue along the river Luga and you will reach the village of **Izvoz (Извоз)** via **Maloye Kuzyomkino (Малое Кузёмкино)**, **Ropsha (Ропша)** and **Keykino (Кейкино)**. Once in **Izvoz (Извоз)**, turn right behind the bus stop onto the unpaved field path. After around 50 metres turn right and continue through the fields and the forest. Follow this path in a sharp left bend. You have to overcome a short bad patch in the path before the path turns into a paved country road. Turn left at **Gospitalnaya (Госпитальная)** and then right at **Petrogradskaya (Петроградская)** to **Ivangorod (Ивангород)** as well as the border. This way, the route cuts out 10 kilometres of the dangerous motorway.

On the left side you will see a cemetery with war graves as well as a monument in honour of those who fell during the Second World War. Continue on road **E 20** along the shores of the river Narva until you reach the border control point. Be-

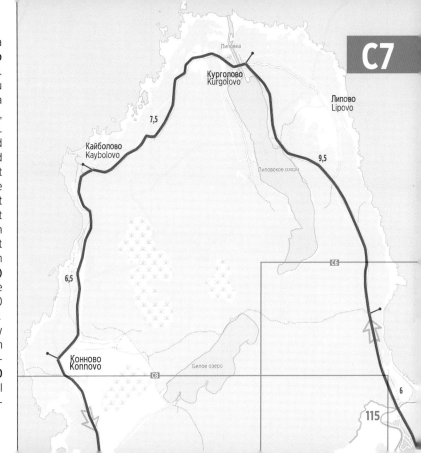

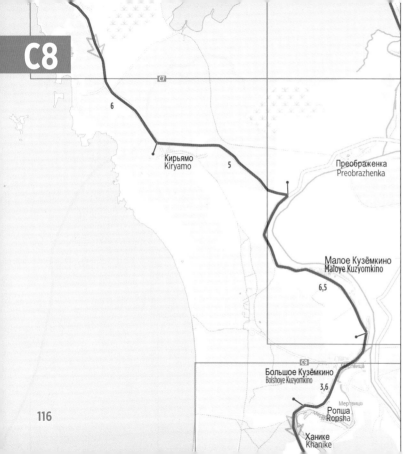

6

Кирьямо
Kiryamo

5

Преображенка
Preobrazhenka

Малое Кузёмкино
Maloye Kuzyomkino

6,5

Большое Кузёмкино
Bolshoye Kuzyomkino

3,6

Ропша
Ropsha

Мертвицы

Ханике
Khanike

fore you get there, the famous fortress of Ivangorod is well worth a visit. Cross the E 20 on **Gospitalnaya** (Госпитальная), then turn left into **Sovetskaya** (Советская) and you will reach the fortress of Ivangorod.

Ivangorod (Ивангород)

The border town of Ivangorod is located on the river Narva, which today marks the border between Estonia and Russia. On both sides of the shore, the Estonian town of Narva and the Russian town of Ivangorod are opposite each other, like twin cities. From 1649 to 1945, Ivangorod was part of the neighbouring Narva. The imposing fortress of Ivangorod and Hermann Castle, erected by the Teutonic Order on the other side of the river shore, are standing today as if they were looking into each other's eyes, just as the soldiers stationed there must often have done in history.

Ivangorod was founded in 1492 by Ivan III, whose name the city bears. The fortress he built still dominates the town today. The way there is unfortunately not well signposted.

After the border control point on the **E 20**, continue on the bridge across the river **Narva** and you will reach the Estonian town of the same name.

Ivangorod Fortress

The history of Estonia

The northernmost country of the Baltic States had a close relationship with the German culture right from the beginning and the area was the subject of a dispute between Denmark and the Teutonic Order, which both influence the population and to bring the country under their control. In the 14th century, the German side finally succeeded in doing so, which led to the settlement of a large number of German vassals, who soon regarded themselves as a separate ethnic group and were called "Baltic Germans". There was also a Swedish minority, known as the "Estonian Swedes".

In the Middle Ages, life in the north of the Baltic States was initially dominated by the membership of many Estonian cities in the Hanseatic League, until Estonia came under Swedish rule in the defence against attacks by Ivan the Terrible during the Livonian War (1558-1583). However, this Swedish period was over in 1710. Under Tsar Peter the Great, the country became part of the Russian Baltic Sea government for more than 200 years. The Russian rulers pursued a strict policy of Russianisation, which reduced the influence of the Baltic German upper class.

After the First World War, Estonia fought for its independence and declared itself an independent democratic republic on 24 February 1918. After its defeat, Germany was forced to withdraw its troops from the Baltic States. Shortly thereafter, the Estonian Liberation War broke out on 28 November with the attack of the Red Army. The war ended on 2 February 1920 with the Treaty of Tartu and the independence guaranteed therein by the Soviet Union.

After that, the country experienced a brief period of prosperity. However, almost 20 years later, its independence was threatened again: The Hitler-Stalin Pact of 23 August 1939 allocated the

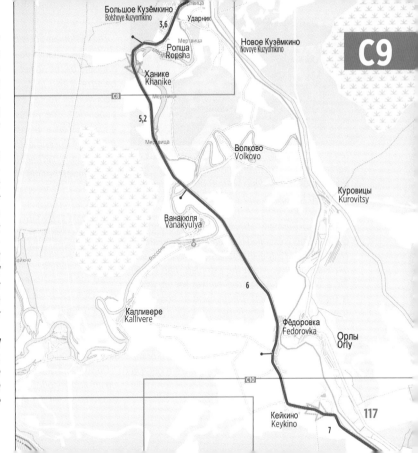

Human chain on 23 August 1989

territory of Estonia to the Soviet Union in a secret agreement, which it then annexed. During the "June deportation" on 14 June 1941, 10,000 people were deported to Siberia, and within a year Estonia lost almost 60,000 of its inhabitants.

After Nazi Germany' attack of the Soviet Union, the German troops expelled the Red Army from Estonia with the help of Estonian partisans. However, instead of independence, which the Estonians had hoped for, a typical occupation regime was set up, which is responsible for both the burning of books and the extermination of the remaining Jews in Estonia.

In order to prevent Soviet troops encircling them, the German troops withdrew in the autumn of 1944 and the Red Army regained control. Of the 11 prime ministers of the inter-war period, ten were killed in Soviet detention and terror after the Hitler-Stalin Pact.

The "Estonian Socialist Soviet Republic" was re-established after 24 years, but extensive areas were annexed by the Soviet Union as a result of borders being re-drawn. In March 1949, 20,000 people were deported to Siberia; Estonia lost 17% of its pre-war population. The Russianisation policy continued and the Estonian population was reduced from 90 to 60% by the end of the 1980s.

The country had been under Soviet control since the beginning of the Cold War, but the relative proximity to Finland and the reception of Finnish radio stations prevented a complete isolation from the West.

Especially in the late 1980s, the Baltic states strove for independence. This quest for freedom came to a head on 23 August 1989 when 2.5 million people took part in the longest human chain ever at the "Baltic Road" on the 50th anniversary of the Hitler-Stalin Pact (see also page 85).

It ran through all three Baltic States over a distance of 600 km between Tallinn, Rīga and Vilnius. They demanded: sovereignty for Estonia, Latvia and Lithuania. The end of the Soviet system had begun.

On 30 March 1990, Estonia declared itself a republic again and renounced further cooperation in the Supreme Soviet of the USSR on 18 December 1990.

Although Mikhail Gorbachev had imposed an economic embargo and still tried to stop this independence movement called the "Singing Revolution" with military force in January 1991, 78% of the electorate voted for independence from the Soviet Union in a referendum on the status of the republic held on 3 March 1991.

After the coup d'état in Moscow on 20 August 1991, the Supreme Council of the Republic of Estonia declared full independence, which was also recognised by the Soviet Union on 6 September 1991.

In the 1990s, the country, roughly the same size as the Netherlands or Belgium and with 1.3 million inhabitants, experienced a remarkable upswing. Skype was developed in "Laptopia" and it is the country with the highest density of internet access and the greatest innovation potential. These were all important factors for the country's accession to the EU in 2004. In the same year, Estonia also became a member of NATO and thus a recognised part of the Western community. Since 2011 it has been part of the eurozone.

There are countless different nationalities in Estonia, almost 70% of the population belongs to the Estonian majority and a quarter to the Russian minority.

The country's culture of remembrance also changed. While during Soviet times the murder of the Jews had been kept secret, people then started to remember their terrible fate. This is why in the area of former concentration camps a monument was erected and the modern synagogue in Tallinn was inaugurated in the presence of the Estonian President Arnold Rüütel. During his visit to Israel in 1998, President Guntis Ulmanis admitted with deepest regret his fellow countrymen's involvement in the Holocaust.

Narva

The third largest and most eastern city of Estonia is located on the river of the same name, which marks the border here. Due to its convenient location, Narva, which was first mentioned in 1171 and granted city rights in 1302, was already an important trading centre in the Middle Ages. Denmark sold the area to the Teutonic Order in 1346. It subsequently came under Swedish rule.

During the Great Nordic War (1700-1721) the "Battle of Narva" took place here on 20 November 1700, during which the Russian army under Peter I suffered a devastating defeat. In 1704, he recaptured the city and incorporated large areas of the Baltic States into the Russian Empire.

In the 19th century, Narva lost its importance as a seaport and developed into a centre for textile production. From 1918 to 1940 the city belonged to the independent Republic of Estonia, then to the Soviet Union until 1991.

The city centre was almost completely destroyed in the Second World War. Only three of the city's inhabitants are said to have survived the war. Only three historical buildings have survived, including the historic town hall. Therefore, today the city is dominated by blocks of flats from the Soviet era. There was a policy to settle Russian immigrants and industrial workers here, while the previously evacuated Estonian population was not allowed to return for a long time. This

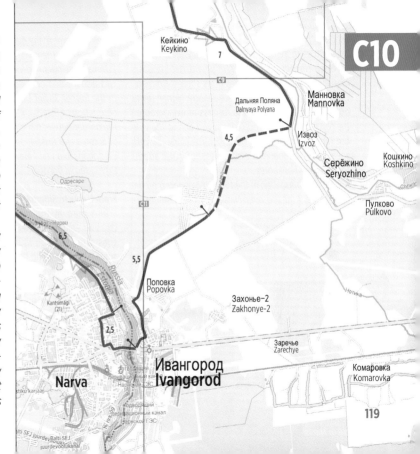

explains the large Russian-speaking population, which is said to be more than 90 percent today.

Also worth seeing is the river Narva with two imposing medieval castles on both sides of its shores. Hermann Castle (Hermaani Linn) with its slightly higher tower on the Estonian side and the fortress of Ivangorod on the Russian side were both destroyed during the war, but rebuilt in the 1950s. This panorama alone is worth seeing – and probably one of the reasons it also adorns the Estonian banknotes.

After the foundation of the town of Ivangorod on the eastern bank of the river Narva, a close relationship

Hermann Castle in Narva

developed over many decades after the Second World War between the two towns. During the period of Estonia's first independence from 1918 to 1940, Ivangorod was also located on Estonian territory, as the border to the former Soviet Union was further east. After the occupation of Estonia in 1940, the river Narva became the border between the former Soviet Union republics of Estonia and Russia. Since Estonia's accession to the European Union on 1 May 2004, the river has been the EU's external border.

From Narva to Sillamäe   37 km

Turn right at the roundabout behind the border crossing – signposted as EV 10 – and you will reach the **coastal road 91**, into which you turn left. Continue on a small bike strip along the river Narva, past a cemetary for German soldiers and many monuments commemorating the First and Second World War. You will also see a border stele of Estonia and a Russian watchtower on the opposite side.

You will reach the famous spa town of **Narva-Jõesuu** with its 10-kilometre-long sandy beach. Follow the signs to the left before the beach. Alternatively, you can continue to the beach and cycle on the quiet **Aia Tn**. AT the end, turn left and then right again onto the **91** until you reach **Udria**. In Udria, turn right into the paved **Rida**

Kühle P. Shortly afterwards, the EV 10 turns into a bumpy gravel street but this later becomes easy to travel on. When you reach the intersection with the **E 20** on your left, turn right onto the paved road and cross a river.

Where the road branches off to the right towards Mummassare, turn left onto the paved road towards **Pimestiku**, which later becomes a mainly comfortable field path, with only a few exceptions. You can hear the sound of the sea but cannot see the Baltic Sea. Just before the farmhouse, continue right towards the coast, where you will find a nicely paved bike path, on which you will reach Sillamäe at the Baltic Sea coast.

Continue on **Ranna Tn.** along the beach – parallel to Gagarini, which was built from 1953-55 and is the town's grandest boulevard as the former "Stalin Avenue". Another avenue branches off towards the town centre on the left. In the centre, you can visit the Culture Palace as well as the church.

Sillamäe

The town of Sillamäe was built after the Second World War by forced labourers. It first became a settlement for uprooted people, who had been driven to Estonia as a result of Stalin's wave of Russianisation. The "secret city" at the Baltic Sea was not included on any map and not was closed to foreigners. Officially it did not exist,

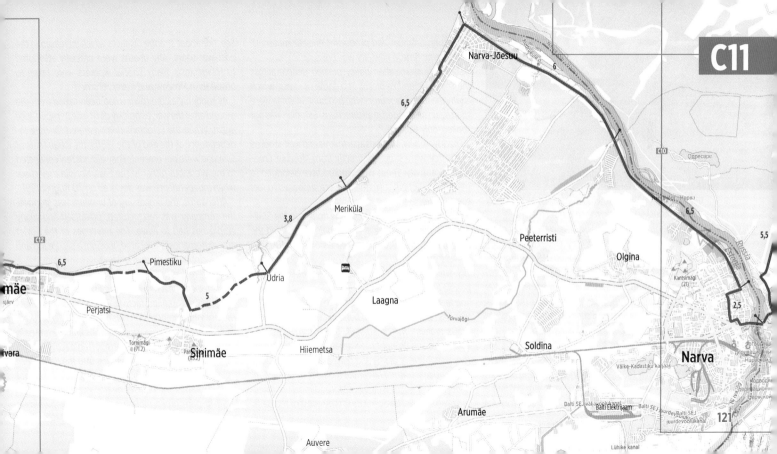

Tank Monument in Narva

because the Baltic Sea town was a centre of the Soviet nuclear industry - and therefore top secret.

The reason for building Sillamäe was the oil shale beneath the surface. The dark grey, clayey sedimentary rocks contained uranium compounds that Stalin urgently needed as after the Americans had succeeded in detonating the first atomic bombs, the Soviets were under pressure. Although their researchers had theoretical expertise, there was a lack of sites to extract and process uranium. Sillamäe was the right place for this.

While in other gulags the people died en masse, the prisoners of war in Sillamäe were treated better. There were additional food rations, and those who worked longer were able to shorten their sentence. Within a few months, thousands of workers built a factory for processing uranium and producing nuclear materials. At the same time, a new city was built.

Stalin's Russianisation policy pushed people across the Soviet Union like pieces in a game of chess, which is why the forced labourers who had built Sillamäe were soon again distributed in all directions. Estonian was not spoken, only Russian.

There were new, spacious apartments and well-stocked shops that were supplied directly from Moscow. Freedom in captivity. Those who worked here belonged to the technical-chemical elite and were supposed to feel comfortable.

The city flourished. Bright yellow houses in the Stalinist style lined the wide avenues, palm trees lined the magnificent stairs leading to the Baltic Sea. 400,000 flowers of all colours adorned the flower beds of the city, which did not officially exist. In 1957 already 10,000 people lived there.

In fact, the uranium content of the Estonian oil shale was less abundant than had been hoped for. In the early 1950s, uranium was additionally taken from other socialist states and brought to Sillamäe in order to enrich it for nuclear power plants and nuclear weapons.

The residents did not talk about the side effects. Neither about nuclear waste, which was stored almost unprotected in an artificial lake directly off the coast of the Baltic Sea, nor about strange diseases which increased in the post-war years. Any deaths were officially attributed to tuberculosis. Many special workers were taken to hospitals in Moscow and never returned.

As suddenly as the town whad been raised from the ground after the war, as quickly did it lose its mportance again. When the Estonians demonstrated for their independence at the end of the 1980s, the inhabitants of Sillamäe were not present. They did not feel connected to the West, but rather to the East. Nor did they cheer when independence was declared on 20 August 1991.

Afterwards, the processing of uranium was stopped, the company was restructured, privatised and many employees had to leave. The privileges of the Soviet era - automatically allocated housing, a secure job and early retirement - were abolished.

And there was another rude awakening: Environmentalists raised concerns about the nuclear waste lagoon of the secret uranium factory. The "lake of death", as the city's inhabitants call it, was not sufficiently secured. Only an unstable, increasingly porous and too low dam prevented 6.5 million cubic metres of radioactive sludge, ash and other liquids from pouring into the Baltic Sea.

Action had to be taken very quickly, but it was not until 2009 that the "lake of death" was sealed. Today, a 50-hectare green mound covers the lake, which is

Valaste

7

6,5

Puhajõgi

Toila

C3

5,7

Voka paisjärv

4,5

Voka

C11

Päite

Ülemine paisjärv

9,5

Sillamäe

Sõtke jõgi

Sõtke paisjärv

Sõtke jõgi

Sõtke jõgi

Vaivara

emägi

kruse

61.6

Jõhvi

Oru

Jõhvi krooa

Viivikonna

regularly inspected, surveyed and checked for radiation. The lake is located at the edge of the port of Sillamäe, in a customs area.

Since Estonia's independence, the city has shrunk from around 20,000 inhabitants to around 14,000. More than 95 per cent of the inhabitants are still Russian-speaking, and only 35 per cent have Estonian citizenship.

The town centre in the style of the "Soviet Baroque" is worth seeing as well as the Culture Palace and Pühjöe church, which was built in 1838 and renovated in 1989.

From Sillamäe to Kunda   94 km

As it is not possible to leave Sillamäe via the coast, turn right at the end of **Ranna** and into **Veski** and then left into **Sötke**. At the end, turn left into **L. Tolstoi**, which leads to **national road 1**, into which you turn right. Cross the railway tracks and once in **Vaivina**, turn right into **Poja Vaivina T.** Follow the signposting of the **EV 10** until you reach the unpaved **coastal road 198**. Continue along the steep coast with cliffs of up to 40 metres height until you reach **Voka**.

At the main intersection, the 198 turns into the **187**. After a few kilometres you will reach the **105**, into which you turn right. Then, immediately turn left onto the **133**, on which you will reach Toila.

Toila

In Toila, the businessman Gregory Yeliseyev from St. Petersburg had a three-storey palace built in Oru Park in 1899. At the beginning of the First World War, he emigrated to France. Estonian industrialists bought the palace in 1935 for 100,000 kronor and donated it to the Estonian President Konstantin Päts, who spent his summers here from 1935 to 1940. Unfortunately, this

Sillamäe Town Hall with the tall clock tower

impressive palace was destroyed in the Second World War, but the impressive park is still there.

In the resort there is a large sanatorium, called "SPA". It has a new EU-supported swimming pool and is very popular.

From Toila, continue on the **133** along the steep coast with a direct view of the Baltic Sea. You will pass **Martsa** and then reach **Valaste waterfall**, the longest in Estonia (25 metres). Then continue along the steep coast on a sandstone plateau. Behind **Saka**, turn right and you will reach the manor house in Saka mõis.

Saka mõis manor house

The manor was first mentioned in writing in the 17th century. Today, there is an inn and a centre for seminars and conferences here.

From the manor house, turn left towards Aa, which also has a former manor house.

Aa manor house

Aa manor house was built by Georg Bogislaus von Wangersheim. It dates back to 1696 and was given its present appearance in the 18th century. The last owners were the Grünenwaldt family until they were expropriated. There is not much left of the interior decoration. A fireplace with blue tiles can be found in the historical museum of Tallinn. Today, there is an old people's home in the manor house.

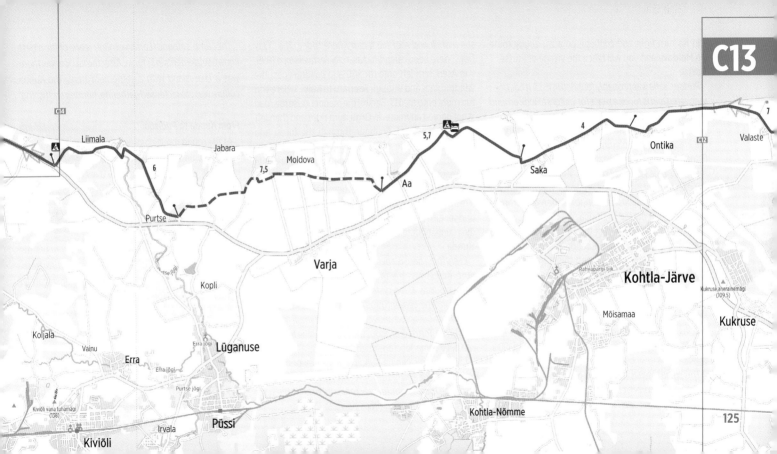

Liimala

C14

Jabara

Moldova

6

Purtse

7,5

Aa

5,7

Saka

4

Ontika

C12

Valaste

7

Varja

Kopli

Koljala

Vainu

Erra

Lüganuse

Erra jõgi

Erra jõgi

Purtse jõgi

Kiviõli vana tuhamägi
(138)

Kiviõli

Irvala

Püssi

Kohtla-Nõmme

Kohtla-Järve

Rahvapargi tiik

Mõisamaa

Kukruse aheraainemägi
(109.5)

Kukruse

In **Aa** turn right and continue on a zig-zaggy route via **Moldova** and you will reach the village of Purtse.

Purtse

Purtse Castle was probably founded in 1533. It has been renovated and is today a place for visitors to look around as well as attend exhibitions and concerts.

The steep Hiiemägi hill is the highest elevation in the area and was probably a sacred site of the ancient Estonians. Since 1992, it has been the site of the "park in memory of the victims of cruelty". Various representatives of Estonia planted oaks here and a "map of Estonian suffering" provides information about the regional origin of Estonians deported to Siberia.

In Purtse the paved part of the route continues. Keep right into the direction of the sandy beach and **Liimala** harbour. Once you have passed this, turn right onto the busy **E 20**, which you follow for seven kilometres until you reach Rannu. Once there, turn right and you will reach Aseri.

On this part of the route you will pass Kõrkküla stone crucifix, a memorial crucifix for the boyar Wassilij Rosladin, who lost his life in the Russian-Swedish war in 1590.

Aseri

This small town is considered to be the capital of clay in Estonia. The production of cement began here in 1899 and stones have been made here since 1922. There is still a brick and roof tile factory here today. The "Clay Days" have been celebrated as a city festival since 1999.

In Aseri, turn left onto the **160** and continue past the windturbines and through **Aseriaru** to **Kalvi**, where you turn right onto the **113**. Behind the manor house the road is not parved anymore. In **Orgu**, turn right and then left behind the S-bend. Continue through the forest and cross the river Vada. At the next intersaction turn right towards the coast and then continue along the coast until you reach **Letipea** lighthouse. Once there, keep left and then turn right onto the 158. Just before the river there is a restaurant with a playground for children. Behind the bridge, turn left into **Rakvere maantee** until you reach the roundabout in Kunda.

Kunda

Everything here is covered with a fine layer of cement dust. Kunda was the most polluted city in Estonia for decades. New filter systems have now improved the situation. The cement production goes back to Baron Girard de Soucanton and the year 1871. A small museum provides information about the history of the town. You can have some food and spend the night.

1.5 kilometres behind Kunda is Malla manor house. It dates from the end of the 18th century and is considered to be the most beautiful in Estonia. Its park at the back is privately owned and drops down to the sea.

The Lamb's Mound (Lammasmägi) is one of the oldest known settlements in Estonia. After the last ice age, there was a lake island with a settlement here. The Kunda culture was characterised gathering, hunting and fishing.

From Kunda to Pudisoo   113 km

At the roundabout, continue south on road **20**, which you follow until you reach the **172**, into which you turn right. Then, turn right onto the **170** and then bear right after the left bend to reach the ruins of Toolse Order Castle at the boast.

Toolse Order Castle

The castle was built in 1471 as a shelter from pirates and was built on top of a former Estonian fortress. The castle was destroyed in the Russian-Livonian War (1558-1582). The ruins are in a picturesque spot, directly by the sea. Today, events are held here for children, and in the distance you can already see the flag of the "pirate ship".

Cross the river Selja in **Karepa**, where you can also visit the Jagraza Paul Museum. Then, continue along the Baltic Sea towards **Rutja**, where you can find a beach café and a watchtower, and you will reach Vainupea.

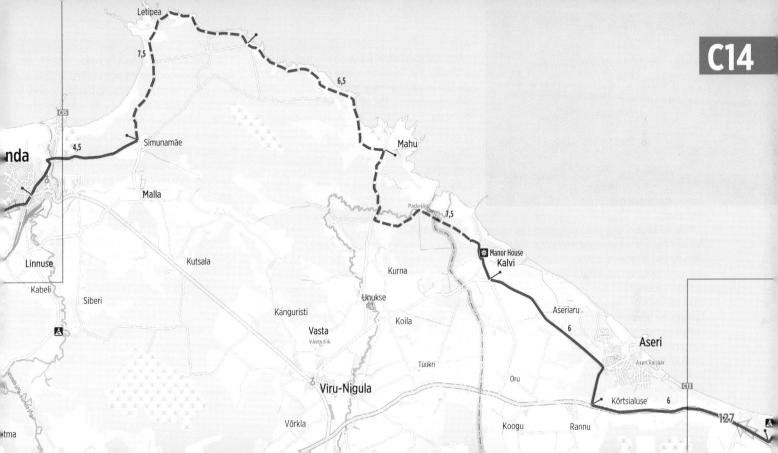

Letipea

7,5

C15

4,5

nda

Simunamäe

Malla

Linnuse

Kabeli

Siberi

Kutsala

Kanguristi

Vasta

Vasta tiik

Viru-Nigula

Võrkla

tma

6,5

Mahu

Pada-jõgi

7,5

Manor House
Kalvi

Kurna

Unukse

Koila

Tüükri

Oru

Koogu

Rannu

Aseriaru

6

Aseri

Aseri karjäär

Kõrtsialuse

6

C13

127

Swamp area in Lahemaa National Park

Vainupea

Since the beginning of the 20th century, this village has been the epitome of summer recreation. The chapel from the end of the 19th century was renovated in 1980 and is the closest sacral building to the sea – at a distance of only 20 metres!

Behind the river Vainupea, turn right onto the **173** towards the beach. You will pass an old lighthouse as well as a pretty church and then turn left into a solid forest path – with a few bumpy parts – along the beach. Continue straight on and cross a river, turn left in **Mustoja** and then later right onto the paved **181**. Cross another river and continue past a restaurant and you will reach the old fishing village of Altja on a slightly hilly road.

Altja

Altja is a typical street village on the coast. The farms of Uustalu and Toomarahva date back to the turn of the 19th and 20th century and have been restored in exemplary fashion. The other buildings are from the 1920s and 1930s. The old fisherman's warehouses are a particularly popular motif for photos.

Lahemaa National Park

The 110-kilometre route leads through Lahemaa National Park, which was founded in 1971. It was the first national park in the Soviet Union and was established to preserve the North-Estonian landscape, its ecosystem and biodiversity.

Its name literally means "bay country", because it includes six beautiful bays worthy of protection. The national park covers an area of 72,000 hectares, of which one third is sea and two thirds are woodland and swamps. Eight of the 62 large boulders in Estonia with a diameter of more than 30 metres are located in the park.

The park has similar problems with the bark beetle as the Bavarian Forest. Today, the previously prevalent monoculture is being replaced with a mixed forest.

Stay on the **181** and you will reach Vergi. The 800-metre long detour from the lighthouse to Vergi sadam is highly recommended.

Vergi

This town used to be famous for building sailing boats. Today, the harbour, which was opened in 1977, is a popular destination for sailors and tourists - especially from nearby Finland. You can visit the lighthouse as well as the old watchtower with two bunkers.

Continue along the coast and you will pass **Lahe** and then reach **Võsu**, the main village in Laheema National Park, where you can eat, put up your tent and stay overnight. Turn right in a sharp angle to get to the beaches, the camping site and the centre of this small, and in the summer quite touristic, village. To get back, go back up the hill to the intersection.

Turn right into **Rakvere tee**, cross the river and then follow the **Mere** in a left bend until you reach the **177**, into which you turn right. Continue through the forest on a nice bike path until you reach Käsmu, which is located at the end of the so-called "middle finger".

Käsmu

From 1884-1934 there was a sailors' school here and 62 captains lived in the little village called "village of captains" between the world wars. At that time, the sailing ships stayed here over the winter. In 1941, many families were deported to Siberia, and in 1944, shortly before the return of the Red Army, about a third of the

Altja

Mustoja

4,2

5,5

Vainupea

3

Haili

C16

Pajuveski paisjärv

Pajuveski

Eisma

Oandu

ndu järv

7

Vihula

Rutja

Karepa

Tiigi

Kiva

Karula

Kosta

Toolse

Mustoja

Paasi

7,5

ndi

Kunda

Kaliküla

C14

Kandle

Noonu

Aaviku

Pehka

2,6

Metsiku

Selja

Kiviküla

Annikvere

Salatse

Marinu

Paasküla

129

Kavastu

Linnuse

500 inhabitants fled across the sea and the town became a restricted area, reinforced by barbed wire.

It was only in 1992 that the beautiful coast was opened to the public again. You can go for a bite to eat and stay overnight here. The building of the former seaman's and border guard school is now home to the Sea Museum. In the so-called General's Chapel there is a photo exhibition about the inhabitants. From the old watchtower you can enjoy beautiful views over the coastal landscape.

In Käsmu, turn left into **Laane tee**. Then, continue on a solid forest path until you reach the coast of the smallest peninsula in Laheema National Park and you will reach the lake. Continue in a south-westerly direction between the lake and the coast. Unfortunately, the route is not signposted towards Eru and has a few very bumpy parts. Turn right twice and after a left bend you will reach **Eru**, where you can go swimming.

Eru bay is one of the many bird breeding grounds in Lahemaa National Park. There are 220 bird species, including 50 to 60 waterfowl species.

Continue straight along the coast, cross a river and you will reach **Tammispea**, where you continue straight on in a left angle and in **Vihaaso** you will reach the **286**, into which you turn right.

Cycle around **Pärispea peninsula**, which was formed from numerous smaller islands – just like other peninsulas in Laheema National Park – which appeared from the Baltic Sea around 8,000 years ago, and you will reach **Kasispea**. Just behind the village, turn

Stone monument in Viinistu

right to the 7.5-metre-tall rock Jaani-Tooma Suurkivi. Those going there should remember to close the gate behind themselves.

Turn right onto the **280**, continue along the coast through Turbuneeme and you will reach Viinistu.

Viinistu

Viinistu is known as the village of the "Kings of the Spirit". In the 1920s and 1930s, local farmers became rich from smuggling alcohol. Today, around 150 people live here, most of them work in the fish factory and the mushroom breeding station. Directly by the sea there is an art museum with a stone monument and artistic sculptures as well as a hotel with restaurant.

Purekkari spit is the northernmost point in Estonia. After the Second World War it was closed due to a Soviet radar station being located here. The only remnants from this time are a dilapidated military facility with a watchtower, radio tower and bunker.

In **Pärispea**, the oldest and once largest fishing village with around 100 households, you can see traditional fishing huts.

In Viinistu turn left onto the **287**, which leads to the **285**, into which you turn left. Continue along the coast via **Suurpea** to Loksa, where you can see an old watchtower.

Loksa

With 3,500 inhabitants - half of them Estonians - Loksa is the largest town in Lahemaa and is known for its brick factory, which was founded by the Count von Stenbock in 1874. Their products were exported to Finland and later a shipyard was added, which is now in Danish hands. The first summer houses were built here at the beginning of the 20th century.

After crossing Walge Jõgi, turn right onto the **283**, past a cemetery and then via **Hara** to the **272**, into which you turn left.

EXCURSION If you would like to see the dilapidated harbour facilities, continue straight on for a further two kilometres.

You will reach **Leesi** on the **272** with great views across the Baltic Sea. Continue through **Kolga-Aabla** – the route continues along the coast here and you can stop for a bite to eat – and you will reach Pedaspea and then Pudisoo.

Pudisoo

From Pudisoo to Tallinn   *90 km*

In Pudisoo turn right after crossing the river and then continue through **Soorinna** until you reach the **260**, into which you turn right towards Kiiu.

CENTRE If you would like to look around Kuusalu town centre, turn left after crossing the river.

Kuusalu

In Kuusalu, Cistercian monks from Kolka built the church of St. Laurentius at the end of the 13th century. Although the order preferred to build its churches on hills, this one was built in a valley. The most valuable piece is a Renaissance

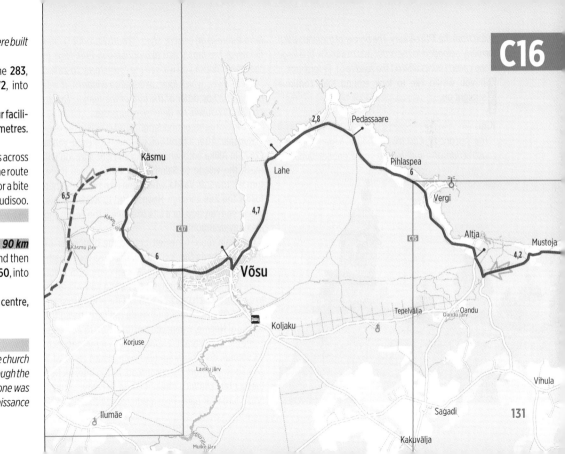

pulpit from the 17th century. The border of the land which formerly belonged to the order was marked with a large stone called Lauritsakivi on the road to St. Petersburg.

EXCURSION If you would like to look around Kiiu, continue straight on.

Kiiu

The history of Kiiu manor house began with the construction of a mill by the von Stenbock family. A

The Church in Loksa

farm estate in an eclectic style ("Youth Baroque") later followed. The family was expropriated in 1919. Next to the manor house you will see the four-storey so-called monk's tower, which looks like a large windmill. It was built in 1520 by order of the lord of the manor, Fabian von Tiesenhausen, for defensive purposes.

The main route continues right after crossing the river in **Kuusalu**. After a bend you will reach **Kuusalu-Valkla (267)** in **Allika**, into which you turn right and you will reach the village of **Salmistu** via **Põhja**. Once there, turn left towards **Valkla**, where you turn right and then follow the **266** through **Haapse** and to **Kaberneeme**, where you can stop for a bite to eat near the beach and also stay overnight.

The main route turns left behind the bridge across the river Kaberla Oja and into an unpaved forest path. You will see a memorial stone "Kaberneeme 1375" here.

Then, immediately turn left again and you will reach a road, into which you turn right. At the end, turn sharp left and continue through **Ihasalu** until you reach the village of **Neeme**, where you can find a few restaurants. Some more restaurants are located directly at the beach.

Continue on a separate bike path, which iss et at a good distance from the quiet road. At the **intersection Ihasalu tee**, continue straight on. In **Punakivi** you will find a large car park. Take a side road with a separate

bike path, which later leads to the **262**, into which you turn right.

Before the left bend in **Jõesuu**, turn right into **Rippsilla tee** and you will reach the suspension bridge for pedestrians. The bridge sways when you cross it but it is just about possible to push your bike across it.

On the other side of the bridge you will find a large golf course. Once you then reach **Ristikangru tee** and the many bungalows, turn right and then stay along the coast. After a bend, continue into **Kivikrive tee**, which leads to **Mesakota tee**, into which you turn left. The road is then called **Maniva tee** and you turn right into **Mäealuse tee**. Just before **Ülgase** the route continues uphill.

After passing the elevation, continue right into Kallavere Ülgase, which is signposed as **EV 10** and **EV 11** but not yet as EV 13. Follow the signposts on the bike path and at the end, turn left in **Maardu** into **Keemikute** and then right into **Orumetsa**, which turns into **Maardu tee**. Stay on there and continue through the new part of Maardu with numeorus concrete housing estates as built during Soviet times.

Maardu

The first stage in the town's development began in 1949 with the opening of the chemical factory. The second stage was initiated by the construction of the power plant in the late 1970s. From 1980 to 1991, Maardu was

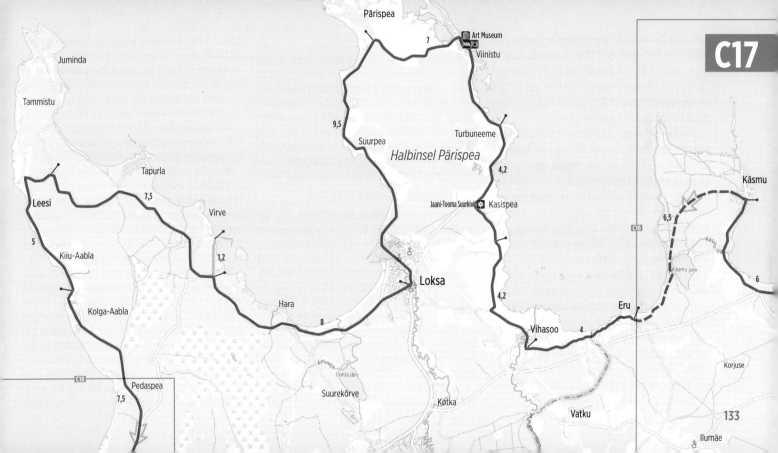

Juminda

Tammistu

Pärispea

7

🏛 Art Museum
Viinistu

9,5

Suurpea

Turbuneeme

Halbinsel Pärispea

4,2

Tapurla

7,5

Jaani-Tooma Suurkivi ✷ Kasispea

Leesi

Virve

5

1,2

Käsmu

Kiiu-Aabla

C16

6,5

Kolga-Aabla

Hara

8

Loksa

Käsmu järv

Käsmu oja

4,2

6

Eru

C18

Pedaspea

Vihasoo

4

Korjuse

7,5

Suurekõrve

Kõtka

Vatku

133

Ämmoja
Lohja järv

Ilumäe

part of the Tallinn district and has been an independent town since 1991. With its 17,000 inhabitants, most of whom Russian, it is the seventh largest city in Estonia.

In the port, which was newly built in 1986, around 90% of the goods are handled. Next to Maardu Manor House, the Orthodox Church is well worth a visit.

Cross the river Kroodi oja and then the railway tracks. After crossing the tracks again, turn right into **Kavallere tee** and then right again into **Muuga tee**. Continue on there and then cross the tracks again. Follow the road until you reach the roundabout, where you turn right onto the **250** and you will reach the village of **Tammneeme** via **Randvere**. Once there, turn right into **Tammneeme tee** and you will find yourself at the coast with great views of the Baltic Sea.

Turn left into **Luhaääre tee** and you will reach **Leppneeme**. In the bend, turn right into **Reinu tee**, on which you bear left and you will reach the **coastal road Rohuneeme tee (251)**, into which you turn left.

Just before **Haabneeme**, you will pass a restaurant with a round roof and a patio and then shortly afterwards Viimsi Vabaohu Museuum. Just behind Haabneme you can still see an old watchtower on the western side. Afterwards, you will pass the Soviet memorial.

Soviet Memorial

The memorial for the victims of National Socialism and especially for the defenders of the city of Tallinn was erected in 1980 on the grounds of a German cemetery, which was built in 1941 by the German Wehrmacht and levelled after the war. The Soviet memorial site with its monumental memorial is located on a small part of the site. Since 1998, a 5.50-metre-high cross made of stone also commemorates the 2,156 German soldiers who were buried here.

Shortly after this you will pass the Estonian History Museum.

The Estonian History Museum

The new museum is located in Maarjamäe Castle, which was built in 1874 by Count Anatoly Orlov-Davidov from St. Petersburg (1837-1905) in the style of historicalism by the St. Petersburg architect Robert Gödicke. The Orlov family emigrated to France after the October Revolution.

After the foundation of the Republic of Estonia, the building was used as the residence of the Dutch envoy. In 1937, the Estonian Air Force purchased the property. Due to the Soviet occupation it became the property of the Red Army in 1940. Later, communal dwellings and communal kitchens were set up there and the building fell into disrepair.

In 1975, the government of the Estonian SSR decided to establish a museum of Estonian Soviet history in the palace. It was intended to complement the monumental Soviet memorial site, which had been built in the immediate vicinity of the palace. The renovation works in the palace, however, lasted from 1983 to 1988, so that was never inaugurated during the Soviet occupation.

Today, the central hall of the palace still has a monumental wall painting in Socialist Realism style from the Estonian artist Evald Okas. The work is from 1987 and has the title Rahvaste sõprus ("The friendship of the people").

Today, the palace contains the modern Estonian History Museum. In addition to a permanent exhibition on Estonian history since the 19th century, there are also temporary exhibitions. A special part of the museum has been dedicated to the first Estonian President Konstantin Päts since 1995. There are also biographies of the other heads of state of the Republic of Estonia.

Monumental Soviet sculptures can be seen in the park. They were erected in Estonia between 1945 and 1990. There is also the Estonian Film Museum.

The **EV 13** stays along the coast and starts getting further away from the main road **Pirita tee** at the Russalka monument, which is dedicated to the sinking of the Russian armoured ship of the same name in 1893. Stay on the signposted bike path and at the end of the road turn left into **Filmi** and then right again into **Nafta**, which turns into **Tuukri**.

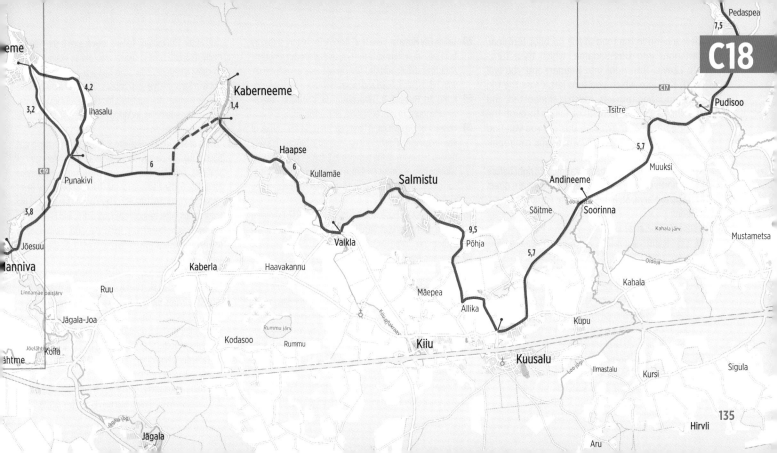

After a bend in the road at the harbour terminal, turn right into **Uus-Sadama**, which then turns into **Laeva**. Turn right into **Kuunari** and you will reach **Kai**, into which you turn left. Cross the big roads and then turn left, which is signposted, and you will reach the old town of Tallinn through the north gate. Not far away, in Uus 33, you will find City Bike (☎ +372 51 11 819), where you can repair or rent bikes.

■ If you would like to get to the station, turn right before the north gate into Rannamäe tee. There are direct trains to Narva, St. Petersburg and Pärnu.

Tallinn

postal code: 11612; area code 6

🛈 **City Tourist Information**, Raekoja Plats 10, ☎ 946946, www.tourism.tallinn.ee

🛈 **Estonian Tourist Board**, Liivalaia 13/15, ☎ 279770

🛈 **Tourist Information Center**, Niguliste 2/Kullassepa 4, ☎ 457777

🏛 **Maritime Museum**, Pikk 70 at Fat Margarets Tower, ☎ 411408. . There is an interesting exhibition on the history of seafaring and fishing in Estonia and you can have wonderful views over the old town and its bay from the tower.

🏛 **Estonian History Museum**, Pikk 17, ☎ 411630. There is a great exhibition on the history of the country – from pre-historical discoveries until today at the Great Gild Hall. There is also a collection of weapons from all over the world.

🏛 **Tallinn City Museum**, Vene 17, ☎ 446553. The history of the city from the 13th century up to the 1990s is explained in a modern, attractive exhibition entitled "The city will never be completed", with videos, slide shows and music.

🏛 **KUMU Art Museum**, A. Weizenbergi 34, ☎ 026000. Award-winning museum with exhibitions on modern art.

🏛 **Museum of Occupation**, 8 Toompea Street, at the corner of Kaarli Boulevard, ☎ 680250. It was opened in 2003 and is a very moving testimony of the suffering in Estonia's recent history. With the help of various exhibition pieces, it provides information on the time of the Soviet and German occupation between 1940 and 1991.

🏛 **A. H. Tammsaare Museum**, L. Koidula 12 A, ☎ 013232. Exhibition on the life and works of the most famous Estonian writer of the 20th century, Anton Hansen Tammsaare.

🏛 **Museum made in USSR**, shows everyday life in the Soviet Union, i.e. the completely normal life behind the "Iron Curtain".

⛪ **Alexander Nevsky Cathedral**, Lossi plats 10, ☎ 443484. This huge Orthodox church was built around 1900 by the then ruling Russians. With its onion towers, it is widely seen as a symbol of the Russianisation taking place at the time. Visitors can not only admire the mosaics and icons, but there are also 11 bells in the tower - among them the largest and heaviest in all of Tallinn, which cannot be overheard.

⛪ **Tallinn Cathedral**, Toom Kooli 6, ☎ 444140. The most important Protestant church in Estonia was built from wood at the begin-ning of the 13th century. Today's appearance is the result of many reconstructions in several eras and an example of the so-called limestone Gothic style. However, the cathedral interior is in Baroque style and contains 107 coat of arms of noble Estonian families. The numerous tombstones of famous seafarers are also interesting, including the tombstone of Catherine the Great's lover.

⛪ **Church of St. Nicholas**, Niguliste 3, ☎ 314330. This church was built in the 13th century for St. Nicholas, the patron saint of seafarers, and at first it was very similar to a fortress. It is famous for its late Gothic altar and for the "Dance of Death" by Bernt Notke, which survived the iconoclasm during the times of the Reformation. After various redesigns, Gothic and Renaissance elements can be found today. Today, the sacral building serves as a museum as well as a concert hall in which weekly concerts take place.

⛪ **Olai Church (13th century)**, Lai 50, ☎ 412241. In the 16th century, this tower was the tallest in the world with its 160 metres. After three major fires, the church was rebuilt again and again, largely in Gothic style, losing 35 metres in the process. It was named after the Norwegian king Olav II, who was also considered the protector of seafarers.

⛪ **St.-Catherine's Monastery**, Vene 16, ☎ 444606. The oldest Dominican monastery in the city dates back to the year 1246.

⛪ **St. Birgitte's Monastery**. This monastery was founded in 1407 and was destroyed 170 years later during the Livonian War. Only

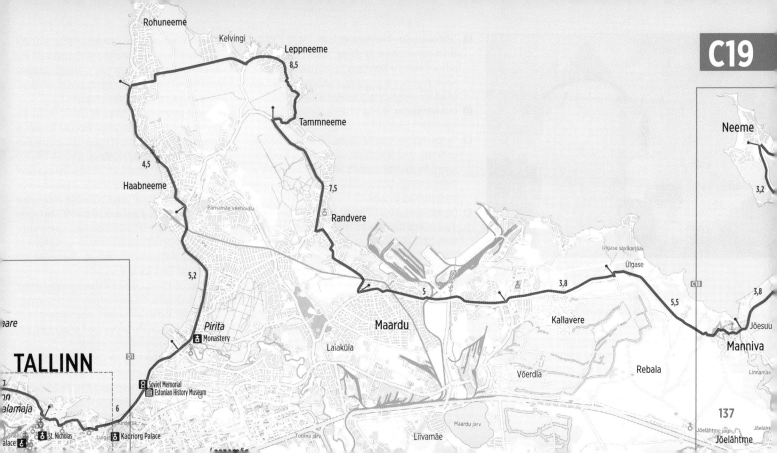

C19

137

Tallinn city wall

the outside walls of the church with its 35m-high west wall remained. The new construction of a convent of the Brigitte Order revives the site.

Toompea Palace (13th century), Lossi plats 1, ☎ 316637. The building in which the Estonian parliament meets today, was used in the past by the powerful rulers at the time, ranging from bishops and knights of the order to Russian governors.

Maiden Tower, Lühike jalg 9 A, ☎ 440896. Built in the second half of the 14th century, it was mainly used as a prison for prostitutes. Today, there is a museum and a café.

Great Coastal Gate & Fat Margarets Tower, Pikk 70, ☎ 411408. This mighty entrance to the city was built in the north of the old town, and in the 16th century the large cannon tower was added. In addition to its protective function, the tower also served as a storage site for gunpowder and as a prison.

Eesti Vabadussoda, Denkmal für den Estnischen Freiheitskrieg (1918-1920)

The town hall dates from the 13th century and visitors can climb up the stairs of the tower for some great views. Just across the street is the town hall pharmacy, which is not quite as old as the town hall but - together with the one in Dubrovnik - is the oldest pharmacy in Europe.

City wall, Gümnaasiumi 3, ☎ 449867. In the 16th century, Tallinn was one of the best protected cities in Northern Europe. Like the rest of the old town, the city wall is still very well preserved. With a width of three metres and a height of 16 metres, it protected the entire old town, with 46 towers spread over four kilometres. Of these, two kilometres and 26 original observation towers still remain.

Kiek in de Kök, Komandandi tee 2, ☎ 446686. The mighty round cannon tower with its three to four-metre thick walls was built in 1475. It got its name "look into the kitchen" because of its height of 38 metres, as from there one could look into the neighbouring houses.

Black Head House, Pikk 26, ☎ 313199. The only remaining Renaissance building in Tallinn was built in 1597 for the Brotherhood of the Black Heads, which was in existence from the end of the 14th century. It was an association of unmarried merchants who were only able to join the great guild as married merchants. Remarkable is the entrance portal with its abundance of colours. Today, the building is mainly used for concerts.

Zoological gardens Tallinn, Paldiski mnt. 145, ☎ 943300. The zoo, which has been in existence for more than 60 years, is home to an impressive variety of species. Its main focus is on mountain goats, sheep, eagles and owls.

Tallinn has 430,000 inhabitants and it is the capital of Estonia. For most of its eventful history, it was known as the German trading city of Reval. In the 14th century the city was surrounded by a wall with 46 towers. The largely intact medieval town centre with its fortified towers and the world's best-preserved Hanseatic quarter - almost 90% of the buildings have survived the war - has been a UNESCO World Heritage Site since 1997.

Of the once 46 towers, 26 are still standing today, and of the originally six gates, the old front gate still exists today, with the cannon tower Fat Margaret, which today houses the Maritime Museum. The largely car-free old town can be easily discovered and admired on foot.

In 1219, it was conquered by the Danish king Waldemar II, who gave it the Estonian name of "Taani linn" - Danish town. The Danes, however, were quickly pushed out again by the order of the Sword Brothers, who tried to attract

German merchants to settle here. Although the Danes soon returned, the urban upper class remained German - as did the official language. After a 150-year period of Swedish rule, the city fell to Russia in 1710.

On 24 February 1918, the independent Republic of Estonia was proclaimed and the name of the town was changed from Reval to Tallinn. Full independence was achieved during the Liberation War (1918-1920) and was recognised by the Soviet Union "for all time" in the Treaty of Tartu on 2 February 1920.

The first Estonian republic lasted from 1918 to 1939. After the Hitler-Stalin-Pact (1939), the German inhabitants in the Baltic States were brought "home to the Reich" by the Nazi Germans and the Baltic States were occupied by the Soviet Union.

In 1941, the German Wehrmacht occupied the country and almost the entire Jewish population of Tallinn and Estonia was murdered. After the return of the Soviets in 1944, the terror was directed against the Estonian people. Every 15th citizen was murdered and every 17th citizen was sent to Siberia for at least 10 years.

In 1991, Estonia reaffirmed its independence and confirmed Tallinn as its capital. Since 2009, a cross made of glass commemorates the successful fight for freedom and two pillars refer to the two dates of independence, 1918 and 1991.

The cathedral hill rises almost 50 metres above the old town, which formed its own town until 1877. It was here that the ruling elite sat and politics is still made here today. The only remains of the old castle are wall residues and three towers, of which the 50-metre-high "Tall Hermann" is the one that attracts the greatest number of visitors.

In 1980, the sailing competitions of the Olympic Summer Games of Moscow took place in the bay of Tallinn. The palace for culture and sports, located near the international ferry port, was built for this purpose – a low and large concrete structure with wide staircases, jetties and a heliport – all of them with visible signs of deterioration. It is here, where the city wants to showcase the traces of its past and at the

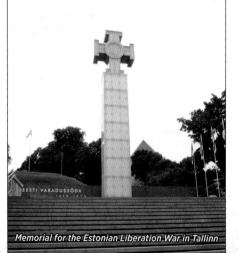
Memorial for the Estonian Liberation War in Tallinn

same time overcome them. The 314-metre-high television tower with a viewing platform was erected to transmit the games. In 1991, there were dramatic scenes when Soviet troops attempted to storm the tower.

The old Hanseatic city (since 1284) on the Gulf of Finland, 80 kilometres from Helsinki, today also wants to redefine itself as a city by the sea. This was not possible during the Soviet occupation because the area between the old town and the water was a military restricted area. The legendary film "Stalker" by Andrej Tarkovski, shot in the 1980s, reminds us of this. Afterwards, the Baltic Sea shore was used as a rubbish tip for many years. As the European Capital of Culture 2011, Tallinn reclaimed the sea with a harbour promenade and a maritime museum.

When the weather is good, you can see Finland (www.teletorn.ee). From the bay you can see the stage of the Estonian singing festivals (Lauluväljak) on the left side of the hill, which is shaped like a sea shell. Since 1865, Estonians have been gathering here every five years to enjoy some folkloric singing. The stage built by Alar Kotli in 1960 offers space for 15,000 singers. It was also the rediscovery of such traditions that ultimately led to the Baltic nations regaining their national independence from the Soviet Union. It is not without reason that we speak of the "Singing Revolution".

From Tallinn to Rīga

845 km

From the Estonian capital, cycle along the Baltic Sea coast route (EV 10) and the Iron Curtain Trail (EV 13) along the Baltic Sea coast, first to Haapsalu and then via the islands of Hiiumaa, Saaremaa and Muhu. You will pass through some coastal regions where the population was not allowed to stay during Soviet times. Back on the mainland, the route continues via Pärnu and Ainazi to the Latvian capital of Rīga.

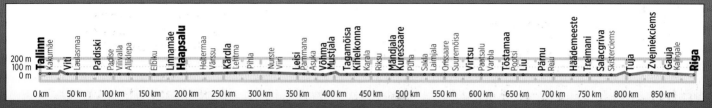

Waterfall in Keila-Joa

From Tallinn to Paldiski   78 km

Leave the old town on **Pikk** and through the north gate, then turn left into **Põhja** and then immediately right again into **Kalasdama**. Then, turn left onto the bike path of **Kalaranna** until you reach **Tööstuse**, into which you turn right. At the end, this turns into **Kopli** and then turn left into **Pelguranna**. At the end, take the bike path along the shore. At Rocca al Mare Museum you will reach **Vabaõhumuuseum tee**, on which the entrance of the museum is located.

Rocca al Mare

On an area of 84 hectares there are 79 popular buildings from the different regions of Estonia dating back to between the 17th to the 20th century – including manor houses, farmhouses, fishermen's cottages and windmills with furnishings and equipment.

At the end of the open air museum, the road continues in a left bend and you will reach **Kalumäe tee**, into which you turn left. Then, turn right into **Vana-Rannamõisa tee** and at the end right again onto the **390**.

Continue through **Tabasalu**, turn right into **Rannamõisa** behind the spot where the **191** branches off to the right and then continue down **Merepigla tee**. When you get to the roundabout, turn left into **Ringtee**, which you follow until you reach the steep coast.

At the end, turn right into **Körgemäe tee** after a left bend. This will take you to **Tilgu tee**, into which you turn right. Continue along the coast, cycle around the police academy and then turn left in front of the gate blocking the road into a forest path. After an S-bend, cross Lõkke tee and then continue until you reach **Lee tee**, into which you turn right.

At the end, turn left into **Tuulmetsa tee**, which will take you to **Kallaku tee**, into which you turn right. Just before the coast, turn left into **Pärtli tee**. After a sharp right turn, continue left into **Kalama tee**, of which only a small section is unpaved. At the end, turn left into **Munakivi tee**. Then, turn right into **Suurupi tee (392)** and then right again after a left bend into **Eerika tee**, which turns into **Soontevahe tee**.

The route then continues to the right into **Aruheina tee** and at the end left into **Matsavahi tee (389)**. Where this continues sharply to the left, keep straight and continue down **Luige tee** and then at the end turn right into **Klooga tee**.

In **Vääna-Jõesuu**, turn right onto the **390**, cross the river Vääna Jõgi and then continue to Keila-Joa via **Türisalu**.

Keila-Joa

Built in 1830 (by the architect A. I. Stackenschneider from St. Petersburg), this farmhouse estate is the only surviving example of "new country estate architecture" in Estonia. The heart of the farm is located on the banks of the river Keila. Windy paths lead visitors through the park and all the way down to the sea. On the way you can see numerous pavilions and sculptures, greenhouses as well as the romantic ruins of Meremõi. Keila waterfall is 6 metres high and 70 metres wide, making it particularly impressive. The estate was handed over from the Soviet government to the Red Army, which let it fall into disrepair.

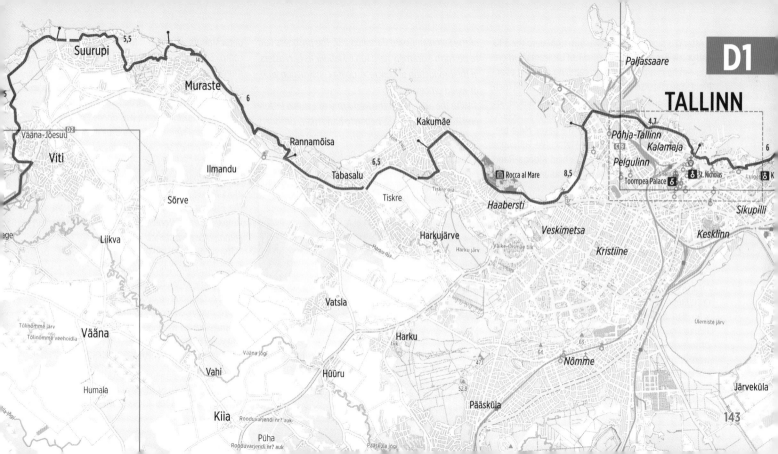

D1

TALLINN

Paljassaare

Põhja-Tallinn
Kalamaja
Pelgulinn

Toompea Palace · St. Nicholas · Luige K

Suurupi

5,5

14

Muraste

6

Rannamõisa

Kakumäe

Vääna-Jõesuu D2

Viti

Ilmandu

Tabasalu

6,5

Rocca al Mare

8,5

4,7

6

Sõrve

Tiskre

Tiskre oja

Haabersti

Sikupilli

age

Liikva

Harkujärve

Harku järv

Veskimetsa

Kesklinn

Väike-Õismäe tiik

Kristiine

Tõlinõmme järv
Tõlinõmme veehoidla

Vääna

Vatsla

Harku

liik

Vahi

Vääna-jõgi

Hüüru

47,1

52,8

Nõmme

64

63

Ülemiste järv

Humala

Kiia

Rooduvarjendi nr? auk

Pääsküla

Järveküla

Pühа
Rooduvarjendi nr? auk

Pääsküla jõgi

143

After crossing the river Keila, turn right onto the **390** and you will reach the coastal town of **Laulasmaa**, where you can have a bite to eat, go camping and stay overnight. You can also visit the palace there. You will then reach **Kloogaranna**, where the small river Treppola has to climb numerous stairs, making it a tourist attraction. Behind the bridge, turn right into the paved **Mere tee**, which takes you to a beach after a left curve. Turn right at the roundabout and then left behind **Klooga-Rand station**. Continue along the railway tracks until you reach the busy **8**, into which you turn right.

EXCURSION To get to the Holocaust Memorial, turn left and then right before the railway tracks.

Holocaust Memorial

The Nazi concentration camp of Klooga was designed for 3,000 male and female prisoners during the German occupation of Estonia. The majority of them were Jews who had been taken from the ghettos of Kaunas, Vilnius and Salaspils in 1943. In addition, some political prisoners, homosexuals and Soviet prisoners of war were also kept here.

The camp had a barbed wire fence around it and the areas for men and women were separated from each other. It was guarded by German SS units and members

of the Estonian Guard Battalion 287. The prisoners had to perform extremely hard forced labour as harvesters, in the production of concrete, doing construction work or wood processing.

With the advance of the Red Army to Estonia in July and August 1944, the SS began to bring many prisoners across the Baltic Sea to the Stutthof concentration camp near Gdansk. The prisoners of the remaining work

Holocaust Memorial in Klooga

detachments were taken to the Klooga concentration camp. On 19 September 1944, 2,000 prisoners were murdered. On 28 September 1944, the Red Army liberated 85 prisoners of Klooga concentration camp who had survived in hiding places.

The Holocaust Memorial was opened in May 2005 by the Estonian Prime Minister Andrus Ansip. In his speech on behalf of the Estonian government, he asked for forgiveness for Estonia's participation in the Holocaust and promised that Estonia would continue to do everything in its power to solve these crimes. On 24 July 2005, the Estonian President Arnold Rüütel and the Israeli Ambassador to Estonia, Schemi Zur, unveiled the marble commemorative stone.

The architects Mari Rass and Diana Taalfeld won the Estonian Architecture Prize for the design of the memorial in 2012. The large concrete blocks on which the texts of the exhibition can be found, symbolise the camp, in which the prisoners had to produce concrete products for the German war industry.

Stay on the busy 8 but then turn right in the left bend and after the sign 41 into **Vaana-Tallina maantee**. Shortly after it becomes unpaved, follow the road in a left and then a right bend. At the next branch in the road, turn right into **Kadaka tee**. Cross Leetse tee on the left and

Vääna-Jõesuu

Viti

Liikva

Naage

Meremõisa

Tūrisalu

Vääna

Lohusalu

Keila-Joa

Adra

Tõlinõmme järv

Tõlinõmme veehoidla

Humala

5,5

5,2

Boulder Kivi Külv

Leetse

9,5

Laulasmaa

Käesalu

Keelva

5,5

4,7

Paldiski

Kersalu

8

Kloogaranna

Tuulna

Illurma

D3

Holocaust Memorial

Laoküla

7,5

Klooga

then follow the road past the nuclear training centre until you reach the coast, where you turn left.

> **TIP** If you want to get to the picnic spot at the beach, turn right at the first possibility.

The main route continues straight on and you will pass the boulder "Kivikülv", the "kissing rock" with a height of 2.20 metres and a diameter of 19 metres. Afterwards, turn right towards the coast. The route continues along

Ruins of Padise Monastery

the 24-metre high cliffs and turns into **Majaka tee**, on which you will reach the cape of the **Pakri peninsula**. The lighthouse there dates from 1889. It is still in operation and is the tallest in Estonia with a height of 54 metres.

Follow **Majaka tee** along the coast, which turns onto the **183**. Pass the port and continue on **Sadama** until you reach Paldiski town centre.

Paldiski

The harbour city of Paldiski was founded by Tsar Peter I in 1718. In 1783, it received city rights under the name "Baltiyski Port". In 1933, it was given the name "Paldiski". During Estonian independence, it was a free port from 1922 to 1939. From 1939 to 1994, the city was the base of the Soviet naval forces and thus a restricted zone. There was an education centre for the nuclear submarine fleet as well as a nuclear reactor as a teaching complex for energy. There are now plans to built a technopark here.

The fortress with its five bastions, also known as Muulamäed, was built from 1718 to 1725 according to plans and under the direction of Peter I.

In the summer of 1912, the German Emperor Wilhelm II and the Russian Tsar Nicholas II met in the former Baltic port for informal talks, in which the French Prime Minister Raymond Poincaré saw ominous signs of a Russian-German partnership.

The Orthodox church of St. George from 1784 to 1787 has a neo-classical main entrance and a Baroque tower dome (renovated in 1899). Tsar Nicholas, patron of the Russian fleet, gave his name to the church of St. Nicholas, which was built in 1841.

The Pakri Islands of Suur-Pakri and Väike-Pakri, which are located three kilometres from Paldiski, were bought in 1345 by five Swedish families. Their descendants were expelled in 1940 when the Hitler-Stalin Pact was implemented. The islands - connected by a dam since 1952 - became a bombing site for the Warsaw Pact. After they had been returned to the Estonian state, it took three years to defuse all the unexploded bombs. Parts of the land were then returned to their pre-war owners, while others were put under protection because of limestone rocks, karst areas and specific flora and fauna.

From Paldiski to Nõva   57 km

From Paldiski, continue along the coast and then past a church, huge gas facilities and the station before crossing the railway tracks. Then, turn right into **Rae põik** and after a right bend you will reach the **E 265**, into which you turn left.

Continue straight into **Paldiski-Padise tee (174)**, on which you cross the river Vasalemma Jõgi and you will reach Madise.

Laoküla

7,5

D3

D2

Langa

Madise

Kurkse

9

Suurküla

Karilepa

6,5

Vintse

Pedase

Vihterpalu

Rabajärv

0,5

8,5

Vilivalla

Änglema

Altküla

Harju-Risti

Padise

4,2

Kõmmaste

6

Määra

Kasepere

Vihterpalujõgi

Pae

Vihterpalu jõgi

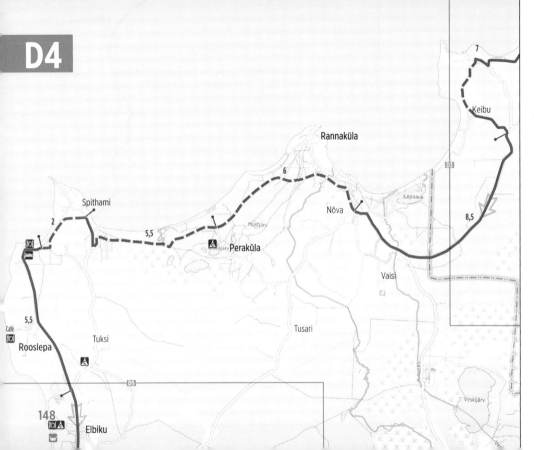

Madise

In Madise, a monument commemorates B.G. Forselius, the founder of the Estonian popular education system who was born here and who - against the resistance of the German-Baltic nobility - founded a teacher's seminar in 1684.

Turn left at the signpost and continue towards the church. You will get to the **174** again, which then leads to the **17**, into which you turn right. Pass **Karilepa** and you will reach **Padise** town centre, where you will find a hotel and a restaurant.

Padise monastery

Padise monastery belonged to the Cistercian order and was built in 1317. It served as a military camp during the Livonian War and was destroyed in 1580, but a walk through the ruins is still very impressive. In 1622, the mayor of Rīga, Thomas Ramm, received some of the monastery land as a country estate. The manor house was built at the end of the 18th century in baroque style. In the 19th century, a second floor was added and around the house a free-style park with pools, ponds (also for fishing) and orchards was created.

Three kilometres behind Padise, the route leaves the 17, turns right and then follows the **230**. Continue through **Harju-Risti** until you reach **Vihterpalu**. Turn right before the river – behind the river you can have something to eat and stay overnight – and then cross the river Vihterpalu jõgi on the left. Don't turn right towards Vintse but continue straight onto the solid forest path. Follow the signposted **EV 10** along the lake shore and you will reach a paved road into which you turn right. Just before **Ristinina**, turn left into **Eravaldus Raasiku**. This is easy to cycle on and is paved from **Keibu** onwards. At the end, turn right onto the **230** and once you have passed **Vaisi** you will reach the village of Nõva.

Nõva

In Nõva you can have something to eat and stay overnight. Just before the village you can also have a cup of coffee and a piece of cake in the information centre. St. Olaf's church from 1750 is the oldest unaltered wooden church in Estonia, although it is also one of the smallest, measuring a mere 13.6 x 7 metres. Its windows from 1836 are made of parchment.

From Nõva to Haapsaluu   57 km

In Nõva, turn right into the **129** and then left behind Nõva jõgi. Continue on a small, unpaved coastal road and through the forest. Behind the river, the path becomes semi-paved. At the next intersection, don't follow the signs of the EV 10 but turn right towards **Spithami**.

Just before the last houses, turn left onto the field path which is signposted **RMC**. After cycling around two gates in the forest, you will reach the **127** in **Dirhami**, where you can stay overnight at the guesthouse and go to a restaurant at the beach.

Turn left and you will reach **Rooslepa**, where you can find a camping site, sauna and a café at the beach. Continue via **Elbiku** – there is also a beach for swimming there – and you will reach **Riguldi**.

ALTERNATIVE At the end of the bay – Hara laht – you can turn right onto the unpaved road, which then leads to a paved road, into which you turn right. You will pass Hosby, Pürksi Birkas and Osterby and then reach

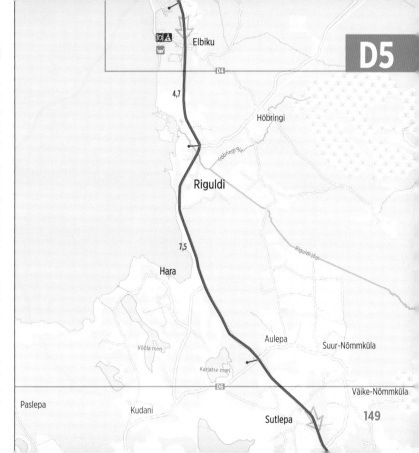

the port, from where you can take a ferry to Haapsalu. You can get information about this ferry connection from Jorma (📞 +372 566 77377).

The northwestern part of Estonia used to be populated by Swedes ("Rootsi"). However, during the Second World War, 60 percent of them fled and left the region to the Soviet troops. As tourists could not access it, the nature here remained untouched with its unique beach landscape and abundance of plants.

Continue straight on the **230** and you will pass through **Sutlepa** and get to **Linnamäe**, where you turn right onto the bike path of the **17** and then reach the **9** via **Kärbla**, into which you turn right.

EXCURSION Those interested in art should take a two-kilometre detour to the left. In a park you will find Kadarpiku estate, the house of the impressionist painter Ants Laikmaa, one of the key figures of the more recent history of Estonian art.

Although you can take the bike path of the busy **9** to Haapsalu, turn left past the bridge across the river Vönnu jögi and towards **Käbi Guest House**. Turn right behind the building and then left again onto the grassy path and then right onto the bike path on the former railway tracks.

Cross a few roads and streams on a nice bike path, then cross underneath the 31, pass a tower as well as

150

Railway Museum in Haapsalu

railway tracks with some rotting trains and you will reach the museum station. Take the **9** on the right until you reach the roundabout. Once there, turn left into **Kalda** and then continue north, past the tourist information centre **(Posti 37)**. Pass the palace ruins as well as the spit with the marina and the picturesque bay with a promenade and spa hall and you will reach Haapsalu old town.

Haapsalu

The city was founded between 1260 and 1270. From the 19th century it was a holiday resort of the Russian tsars and aristocrats. The Bishop's Castle with its park and lake and a perimeter wall of 803 metres in length is the most important medieval building in Haapsalu and one of the best-preserved in Estonia. The Cathedral Church also belongs to the castle complex and is one of the largest single-nave cathedrals in the Baltic States. It was completed around 1270 and is known for its good acoustics.

In August, a mysterious white lady appears in the middle window of the baptistery in the light of a full moon. This is the reason for the annual festival "Time of the White Lady" (Valge daami aeg). The 38-metre high church tower offers one of the best views over Haapsalu.

The city is famous for its scarves, which are all handmade. Ilon Wikland also lived here, who illustrated Astrid Lindgren's

book "Us children of Bullerby". Pyotr I. Tchaikovsky composed his 6th symphony, the "Pathétique" in his summer house here.

The station (Raudtee 2) was built in 1906. At 216 metres, it has the longest covered platform in Estonia. It was built especially for the tsar's visits and measured exactly the length of the tsar family's private train. However, trains have not run here for a long time and so it is now used as the Estonian Railway Museum (Raudteemu Museum) with its old locomotives and wagons.

In this district town with 10,000 inhabitants you can stop and spend the night. Interesting is also the second oldest building, the church of St. John (Jaani) behind the town hall, and "Peter's House" on the corner of Linda/Rüütli, where the Russian tsar Peter I slept in 1715. A walk along the beach leads to the spa hall, which was built in 1898, to the music pavilion (Promenaadi 1) and to the Tchaikovsky Bank. Numerous Art Nouveau villas also date back to the time this town was flourishing as a spa town.

Endel Nelis

The fencer Endel Nelis (1925-1993), who was popular in his home country, won many titles and founded the internationally renowned fencing school "En Garde" in Haapsalu at the beginning of the 1950s. The fencers he coached won many important prizes.

D9

Kap Tahkuna

Tahkuna

6

Lehtma

6,5

7

3,6

Kodeste

Reigi

Risti

Kärdla

Rootsi

Nuutri jõgi

D10

Hausma
4

Kidaste

Port Roograhu

Kanapeeksi

6,5

Linnumäe

6

õrgessaare

4,7

Pihla

Koidma

Koima

Pal5

D8

Kukka

153

Heigi

Lauka

Paluküla

Hopi järv

Lighthouse at Cape Tahkuna

The Finnish director Klaus Härö tells his life story in the film "The Children of the Fencer": As a teacher, he slowly becomes a father substitute for his pupils, who include war orphans and children whose parents are in Soviet captivity. The school principal, a devout Communist party comrade, rejects fencing as he perceives it to be a feudal relic and instead demands a more proletarian sport is taught. However, he was unable to assert himself against the resistance of the parents.

ALTERNATIVE If you don't want to pass the idyllic Estonian islands, follow the 31 in Haapsalu for nearly 40 kilometres until you reach the 10. Once there, turn right towards Lihula and Virtsu. Continue through a sparsely populated, flat landscape and after 75 kilometres, you will reach Pärnu..

From Haapsaluu to Kõrgessare	**73 km**

Turn left at the Railway Museum onto a nice bike path that was built on the former military road connecting the tsar railway station with the harbour. Near the train station is Kiltsi Airport, which served as an administrative station for MiG military jets during the Soviet era. On a wonderful forest path, you will pass the ruins of Ungru Castle of the pirate Baron Ewald von Ungern Sternberg. It was built in 1896 for the Baron's mistress and was intended to look like Merseburg Palace, but it was never finished because the lady died before it was completed. After about 10 kilometres you will reach the **ferry port of Rohuküla**, from where you can take a boat to Hiiumaa almost every two hours. The journey takes 75 minutes and the exact departure times can be found at www.praamid.ee.

Hiiumaa

The Estonian islands in the Läänemeri, i.e. the West Sea - this is how Estonians call the Baltic Sea - were used as outposts of the Soviet Union for many years and therefore a military restricted area. Due to the danger of people escaping, visitors were practically banned from entering. Of the once 3,000 inhabitants of the island of Vormsi, for example, only about 200 remained after the Second World War - and these were mostly soldiers. The islands of Hiiumaa and Saaremaa share a similar story.

Today, there are still 200 animal and 400 plant species in these areas, e.g. wild orchids and buttercups next to juniper trees and berry bushes. In terms of wildlife, you can see brown bears, moose and lynx roaming around.

After leaving the ferry in the port of **Heltermaa**, continue straight on the **80** and you will reach Suuremõisa.

Suuremõisa

The church of St. Lorenz is the oldest church in Hiiumaa. It was completed around 1259 and contains the grave of Ebba-Margaretha Stenbock (1704-1776), whose great-grandfather once owned the whole island and who is buried in the churchyard next door. There is also the best preserved manor house complex in Estonia, which is today used by two schools.

Turn right before Suuremõisa onto the **167** – a solid forest path – and then at the end left onto the **102**. In **Hellamaa**, turn right onto the **104**, which turns into the **106**. In **Harju**, turn right onto the **108**, which is easy to travel on, and you will reach **Kukka**. Continue along the coast and past the airport until you reach the **port of Roograhu**, where you can also find a restaurant.

From the port, the route continues back onto the **110** and to the golf course, where you turn right onto the

Kõrgessaare

4,7

Heigi

Lauka

Kurisu

Napi

Isabella

Jõeranna

8,5

Paope

Palli

Luidja

Kõpu Lighthouse

Villamaa

3

Puski

Heiste

6

Kõpu

Kiivera

Hüti

6

Laasi

Tammistu

Sülluste

Kiduspe

4,7

Nõmme

Vanajõgi

Jõesuu

paved **165**. Continue on there and along the coast until you reach Kärdla, the capital of Hiiumaa.

Kärdla

The city of Kärdla was first mentioned in 1564 and with its 3,000 inhabitants it is the only city on Hiiumaa and one of the greenest cities in Estonia. It is located in the pit of a meteorite that fell to earth around 400 to 500 million years ago.

The museum of Hiiumaa is located in the so-called "Long House", a former cloth factory, which was built around 1830 by the factory owner Robert von Ungern-Sternberg as a residential building. The exhibition and science centre is also located here. In Kärdla you can stop for a bite to eat and spend the night.

After the left turn, the **165** turns into **Uus** and you then turn right into **Posti**, which turns into **Vabrikuväljak**, on which you will reach the museum. From the museum, turn left into **Lubjaahju** and then right into **Vabaduse**, on which you will reach the **80**, into which you turn right. Just before you turn right onto the **82**, Ristimägi is well worth a visit.

Ristimägi

Ristimägi is a hill covered with crucifixes on both sides of the country road, which was created in connection with the deportation of the Swedes living in Reigi. Catherine the Great of Russia signed a decree according to which the Swedes should resettle south of Ukraine.

Before their deportation, the Swedes gathered on 20 August 1781 for a final worship service in the place known today as Ristimägi. Everyone built a cross before leaving the island and said goodbye to the place that had been their home for 400-500 years. Today, the opposite is true: visitors who come to Hiiumaa for the first time add their cross on the hill.

Just before Risti, the main route turns right onto the **82**, which leads around the Tahkuna peninsula.

Tahkuna

The Tahkuna peninsula is a sandy area with pine and spruce forests and is rich in berries and mushrooms. On the cape there is a 43-metre-high lighthouse, built in France in 1874. On the beach there is a monument by Mati Karmin, which remembers the children who lost their lives when the ferry "Estonia" sank in 1994.

The island was occupied by German armed forces during the First and Second World War. Fierce fighting took place in October 1941, which is commemorated by numerous war memorials in the woods and beaches on Hiiumaa.

You will reach **Lehtma** on the **82**. Then, continue on the unpaved path along the coast and you will reach Tahkuna, where you can have something to eat. Turn right at the cape to visit the lighthouse.

From the cape, continue on the **113** to **Malvaste**, where you turn right onto the **114** – a little bit further down on the 113 you will find the Mihkli Talumuuseum – and you will reach **Reigi**.

Mihkli Talumuuseum

The museum consists of a well-preserved farm. There are eight different buildings, one of which is a steam sauna from the 18th / 19th century. The inhabitants were Swedes who had settled in the north and west of the island.

In Reigi turn right onto the **80**, from where you turn right again towards Kõrgessare.

Kõrgessaare

This place was mentioned in writing as early as 1532. From 1909-1914, the Belgian company "Viscosa" operated a factory for artificial silk here, but because of the war that began in 1914, it could only be put into operation for a short period of time. In the village you can stop for some food and spend the night.

From Kõrgessaare to Leisi   40 km

From the **80** continue to **Luidja**, where you turn left into **Emmaste Luidja (84)**.

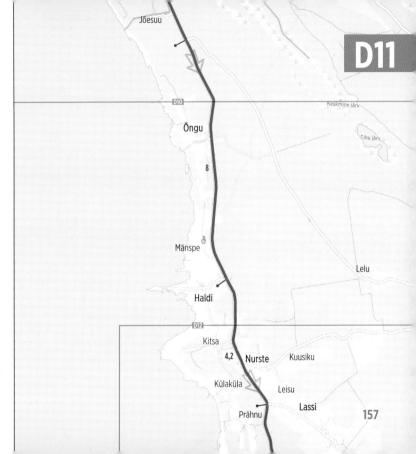

ALTERNATIVE If you would like to visit the Kõpu peninsula, turn right into Puski-Kõpu-Ristna and follow the signposted route.

Kõpu

The western tip, the peninsula Kõpu, should not be missed when you are on Hiiumaa. It was once a separate island. The landscape is picturesque with beautiful beaches, marshes and dunes. At the cape of the peninsula you will find a surfers' paradise with high sea waves. The world's third oldest lighthouse is the symbol of the island. As early as 1490, the Hanseatic League called for the construction of a lighthouse, which was completed in 1531. It was not until 1819 that stairs were included and the upper part was added so that you can look down to Hiiumaa from a height of more than 100 metres.

Continue straight on the **84** and at **Jõesuu** you will see the 10-metre deep valley of Vanajõe in the otherwise flat landscape.

Vanajõe Valley

At the bottom of the valley there is a small stream. The water is very clean as it is fed by numerous springs.

Continue on the **84** towards Emmaste. Pass through **Õngu** and **Nursti** and you will reach the village of **Metsalauka**, where you turn right onto the **133** and then left onto the **132** and you will reach Sõru.

Sõru

The harbour with the lighthouse of Sõru was built in the 19th century. Visitors of the National Museum can learn a lot about the life of the people on the coast as well as about the yacht "Alar". The main function of the port is the operation of the ferry line between the islands of Hiiumaa and Saaremaa www.veeteed.ee.

Saaremaa

Saaremaa is the main island and it is connected with neighbouring Muhu by a dam on which it is possible to travel. There are ferry connections to the mainland port of Virtsu. With 36,000 inhabitants, three percent of the Estonian population live

D11

157

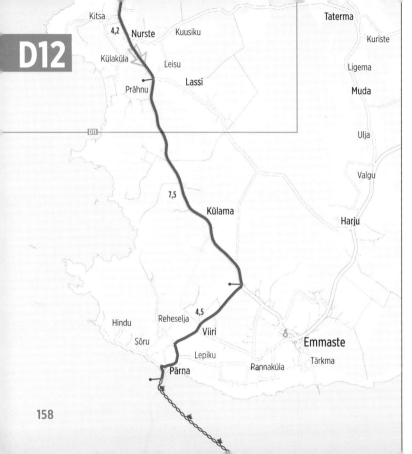

on Saaremaa island. Its isolated location left the island relatively unaffected by the Russianisation policy during the Soviet occupation period. The main town of the island is Kuressaare with about 16,000 inhabitants.

Roomassaare has the only airport on the island. The 1,300-kilometre-long coastline is characterised by large peninsulas and 600 smaller islands offshore. The Sõrve peninsula extends up to 30 kilometres into the Gulf of Riga. The southernmost point is marked by the 52-metre-high lighthouse near Sõrve. It was built in 1960 but its origins go back to 1646.

Saaremaa has a rich flora and fauna. In addition, it is located in the migration area of numerous bird species, that use the island as a stopover on their journey in spring and autumn.

With the beginning of the expansion policy of the Teutonic Order in the 13th century, Saaremaa came under foreign rule. However, the German order soon had to leave parts of the island to the diocese of Ösel-Wiek, which led to con-

stant armed conflict. Despite numerous uprisings against the occupying power, the Order was able to maintain its rule over the island until 1559.

During the Three-Crown War (1563-1570) between Poland, Sweden and Denmark, Saaremaa fell under Danish rule. After that, the rule over the island changed constantly until 1710, when it was taken over by the Russians in the Great Nordic War.

During the First World War the island was an important base of the Russian fleet. At the end of 1917 it was conquered by the Germans, who withdrew again after the armistice of 1918. After gaining independence in 1918, the island became part of Estonia.

During the Second World War the island was occupied by the Germans and many inhabitants were deported in 1944. On the Sõrve peninsula there was a fierce battle between the Germans, who withdrew from Saaremaa, and the Soviets, who were advancing from the east. Today, a 21-metre-high memorial at Tehumardi in

Pammana

Soela

4,5

7,5

Meiuste

Poka

6,5

Liiküla

Asuka

3,4

Metsküla

5,5

Parasmetsa

3,8

Triigi

Panga Cliff

1,8

Panga

5

Liiva

Pahapilli

Laugu

Leisi

Oitme

Võhma

4,5

Põitse

Nurme

Veske

Mäeküla

Aru

6,5

Paatsa

Angla Tuulikumägi

Angla

159

Linnaka

the form of a broken sword reminds us of this confrontation, which claimed thousands of victims.

During the fights until the end of November 1944, almost the entire peninsula was razed to the ground. Old gun facilities and dilapidated fortifications can still be found on the southern tip of Sõrves. The devastation of the war, deportations and evacuations reduced the island's population by more than 30%.

In the post-war period, Saaremaa was almost isolated from the mainland, even Estonians needed permission to enter the island. With the Estonian declaration of independence in 1991, Saaremaa gained the right of self-determination and was able to develop.

After reaching the port of **Triigi**, turn right after a few kilometres and you will reach Leisi.

Leisi

The historical parish of Karja in the area of today's Leisi was first mentioned in documents in the 13th century. The early Gothic church of Karja from the 14th century and the Orthodox churches of Leisi and Metsküla from the 19th century are well worth seeing.

If you would like to visit the five windmills in the village of Angla, turn left in Leisi and you will reach them after five kilometres.

From Leisi to Karala   100 km

Follow the paved **129** until you reach **Meiuste**, where you turn right onto the paved coastal road. This will take you directly along the Baltic Sea shore and it is easy to get to the sandy beaches from here. The **128** will take you to **Murika**. Afterwards, continue until just before **Metsküla**, where you turn right onto the paved

Viewing tower at the cliffs of Panga Pank

129 at the main intersection. You will pass the Russian-Orthodox church, which was built in 1911. Pass through **Asuka** and you will reach **Pahapilli**, where you continue straight on the unpaved **127**. Shortly afterwards you will reach a mustard production place which was opened by Germans from Dortmund. They also offer a mustard tasting sessions.

Cross the river Rossa oja and you will reach **Panga**, where you can have something to eat and spend the night. The main route continues left towards **Võhma**. Turn right to get to the very impressive limestone steep coast of Panga Pank. You can go for a bite to eat there and climb a viewing tower.

In Võhma turn right and after cycling along the bay for 12 kilometres you will reach **Mustjala**. Once there, turn left towards **Silla**, where you turn right and then continue through the river valleys of **Küdema** and **Lepakõrve**, the most beautiful and interesting on the island. In **Pidula** there is a Baroque manor house which is regarded as the most beautiful in Estonia and which has adjoining buildings in which you can spend the night. The surrounding park is also designed in Baroque style.

In **Kallaste**, continue straight on and then cycle along the bay to **Veere** and **Tagamõisa**. Then, continue straight on again and take the **78** until you reach **Kurevere**. Once there, turn right onto the unpaved **182** and you will reach

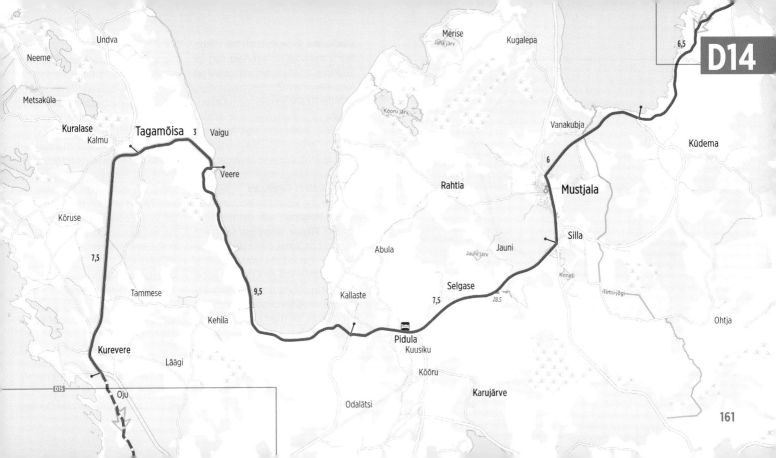

Neeme

Undva

Metsaküla

Kuralase
Kalmu

Tagamõisa

Vaigu

Veere

Kõruse

7,5

Tammese

9,5

Kehila

Kurevere

Läägi

Oju

D15

Merise
Jaha järv

Kugalepa

Kooru Järv

Rahtla

Abula

Kallaste

Pidula
Kuusiku

Kõõru

Odalätsi

Selgase

7,5

Jauni

Jauni järv

28.5

Karujärve

Vanakubja

6

Mustjala

Silla

Konati

Tirtsi-jõgi

Küdema

Ohtja

6,5

161

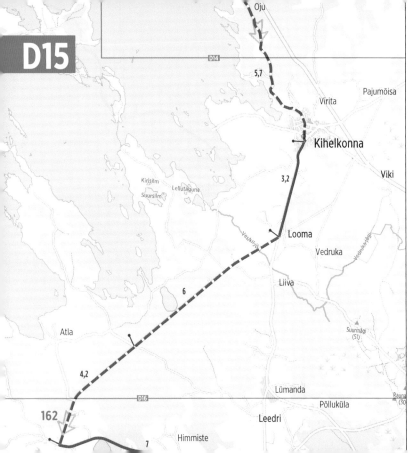

Kihelkonna. Cycle through the village, which was once an important port for Saaremaa, then turn right and you will get to **Loona** on the **102**, where you turn right onto the **112** and you will reach Karala.

Karala

In 1953, a 28-metre high lighthouse was built in the village of Karala with its 74 inhabitants, 42 metres above sea level.

From Karala to Kuressaare   45 km

Follow the **112** in the left curve and behind **Metsapere** you can turn right towards **Pilguse**, where you can spend the night. In **Varpe**, turn right onto the **102** – on the left in Lümanda there is a restaurant – and pass through **Koovi** and **Risku** until you reach **Toomalõuka**.

ALTERNATIVE If you would like to cycle around Sõrve peninsula, turn right onto the 108 and cycle to Möldri.

Sõrve

In 1944, a devastating battle between the retreating German Wehrmacht and the advancing Red Army took place on the adjoining peninsula in the south.

Some military buildings and the Soviet memorial on the beach near Tehumardi are reminders of this. Due to deportations to Germany or Russia and the devastation of the war, the island lost more than 30 percent of its population.

The **102** branches off to the left behind **Toomalõuka**. Pass through **Lõmala** and **Suurna** and you will reach **Tehumardi**, where you can have a bite to eat and spend the night. Turn left onto the busy **77** and you will reach **Mändjala**. The separate bike path starts here and this will take you through **Nasva** and all the way to Kuressaare, the capital of Saaremaa.

Kuressaare

The townscape of Kuressaare with its 16,000 inhabitants is dominated by magnificent buildings from the 17th and 18th century, including many wooden villas. In the second half of the 19th century, healing mud was discovered nearby, which led to the construction of a spa centre. The restored 1889 spa house with its concert hall is the main building

Kogula

Käesla

Leedri

Himmiste

Karala

D15

7

Metsapere

Nigu laht

Pilguse

Jõgela

Varpe

Kõrkküla

Paadla laht

Hirmuste

Kipi

Koki

Koovi

7

Vägara laht

Koimla

D17

Kotlandi

Taritu

7

Riksu

5,7

Järve

Lahetaguse

Toomalõuka

Lõmala

Tiirimetsa

Suurna

Järve järv

Möldri

8

Tehumardi

Salme jõgi

Sõrba jõgi

163

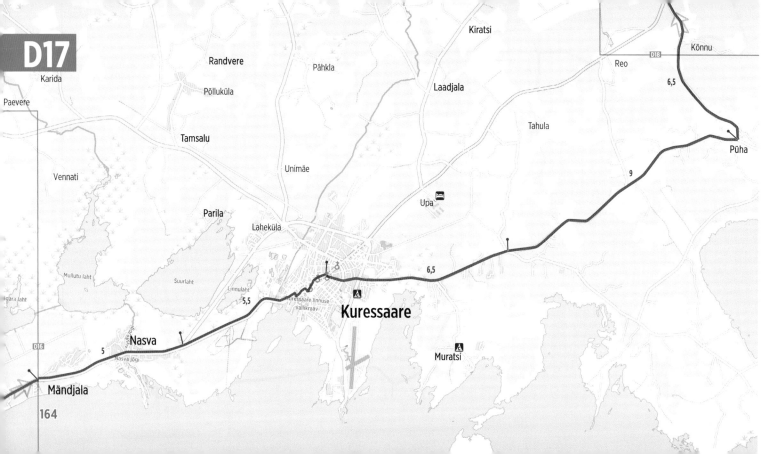

Karida

Paevere

Randvere

Põlluküla

Pähkla

Kiratsi

Laadjala

Kõnnu

Reo

6,5

Tamsalu

Tahula

Vennati

Unimäe

Upa

9

Parila

Laheküla

Püha

Mullutu laht

Suurlaht

Linnulaht

6,5

igara laht

5,5

Kuressaare linnuse
vallikraav

Kuressaare

D16

5

Nasva

Nasva jõgi

Muratsi

Mändjala

Audla
Ridala
D19

Haeska
Löve-Jõgi
Jõõri
Kõnnu
Koksi
Kuiste
6,5
Lööne
Rahu
Männiku
Laimjala
D18
Valjala
Röösa
Kahtla
Rannaküla
Tõnija
Asva
Liiva-Putla
Reeküla
Eiste
Kalli
Jursi
8,5
Kõiguste
Kaali
Kaali järv
Kõljala
Kallemäe
Rannaküla
Ruhve
6
Kangrusselja
4,5
1,5
0,2
Sakla
D17
Nurme
Kungla
Metsaküla
Väljaküla

Kõnnu

Sculpture at Kuressare marina

of the town park. Chamber music and opera festivals are held here every year. The centre has retained its old structure: Opposite the town hall from 1654/70 is the Wiegehaus, which later became a shop, as well as the market square.

Built in 1380 by the Teutonic Order in Kuressaare, Arensburg is considered the best-preserved medieval castle in the Baltic region. It is dominated by the 29-metre-high tower Pikk Hermann (Long Hermann). Today, it is home to the Saaremaa Museum, which introduces visitors to the island's history and nature.

From Kuressaare to Orissaare   61 km

Follow **Talinna 77** and then turn right into **Pihtia tee (133)**, which turns into **Kuressaare-Püha-Masa**. Cross the 76 and you will reach **Püha**, where you follow the sharp left turn until you reach the **10**, into which you turn right.

EXCURSION If you would like the famous meteorite crater of Kaali, turn left into Masa-Kaali and continue past Kõljala manor house.

Meteorite crater

The main crater (Kaali Meteoriidikraater) is a greenish pond of about 50 metres in diameter, surrounded by a 16-metre-high earth wall with a diameter of 110 metres. There are a further eight secondary craters in the vicinity of the crater created by the main impact. They are considerably smaller with diameters between 15 and 40 metres. The meteorite that probably struck 4,000 years ago sparked many myths in the population. The small crater lake is surrounded by a wide forest belt, with a path running through it: "Lovers' Boulevard".

There is also a museum, where you can stop and spend the night.

Kõljala Manor House

The manor house which was first mentioned in 1509 is in Baroque style and surrounded by a park.

The main route continues on the **10** towards **Masa**, where you turn right into **Masa-Laimjala-Tumala**, on which you will reach Sakla.

Sakla

This village with its 100 inhabitants was first mentioned in 1645. Around the middle of the 18th century, the "Crown Estate of Sackla" was built on local farmland.

After the Soviet occupation of Estonia, the first collective farm of the Estonian SSR was founded in Sakla in 1947. It was named after the Estonian communist Viktor Kingissepp (1888-1922), who came from Saaremaa.

In the local library, a small museum provides information on the history of the forced collectivization of agriculture in the region. There is also a private museum with historical radios and TVs in the village.

Pass through **Laimjala** and you will reach **Puka**. If you turn right, you can visit the 40-square-kilometre-big Koigi moor in Oti with Lake Koigi and in Pöide the largest church in Saaremaa.

Pöide

This church was one of the first stone churches in Estonia. Its fortified appearance dates back to the occupation of the island by the Livonian Order, which sought to consolidate its dominance.

Cross the 10 again and you will reach Orissaare.

Orissaare

In this rural community with more than 2,000 inhabitants there is a library and since 1946 also a grammar school. Since 1896 the town has been connected with the island of Muhu by a dam. There are overnight stays and refreshments available. The curiosity of Orissaare is an oak tree standing in the middle of the local football field. When the stadium was expanded in 1951, the Soviet construction workers were unable to remove the roots. Footballers have got used to it - in 2015, the oak tree was voted to become the "European Tree of the Year".

From Orissaare to Virtsu   **27 km**

Continue through the village on the **75** and you will reach the island of Muhu by cycling on the busy dam.

Muhu

Estonia's third largest island has 2,000 inhabitants. In the north there are steep cliffs. Together with the islands of Saaremaa, Hiiumaa and Vormsi as well as a number of smaller islands, Muhu is part of a UNESCO biosphere reserve with an area of 4,000 hectares and 11,000 square kilometres of water.

Behind the dam, turn right and then keep right – all unpaved but easy to travel on – and you will reach **Nurme**, where you continue on **Liiva-Suuremõisa-Piiri** and then turn right at the next intersection. Behind **Suuremõisa** and before **Laheküla**, turn left and you will reach the unpaved **154**, into which you turn right. In **Pädaste**, follow the road in a sharp left turn towards **Kuivaste**, where you turn right and will then reach the port. From there, you can take the ferry to Virtsu.

> In winter, when the ice on the straight between Virtsu and Kuivastu is deep enough, the island can be reached by land vehicles via a track marked on the ice.

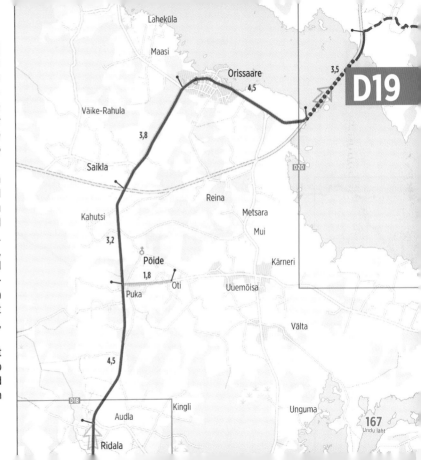

Virtsu

Virtsu on the peninsula of the same name is a village with 600 inhabitants, which was founded in the 19th century around the only and important ferry port to Muhu/Saaremaa, from which it also derives its meaning. Today, the town is also known for its wind farm owned by the Estonian energy company Eesti Energia.

About three kilometres from the port you can see the remains of a vassal castle of the diocese of Ösel-Wiek, which was already destroyed in 1534.

To the south of the peninsula is the small island of Puhtulaid, to which a dam leads. The owner of Virtsu Palace had an English park created here, which is completely neglected today. However, Puhtulaid offers the best conditions for bird studies and cyclists are allowed to pass through.

> **TIP** You should stock up on some food supplies before leaving the village as the nearest bigger supermarket is 50 kilometres away.

Von Virtsu nach Tõstamaa 50 km

Immediately after leaving the harbour, continue straight on and past the petrol station and the supermarket. After the bend, the route continues right, with signposts towards Tõstamaa, into the road **Tammi tee**, which is signposted as **Bike Path 1** and **EV 10**. The road is paved, marked in red but very quiet.

Behind the bridge and a right bend turn right – in the opposite direction of the signposts – into **Hanila-Hõbesalu** with little traffic. Pass through **Rame** and you will reach **Pivarootsi**, where you can see the windmill on the right side and where you can spend the night and have something to eat.

At the village exit, the pavement stops and the route continues on the solid path. Follow **Hanila-Hõbesalu** in

Windmill in Pivarootsi

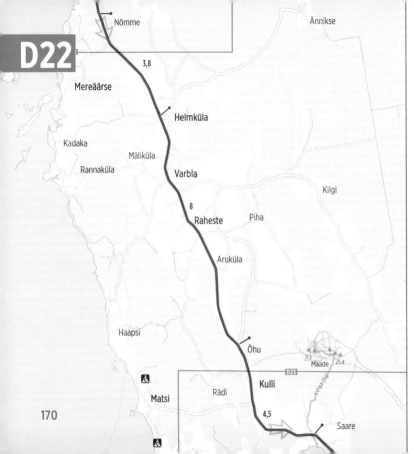

a sharp left turn until you reach the end in **Hõbesalu**, where a memorial stone commemorates Jaan Teemant.

Jaan Teemant

Jaan Teemant (1872-1941) was Head of State of the Republic of Estonia from 1925-27 and 1932. He was a member of the Tallinn City Council, took an active part in the 1905 revolution and was forced to go into exile in Switzerland. He was sentenced to death in absentia by a tsarist court. In 1908, he was able to return to Estonia, but he spent one and a half years in custody.

From 1919-1920 he was a member of the Constituent Assembly of the newly established Republic of Estonia and a long-standing member of the Estonian Parliament (Riigikogu).

After the Soviet occupation of Estonia, Jaan Teemant was arrested by the NKWD on 23 July 1940. It remains unclear to this day what happened to him. It is possible that he was executed in Tallinn in the summer of 1941.

Turn right into **Rame-Paatsalu**, which is signposted as **EV 10** and **Bike Path 1**. Cross Paadrema jõgi on the quiet road and you will reach Paatsalu.

Paatsalu

Paatsalu is a village with 70 inhabitants and is located at the Gulf of Riga. The south-eastern part of the village belongs to the Paadrema nature reserve. Jaan Teemant was born in Illuste, which today belongs to Paatsalu.

Puhtu-Laelatu wetlands and Nehatu moor

This wetland area consists of a succession of open or overgrown lagoons and is of great importance for passing waterfowl. The moor with its two-metre-thick layer of peat consists of shallow ponds, swamps and forest meadows and thus offers welcome resting places for geese and cranes. One of the oldest international treaties on environmental protection, the Ramsar Convention of 1971, already lists this region among the protected wetlands.

Rädi

Kulli

Ermistu

Soomra

Ermistu Järv

4,5

Saare

D22

Vaiste   4,5

Rammuka

Lõuka

Kastna

Karuga

Ranniku

6

Tõstamaa

Värati

Tõlli

6,5

Seliste

D24

Kõpu

5,2

4,7

3,5

Pootsi

Kavaru

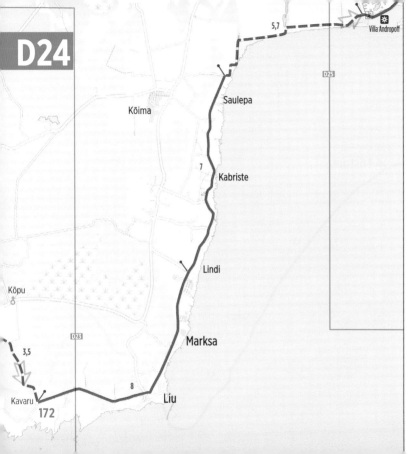

Kõima

Saulepa

7

Kabriste

Lindi

Kõpu

Marksa

D23

3,5

Kavaru

172

8

Liu

5,7

Villa Andropoff

D25

You will reach **Varbla** on the quiet road. At Raheste bus stop, a memorial stone commemorates the writer Karl Ristikivi (1912-1977), who was born here and who fled to Sweden during the Second World War and fought for Estonia's independence.

The next ca. 40 villages all belong to Varbla parish, which has a 60-kilometre-long beach and is therefore very popular as a holiday destination. The most popular is Matsirand in the south, near Saulepi.

You will reach Tõstamaa by continuing on the main road.

Tõstamaa

Tõstamaa was first mentioned in 1553 and today 1,500 inhabitants live in the rural community. It is the historical centre of the region, an old bishop's estate that grew into a village. Here you can stop for a bite to eat, spend the night and go shopping.

From Tõstamaa to Pärnu   50 km

Continue straight on the **101**, follow the signposts to Pärnu and behind Tõstamaa

Accordion sculpture in front of Pärnu Spa Hall

you will pass a petrol station, where you can go shopping and have breakfast. You will reach **Pootsi**, where you can find a restaurant that is open from 10am-6pm.

EXCURSION If you want to get to the islands of Manõja and Kihnu, turn right onto the road towards Munalaiu harbour.

Kihnu

The largest island in Rīga Bay (16.3 km²) is located 12 km from the mainland and has been the location of four villages since the 15th century. The church was built in 1642. The culture of the inhabitants developed independently for 600 years and differs in language, dress, folk songs and marriage traditions. Some women still wear traditional clothing. On the island there is an ethnographic museum and a memorial stone for the legendary ship captain Kihnu Jõnn at his birthplace. At the top of Pitkana there is a 31-metre-high lighthouse.

Manilaid

The 4.5-kilometre-long sandy area is not suitable for forests or meadows and is only one kilometre away from the mainland. People have only been living here since 1933, when the lighthouse was built.

As there is a gap of 100 metres, it is not possible to cycle from Pootsi directly to **Kavaru**. Therefore, follow the **101** towards **Kõpu**, where you turn right behind the bus stop "Maria" onto a solid field path which is

Tallinn Gate in Pärnu

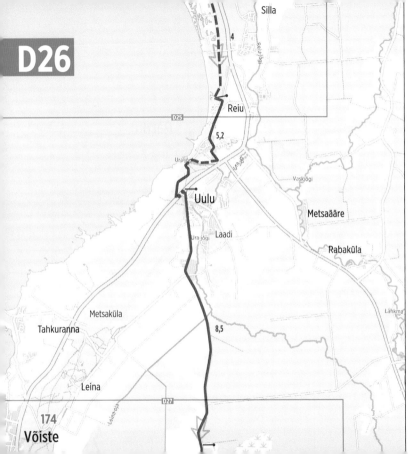

Silla

4

Reiu

D25

5,2

Uralj

Vaskjõgi

Uulu

Metsaääre

Laadi

Ura jõgi

Rabaküla

Lähkma

Metsaküla

Tahkuranna

8,5

Leina

D27

signposted towards Kavaru. In **Kavaru**, you will reach a paved road with very little traffic, into which you turn left and continue along the lake until you reach **Liu**. Continue past holiday homes and a bus stop. Where the road continues left towards Lindi, there is a shop on the right side where you can stock up on supplies.

Stay along the coast – a great, paved road with very few cars – and you will pass through **Kabriste** and **Saulepa** before you reach the river Tuuraste oja, behind which the paved part of the road stops. The route then continues on a not very comfortable gravel road, from where you can hear the sound of the Baltic Sea until you reach **Audru**.

Go straight at the intersection into the paved **Valgeranna**. The long beaches are protected from the cold northern wind by pine forests. Continue past the large White Beach Golf Course.

EXCURSION If you want to get to the Andropoff villa, where you can have something to eat and spend the night, turn right just before the bridge across Audru jõgi into Ranna tee.

Behind the bridge, turn right into **Elu tee**, cross the big road which has the right of way and then continue straight on. At the end of Elu tee, turn left and then immediately right again into **Nooda tee**. At the end, turn right into **Mõrra** and then left into **Kest**, which you follow on the right. At the end, bear left to get to the main road, into which you turn right.

Cross the river Sauga on the joint pedestrian/bike path and then turn right at the next intersection and cross Pärnu jõgi on a bridge.

To get to the **station**, turn right directly behind the bridge and then continue underneath the bridge along the river bank on a nice - and even lit – bike path which is signposted **EV 10** and **1**. After crossing underneath the main road and the railway tracks, turn right and you will reach Pärnu station. From there, you can take direct trains to Tallinn.

TIP If you want to get to Pärnu information centre, continue straight into Akademia, then left into Rüütli and at the corner of Uss, left again into Nikolai.

Pärnu

- **Yekaterin Church**, Vee 16, is the most beautiful Baroque church in Estonia. It was built from 1746 to 1768 at the request of Catherine II and has had a strong influence on the architecture of the Orthodox churches in the Baltic States.
- The construction of the **Church of St. Elizabeth**, Nikolai 2, was financed by tsaress Elizabeth in 1744-47, which explains the name of the church. The organ concerts are particularly recommended.
- The **Red Tower**, Hommiku 11, is the only remaining bastion of the former city wall and the oldest building in the city. Before it was reconstructed from 1973-80, it had various functions; among other things it served as a prison and a city archive.
- The **town hall**, Uus 4, from 1797 was once the residence of a merchant. After his death it was bought by Alexander I and then converted into a commander's house. It has been a town hall since 1839.

- The **Tallinn (Reval) Gate** is the only completely remaining city gate in the Baltic States. The bridge used to provide access to the city across the gateway moat. It was known as Carl-Gustav Bridge until 1710. Similar king's gates can be found in Narva and Rīga. The building was restored from 1977-1980.

Pärnu, named after the longest river of the same name in Estonia, has been the so-called "summer capital" of Estonia since the opening of the first swimming pool in 1838. At this time of year, it turns into a place of entertainment. There are concerts, shows and sports competitions every day. In good weather, the beach is the most popular place and can get crowded. The recreation centres are also famous. The parks are good for walking and cycling. If you want to see architectural monuments, you should have a wander around the relatively small town centre.

Soomaa National Park

Soomaa National Park, also called the "land of marshes", is located 35 kilometres east of Pärnu and is the second largest in

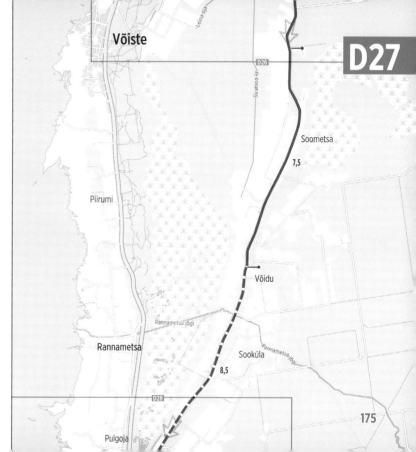

175

Pulgoja

Papisilla

Arumetsa

Häädemeeste

6,5

Jaagupi

Krundiküla

Penu

Häädemeeste jõgi

Urissaare

7,5

Kabli

Massiaru

D29

Estonia after Lahemaa National Park. It is home to the largest high moor in the Baltic States and one of the largest in Europe. 400 square kilometers of heather, pine and birch trees.

The park was created to protect its extensive high moors, floodplain meadows, forests and meandering rivers. Soomaa is also home to rare animals such as moose, wild boars, beavers, wolves or brown bears and is also an important breeding ground for golden eagles, black storks and capercaillies.

In the flat landscape of south-western Estonia there is an interesting water world: The national park comprises five moors, separated by dense forests and vast floodplains, fed by countless small rivers. The so-called "fifth season" is unique: Each year when the snow melts or during heavy rainfall, huge quantities of water flow down from the nearby Sakala plateaus into Soomaa National Park, where they flood an area of several hundred square kilometres. A rise in the water level of individual rivers of up to six metres was measured during the flooding season. The stables of the region's farms have two storeys to keep the animals safe on a higher level. During this time, the national park is transformed into an inaccessible water wilderness. During this time, the only means of transport is the canoe. Guided canoe trips are offered for tourists.

From Pärnu to Ainaži   69 km

Behind the bridge across Pärnu Jõgi, the main route continues right and across the car park. Cross the river Walikäa on a small bridge and then turn right into **Lootsi** and follow the bike path along the coast. Continue past the viewing tower and through the park until you reach the spa hall with a sculpture of an accordion player.

Turn right at the road and then left and continue along the beach, where you can see numerous stone sculptures.

Turn left behind Hedon Spa Hotel and then right into **Ranna puiestee**, which you take parallel to the beach promenade, past an old watchtower and a climbing adventure park.

At the end of the road, take the bike path at **Papiniidu**, which turns into **Kalevi puiestee**. At the end, turn left behind **Ranamaetsa tee** onto the unpaved forest path and then right into **Golfi tee**, past the golf course.

The path is easy to travel on and only bumpy in parts. However, in comparison to the main road, where you are overtaken by many lorries at a high speed and little distance, it is very comfortable.

Golfi tee is then paved for a small stretch and you will cycle past the golf course, which stretches for quite some distance. Behind **Rae tee**, the paved part stops and you continue past the golf course and through the forest until you reach **Kulla Villa** directly at the coast.

Once there, turn left into **Kulla tee**, which takes you to **Posti tee**, into which you turn right. This quiet residential street is paved. After the next intersection it is called **Mereküla tee**. The route continues past a holiday camp for children and into

Karu tee, that leads to the **E 67** after a right and then a left bend.

Just before, turn right into **Kanali tee**. This first takes you past holiday houses and then continues as a bike and pedestrian path behind the bridge. Keep right where the paved part stops and follow the wide forest path. You will see Uulu Canal and the path then continues downhill across a small bridge. At the other side of the canal it is quite difficult to get to the wide forest path.

Turn right at the next intersection into **Kösti tee**. Continue past Puhkemaja holiday resort, then turn left at the next opportunity and in **Uulu** you will get to the busy **E 67**, into which you turn left. After a few metres, turn right at the petrol station onto the **333**.

Continue on the quiet road along Rannametsa-Soometsa conservation area and across a small river until you reach **Soometsa**, where there are no shopping or dining possibilities.

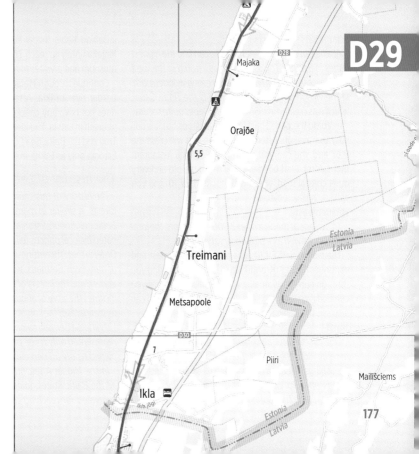

Rannametsa-Soometsa

At a height of 40 metres, here you can find the highest dunes in Estonia. Tolkuse swamp is located in the west and is accessible via a two-kilometre long wooden path. In the village of Rannametsa there is the Timm Canal, which was created in 1858 and today looks quite natural.

In **Võidu** the paved part of the road stops but it is still easy to travel on. After 6 kilometres you will cross the E 67 and you can find a shop as well as a restaurant there. After a left bend you will reach the old and very quiet coastal road, which is signposted **EV 10**, and you will reach Häädemeeste.

Häädemeeste

This village at the beach has 2,000 inhabitants, the local museum as well as a bird observation point.

The signposted **EV 10** runs parallel to the coast and continues through **Krundiküla** to Kabli, while taking you through numerous smaller coastal villages, where you can find nice camping sites and hotels. In Kabli you can also see the Baltic Sea from a viewing tower.

Kabli

One of the first long-haul sailing yachts was built here in 1861. The ship owner J. Markson's house and furnishings has been preserved in its original condition and is open to visitors. It is located directly in Kabli directly along the route.

Behind Kabli, follow the signposted **EV 10** through **Majaka** until you reach **Treimani**, where you can visit a museum and a water tower.

Continue through **Metsapoole** and you will reach the border river in **Ikla**. After crossing the border, which does not have any checkpoints anymore, you will find yourself in Latvia. The identical route of the Iron Curtain Trail and the Baltic Sea Coast Bike Path is signposted in Estonia only as EV 10, in Latvia only as EV 13.

The history of Latvia

The history of this country, rich with waterways and forests, is similar in many respects to the history of its Baltic neighbours Estonia and Lithuania. The land dominated by local princes fell under the rule of the Teutonic Order in the 13th century, which resulted in the settlement of numerous Germans, who back then belonged to the upper class. The history of the castles and knights' estates includes the story of about a hundred Baltic families, the descendants of the knights and sword brothers who ruled Latvia like a German colony for 700 years. Although they represented only three percent of the population, they owned nearly 50 percent of the country.

In the Middle Ages, numerous Latvian cities, like in all the Baltic States, joined the Hanseatic League and cultivated far-reaching trade relations. As a result of the Reformation, the Holy Order was transformed into a duchy. After the end of the Livonian-Lithuanian War, the country experienced numerous changes of territory before Sweden gained control over most of the country's territory in 1629 with the conquest of the territory of Livonia.

The next change took place as early as the beginning of the 18th century, when Latvia became largely Russian, following the Great Northern War. In the 19th century, and particularly in the 20th century, the desire for independence began to grow.

After the Russian Revolution and the First World War, Latvia declared its independence on 18 November 1918 and was able to defend its independence against Soviet Russia in the Latvian War of Independence (1918-1920). As part of the Peace of Rīga in 1920, the Soviet Union recognised Latvia's independence "for all time". The Hitler-Stalin Pact, however, made the country once again "fair game" for foreign powers in 1939, when the two dictators divided Eastern Europe among themselves, "the northern border of Lithuania also constituting the frontier of the interests of Germany and the USSR."

On 17 June 1940, Soviet troops occupied the Latvian territory under Soviet force, installed a puppet government, and made it the 14th Soviet Republic. Following this, about 100,000 Latvians were deported to Siberia.

Just one year later, on 22 June 1941, Nazi Germany attacked the Soviet Union. With the so-called "Operation Barbarossa" attack, German troops brought Latvia under their control and wasted little time in beginning the elimination of the Jewish population. About 70,000 were murdered. In the forest of Rumbula alone, 25,000 Jews were shot. According to the report by the International Commission of Historians (2005), the Germans were aided in this atrocity by the Latvian authorities.

After the defeat of the German troops at the end of the Second World War, the Soviet Union returned to power, and the country became a part of the Soviet Union as the "Latvian Soviet Socialist Republic" (LSSR). The initial resistance was broken in very little time and extensive deportations to Siberia followed. At the same time, massive immigration waves from other parts of the Soviet Union threatened to make Latvians a minority in their own country.

The struggle for independence from the Baltic states became obvious on 23 August 1989, the 50th anniversary of the Hitler-Stalin Pact (see also on page 85). On that day, 2.5 million Estonians, Latvians and Lithuanians formed a human chain across 600 kilometres of the "Baltic Way" through the three Baltic states from Tallinn via Riga to Vilnius, in a call for independence and a rally against the communist regime. This was the longest human chain of all times. The fall of the Soviet empire had begun.

On 4 May 1990, the Supreme Council of the LSSR decided to restore the Republic of Latvia and declared its independence from the Soviet Union. The "Singing Revolution" however, could not stop Soviet troops being sent to Vilnius and Rīga by order of Mikhail Gorbachev in January 1991.

Following the call of the "Latvian People's Front" (Latvijas Tautas fronte), thousands of people built barricades around the parliament building, squared up to the Soviet troops and thus defeated

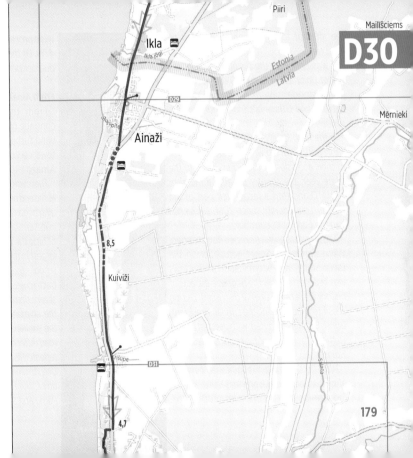

the attempt to regain control initiated by Moscow.

It was only with the disintegration of the Soviet Union on 21 August 1991 that the parliamentary decision to recognise Estonia's, Latvia's and Lithuania's independence succeeded.

In the 1990's, Latvia experienced a remarkable upturn, which was an important factor in their accession to the EU in 2004. In the same year, the country became a member of NATO and thus a recognized part of the Western community. Since 2014, Latvia has had the Euro as its currency.

The way history was recorded also changed. While during the Soviet occupation in the Baltic States, the extermination of the Jews was kept secret, now the negative aspects of history were being openly discussed. During a visit to Israel in 1998, the Latvian President, Guntis Ulmanis admitted, with deepest regret, to the participation of his countrymen in the Holocaust.

With its two million inhabitants, Latvia is almost as large as Bavaria and has a 500-kilometre-long coastal strip with a 300-metre-

Lighthouse in Ainazi

wide protection zone and a forest area of 47%. Of the two million inhabitants, one quarter belongs to the Russian minority.

From Ainaži to Saulkrasti   87 km

From the Estonian-Latvian border, continue on the old country lane, past a wind turbine and   you will reach Ainaži town centre.

Ainaži

The town of Ainaži gained some importance at the end of the 19th century, when shipbuilding began due to the large amount of wood in its surrounding area. Within a short period of time the port grew to become one of the largest in the country. The first Latvian naval school - today a museum - added to the attractiveness of the town. However, it suffered severe damage during the First World War, the shipping industry was destroyed and the sunken ships were blocking the access road. After its reconstruction, the town's fate repeated itself during the Second World War. Despite renewed reconstruction during Soviet times, the town lost important functions to Pärnu and Salacgrīva.

In addition to the museum, there is an old sailors' cemetery, the slim white lighthouse from 1930 and the Orthodox church from 1895. The hike on the northern breakwater, which is composed of coarse stones, is a real nature experience. It first leads through a sea of reeds before it reaches the open water.

Cycle through the town on the old and quiet street, past the lighthouse and the marine museum as well as Nordvidzeme Biosphere Reserve.

Nordvidzeme Biosphere Reserve

With an area of 4,600 km², Nordvidzeme Biosphere Reserve covers around six percent of Latvia's territory and consists of mixed forests, high moors, dunes, coastal meadows, lakes, rivers and sandstone cliffs.

Valdemāra iela will take you to EV 13, which is signposted Via Baltica (A 1), into which you turn right. After one kilometre, turn left and continue on the old paved road again. Just before this leads to the new road, turn left onto the signposted but unpaved forest path. Continue along a stream and parallel to the A 1. Just before Krišupe, turn right onto the bike path which is signposted as EV 13. Continue past Kapteinu osta and all time cycle parallel to the A 1. Cycle on the separate bike path (purple) along the main road for about 3 km and then turn right into Pernavas iela. This continues parallel to the main road until Salacgrīva. You will pass a war memorial with the inscription 1914-45 and at the end of the road after a left bend – the harbour is located on the right – you will reach the **A 1** again, into which you turn right. In Salacgrīva you will cross the river Salaca on a separate bike path.

Salacgrīva

This port town with 3,000 inhabitants is the centre of the administrative district of the same name, which merged in 2009 with the town of Ainaži and the three rural communities (pagasts) of Ainaži, Liepupe and Salacgrīva to form one joint administrative community. A total of 9,000 inhabitants live here on an area of 640 km².

The area was inhabited by the Lives. From 1207 onwards, a trading post of the Archbishop of Rīga existed at the estuary of the Salaca river, which was secured with a castle from 1226 onwards. After 1561, the area belonged to Poland-Lithuania. The castle was destroyed in the wars with Sweden. After the town became part of the Russian Empire in 1721, the Livic language slowly died out. In 1870, the riverbed was made deeper and a harbour was opened. This led to the settlement of industrial companies and craft businesses. However, the town became less important when in 1903 another port was opened in neighbouring Ainaži, which received a railway connection (narrow gauge) in 1912.

It was not until after the Second World War that the number of inhabitants increased again after a large fish processing factory was built.

Immediately behind the bridge turn right and then left into **Rīgas iela**, which turns into **Sila iela** behind the church and the tourist information centre. Continue on the forest path which is signposted as route **101** and becomes unpaved later. After 7 kilometres, cross the river Svētupe, where you can put up your tent and go for a bite to eat. Then, turn left, continue for 1 kilometre on a gravel road leading to the A 1 and then continue parallel to the **A 1** for three kilometres. The route continues for 3 kilometres on the A 1 until you reach the river Vitrupe. Continue on

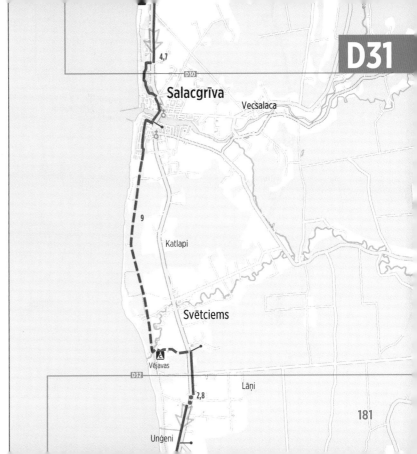

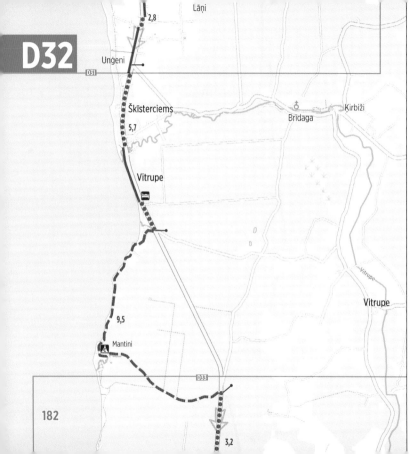

the bike path for 2 kilometres and from the car park, turn right off the A 1 after one kilometre without a bike path. The route continues on a quiet and paved road along the coast and then on a solid forest path along the "rocky coast". In **Berzini** you can stay overnight directly on the beach and in **Mantini** you can find a large camping site.

Hurricane Gudrun

Hurricane Gudrun swept across Northern Europe in January 2005 with wind speeds of up to 145 km/h. It claimed 15 lives and threatened coastal towns in Finland, Russia and Estonia due to high water levels. Parts of the bike path also disappeared. Since the owner of the adjoining property does not allow the bike path to run across his land, cyclists have to choose between a detour of seven kilometres along the main road and a bad gravel road or to push the bike along the beach for one kilometre.

Continue on the coastal path, turn left behind Mantini camping site onto the **A 1**. After 3.5 kilometres, turn right and after a further 3 kilometres you will reach the coast. Continue for another 5 kilometres and you will reach **Tuja**, where the road is paved and you keep right along the coast. The paved part of the route stops then and you will reach the fishing village of **Lembuži**, where you turn left and will reach **Via Baltica**, into which you turn right. Stay on the bike path and once in **Liepupe** you will pass the church in which Münchhausen got married. You will also find a 4* hotel there with a good restaurant. Behind Liepupe, continue for 6 kilometres on the **A 1** until you see the sign for the Münchhausen Museum. Turn right behind the sign and continue on the paved road until you reach the Münchhausen Museum in **Dunte**.

Münchhausen Museum

Most people in Germany have heard of the "baron of lies", who allegedly flew around on a cannonball, pulled himself and his horse out of the swamp by his own head or is said to have caught ten ducks with bacon tied to a leash.

Münchhausen Museum in Dunte

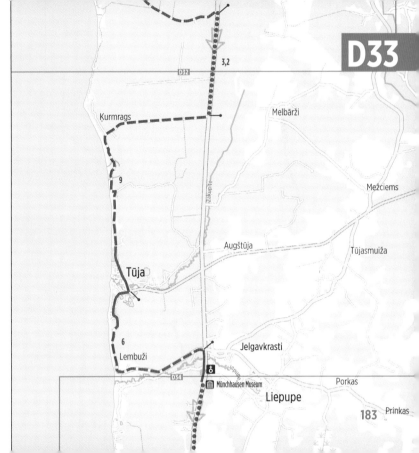

Hieronymus Carl Friedrich Freiherr von Münchhausen (1720-1797) was stationed as an officer in the garrison town of Rīga, which at that time belonged to the Russian Empire, and found the love of his life in Jacobine von Dunten. The couple lived on the family's estate in Livonia for six years before moving to Lower Saxony in 1750. The museum was opened in the rebuilt manor house in 2005.

The route continues from the museum on the paved road back towards **Via Baltica**, into which you turn right. After 1 kilometre you have to decide how to continue: You can either turn left and continue for 10 km on a road with a gravel and asphalt surface or you continue for 6 km on Via Baltica with heavy traffic.

From there, turn right into the paved road **Tallinas iela** (red) and after crossing the river Age you will reach the coastal town of **Zvejniekciems**. Continue along the coast to Saulkrasti.

Saulkrasti

This small town with 3,000 inhabitants extends over a length of 17 kilometres. You can have a bite to eat at Hotel Minhauzena Unda and also spend the night.

Continue on the bike path, which is located at a good distance parallel to the road and signposted as **EV 13**, and at the Lutheran church, cross the river Pēterupe.

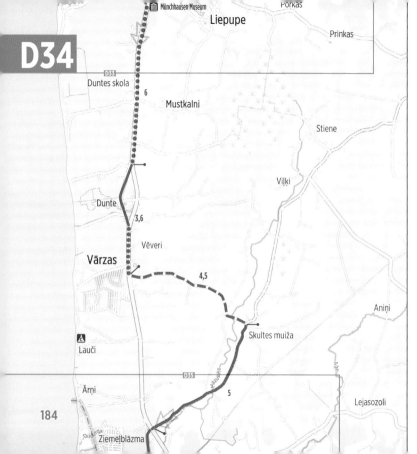

Münchhausen Museum
Porkas
Liepupe
Prinkas
D33
Duntes skola
6
Mustkalni
Stiene
Viļķi
Dunte
3,6
Vēveri
Vārzas
4,5
Aniņi
Skultes muiža
Lauči
D35
Ārņi
5
Lejasozoli
Ziemeļblāzma

In **Pabazi** you will pass the bicycle museum, the only one in the Baltic States.

Bicycle Museum

There is a great variety of Latvian bicycles on display, with beautiful flower decorations, nickel-plated mudguards and the typical half-racing handlebars. Of course, you can also find famous Latvian brands such as "Erenpreis" or "Leitner" as well as some foreign import bikes, among others from Germany. However, there is also some information on the sad legacy of the German invasion: a "Brennabor" foldable bicycle of the German Wehrmacht.

At the mouth of the river Incupe, you can see the White Dune, from where you can enjoy wonderful views over Rīga Bay.

The memorial for Finnish fighter pilots who died here on 23 April 1943, is located at a petrol station. It was built by Finnish war veterans on the 70th anniversary.

From Saulkrasti to Rīga   51 km

Continue on the quiet **Rīgas iela** and parallel to the railway tracks, which you cross along with Via Baltica. The quiet street is inaccessible to lorries and you will reach the bike path of Via Baltica, into which you turn left. You can also take the train from Saulkrasti to Lilaste. Cross the river Lilaste and then turn right. Then, cross the railway tracks and continue the journey parallel to the tracks.

Behind **Lilaste** station, turn left, cross the tracks and then turn right again. Continue along lake Ummis and parallel to the tracks. At **Carnikava** turn right, cross the tracks and then continue on

Sculpture at Münchhausen Museum in Dunte

Bicycle Museum in Pabazi

the western side of the railway line on the new bike bridge across the river Gauja. Continue parallel to the tracks until you reach **Garupe** station, where you cross the tracks again.

You will get to **Mežgarciems**, which used to be a settlement of the Soviet army, who carried out air defence trainings here. There are still some bunkers here today.

The route continues from the station in **Garciems** on an unpaved forest path and then again on the country road **P 1**.

Once in **Kalngale**, turn right into **Vanagu iela**. At Kalngale station cross the tracks and then continue for 1 kilometre to Vecāki beach. Continue for 3 km along the Baltic Sea, then turn left and you will reach **Vecāki**. Staying parallel to the railway tracks, you will pass the stations of **Vecdaugava** and **Ziemelblazma**, then cross the river Milgravis and then turn left into **Ostas Prospects**. This will lead you through the Mežaparks – where open air festivals with up to 100,000 visitors sometimes take place – and you will then reach **Atputas aleja**, into which you turn right and which later turns into **Kokneses Prospects**. Pass the zoo and at the end you will reach **Kisezera iela**, into which you turn right. Cross underneath the main street, continue on **Gaujas iela**, then cross the railway tracks under the road bridge at **Brasas** station. Then, continue on **Miera iela** until you reach **Senču iela**, into which you turn right. Then turn left into **Krisjana Valdemara iela**.

Behind the hospital the route continues left into **Bruninieku iela** and then im-

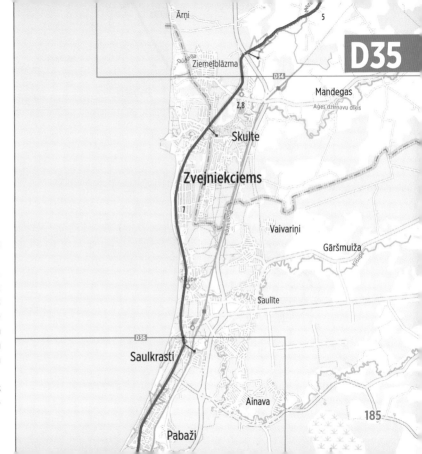

185

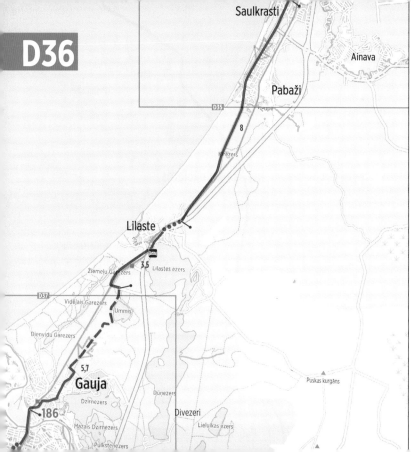

mediately right into **Skolas iela**. Behind **Elizabetes iela** continue straight through the park into **Reimersa iela**. At the end, turn left before the channel into **Raiņa bulvāris**, pass the freedom monument and you will reach Rīga station.

Rīga

postal code: 1050; area code: 72

- 🛈 **Tourism information office**, Kalku iela 16, ☎ +371 672 27 337, www.liveriga.com
- 🛈 **Tourism information office**, Rātslaukums 6, ☎ +371 670 37 900, www.liveriga.com
- 🛈 **Tourism information office**, at the main station, ☎ +371 672 20 555
- 🏛 **Church of St. George (13th century)**, Skārņu iela 10/20. In the oldest sacral stone building of Rīga you can today find an interesting arts and crafts museum.
- 🏛 **Pharmaceutical Museum**, Riharda Vāgnera iela 13/15, ☎ 13008. You can find out everything there is to know about the history of drug production. Guided tours are also available in English.
- 🏛 **Mentzendorf House**, Greciniek iela. Original furnishings are on display and give an impression what the typical patrician houses looked like in the 17th and 18th century.
- 🏛 **Black Head House (Melngalvju nams)**,, Rātslaukums 7, ☎ 70/44309. Rebuilt several times after fire and destruction, the Brotherhood's house for unmarried businessmen has now been renovated according to its original style and its sculpture jewellery is well worth a visit. For those interested in an exhibition on the first floor also offers a brief overview of the history of the house.
- 🏛 **National Museum of Art**, Krijšāņa Vāldemara iela 10A, ☎ 73/25051. More than 52,000 works by Latvian artists are collected here and provide an overview of Latvian art from the 18th century to the present day.
- 🏛 **Rīga Ghetto and Holocaust Museum**, Maskavas iela 14a. This commemorates the Jewish community in Latvia and the tragedy of the Holocaust. It was opened in 2010 and contains a memorial wall with over 70,000 names of Latvian Jews who died in the Holocaust.
- 🏛 **Museum of Occupation**, Latviešu strēlnieku laukums 1, ☎ 72/12715. Several exhibition rooms document the occupation of the country and the crimes committed by Nazi Germany and the

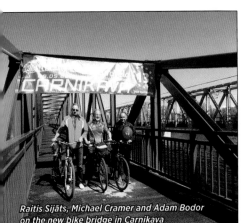

Raitis Sijāts, Michael Cramer and Adam Bodor
on the new bike bridge in Carnikava

former Soviet Union. For Latvia, this is an important contribution to
the search for today's national identity and sovereignty.

- 🏛 **Museum of Urban History and Maritime History**, Palasta iela 4,
  ☎ 735/6676. Upper floor of St. Mary cathedral monastery. Topic:
  Development of the Hanseatic city of Rīga.
- 🏛 **State Art Museum**, Torņa iela 1, ☎ 72/13695. This displays numerous works by Latvian and Russian artists.
- 🏛 **Art Nouveau Museum**, Alberta iela. In the same street there are still
  several houses, richly ornamented with heads, monsters and lions,
  that stemp from the time of the formerly flourishing Art Nouveau

style in Rīga. Next to Vienna, Paris and Barcelona, Latvia was the most important centre of the European Art Nouveau style.

🏛 **Museum of Barricades from 1991**, Krāmu iela. This has been located in the old town since 2001 and shows the permanent exhibition "The Barricades of Rīga - the struggle for the restoration of the independence of the Republic of Latvia in 1991". The restaurant Rozengrāls is located in the vaulted cellar of the building dating from 1307, where you can enjoy medieval-style dining.

🔱 **Order Palace (Rīga pils)**. With its Holy Ghost Tower and Tin Tower, the palace dominates this part of the townscape. Situated on the banks of the river Daugava, it is located in an important strategic location that was used as a seat of government by both the religious state as well as later on by the occupying powers. A small part of the palace is now used for exhibitions: Museums of Latvian History, Literature, Theatre and Music.

🔱 **Rīga Cathedral**, Herderer laukums 6. The largest church in the Baltic States was built at the beginning of the the 13th century. Originally Romanesque, Gothic chapels were built into the side aisles later on. In order to surpass the Basilica of St. Peter, the steeple was raised to 140 m and the interior was decorated with precious paintings, carvings and a Romanesque cloister.

🔱 **Church of St. Peter (13th century)**, Pēterbaznīcas iela. This is the landmark of the city and it has the highest wooden tower in Europe. It was destroyed several times by lightning or during wars, but rebuilt again and again. Today, you can take a lift up to the second tower gallery and enjoy beautiful views of Rīga. Next to

this Baroque tower there is a three-nave Gothic basilica, which is used as an exhibition space on weekdays. Church services are only held here on Sundays.

🔱 **Church of St. John (13th century)**, Jāna iela 7. This one-nave brick church was rebuilt several times and today contains a mixture of Gothic and Renaissance styles. In the church there is a remarkable Baroque altar and a stone mask, which legend has it, used to preach about a Christian life without sin.

🔱 **TV Tower**, not only an architectural feature, it offers the best view over the city at a height of 97 metres.

Freedom Monument in Rīga

🔱 **Freedom monument**, Brvbas piemineklis. This monument was inaugurated in 1935 on Independence Day, which is 18 November. The bronze statue "Milda" with its three golden stars symbolizes the three regions from which today's Latvia originated: Kurland, Latgalia and Livonia. It survived the Soviet era despite the Central Committee of the CPSU in Moscow having decided to demolish the monument.

✼ **Reutern House**, Mārstaļu iela 2/4. This magnificent historical office building was built at the end of the 17th century for the merchant Johann Reutern. Corinthian columns and several portraits of the family adorn the building, which was built in Nordic baroque style. Typical for historical office buildings, of which only a few still exist today, was the division of the property into business premises on the ground floor, storage space under the roof and the use of the rooms in between by the merchant family.

✼ **Dannenstern House (17th century)**, Mārstaļu iela 21. Relatives of Johann Reutern tried to outdo the Reutern House with this building. The remarkable façade design is the most striking feature of this Baroque building.

✼ **House of the Livonian Knighthood (19th century)**, built in the Italian Neo-Renaissance style. Today, it is the seat of the Latvian parliament.

✼ **The Swedish Gate**, Zviedru vārti, Torņa iela 11, built in the 17th century under Swedish rule, this is the only remaining city gate. The city's executioner lived in the adjoining Jürgen's Tower.

- ✿ **Cat House**, Meistaru iela 19. Built at the beginning of the 20th century by the Latvian merchant Plme, after both guilds had refused to accept him. To show them that he was serious in turning his back on them, he placed two black cats with arched backs on both corner towers.
- ✿ **National Opera House (19th century)**. Originally built as the seat of the Deutsches Theater.
- ✿ **"Three Brothers"**, Mazā Pils iela 17, 19, 21. Building ensemble from three different centuries. All three houses show the way of life of their time - from the 15th to the 18th century.
- ✿ **Central market**, Centrltirgus. The 72,000m² market hall was built from several German Zeppelin halls.
- ✑ **Fans Sport**, Garozes iela 1
- ✑ **Burusports**, Aleksandra Čaka iela 149, ✆ 73/17777

The 730,000 inhabitants of Rīga and its suburbs make up the largest urban area in the Baltic States, where half of Latvia's population lives. Even though the population has fallen by 180,000 since independence in 1991, particularly as a result of the migration of Russians, more than half of the population are still Russian native speakers.

The old Hanseatic city on the river Daugava, the "Paris of the East", is located near Rīga Bay, which cuts deeply inland. It is the political, economic and cultural centre of the country. The well-preserved city centre is dominated by brick Gothic, Renaissance and Art Nouveau styles and you can find old and splendidly rebuilt Hanseatic

architecture, as well as some more sad looking Soviet remnants and bold garlands in Art Nouveau style.

The stone Roland in front of the town hall testifies that the city was founded in 1201 by Bishop Albert von Buxhoeveden, a Bremen-born bishop. Until 1561, it was the seat of an archbishop who shared the power of government with the Council of Merchants. By attracting Germans to move here and with military help from the Sword Brothers and German Orders, the city experienced a rapid upswing and played an important role in the Hanseatic League from 1282 onwards. As the Order and the archbishop became increasingly entangled in trade relationships, the citizens were gradually able to emancipate themselves from the archbishop. The Reformation finally put an end to his rule. For the next 100 years the city came under Polish-Lithuanian influence until it was conquered by Sweden's Gustav II Adolf in 1621. Almost 100 years later, during the Great Nordic War (1700-1721), Rīga fell to Russia and became one of the largest ports of the tsarist empire. The upper class as well as the official language until 1891 remained German. Gradually, however, a Latvian middle class emerged and with it the first signs of a national identiy. After the invasion of German troops during the First World War, on 18 November 1918 it declared an independent Latvia

Museum of the Occupation of Latvia in Rīga

- with Rīga as its capital - which was recognised by the Soviet Union "for all time" in the Peace of Rīga in 1920.

As a result of the Hitler-Stalin Pact of 1939, the German population was relocated to Germany and the city was occupied by the Soviet military, but then conquered by German troops in 1941 after the attack on the Soviet Union. After Soviet troops had conquered it again in 1944, the old town was severely damaged. Rīga has been the capital of the sovereign Latvian state since August 1991.

Rīga is a town characterised by Art Nouveau style buildings. The old town was shaped by its architect Michail Eisenstein (1867-1921) with many Art Nouveau style buildings, and has been a World Heritage Site since 1997. Its dominant feature is the Church of St. Peter, which was first mentioned in 1209, with its 123-metre-high tower and a portrait of Martin Luther. It was redesigned many times, often with the money from the merchants'

guild, who wanted to outdo the archbishop's cathedral. The prominent wooden tower was destroyed and rebuilt several times. The last time was in 1973, when Soviet engineers installed a lift, which takes the numerous visitors of the church comfortably to a height of 72 metres, from where they can enjoy far-reaching views over the city and the river.

The 108-metre-high cultural palace was built in 1952-58 in the style of Socialist Classicism. "Stalin's Birthday Cake" was originally intended as a house of collective farms, but has been home to the Latvian Academy of Sciences since 1960.

Leaving the tower, you will almost be standing on the town hall square with the Roland statue. On the left you will see the red, manneristically decorated gables of the Black Heads House. This was used by the "Great Guild" as an assembly building from 1334 and was later redesigned in Dutch style. The company of the Black Heads was a brotherhood of young unmarried trainee merchants who had St. Mauritius as their patron saint. It was destroyed by German bombardment in 1941, blown up by the Soviets in 1948 and finally rebuilt in 1999 true to detail, including all German inscriptions. As if the master builders of 1600 had been clairvoyants, they wrote:"Should I fall down one day / so build me up again".

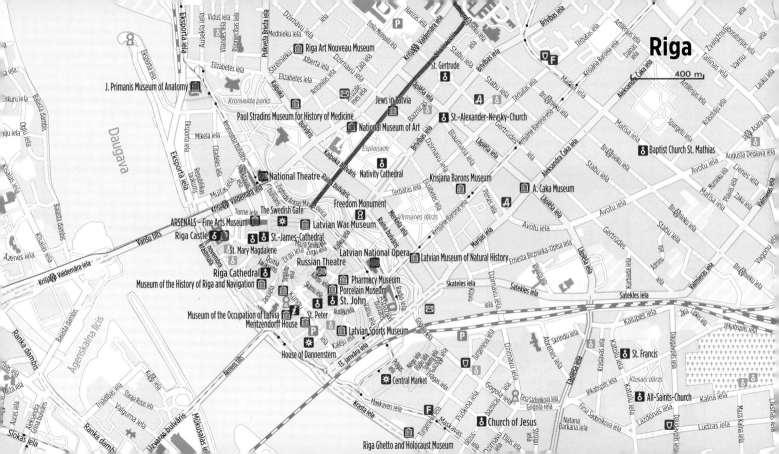

Riga

400 m

Daugava

Eksporta iela

Kronvalda parks

Esplanade

J. Primanis Museum of Anatomy

Riga Art Nouveau Museum
St. Gertrude
Paul Stradins Museum for History of Medicine
Jews in Latvia
National Museum of Art
St.-Alexander-Nevsky-Church
Baptist Church St. Mathias

National Theatre
Nativity Cathedral
Krisjana Barons Museum
A. Caka Museum

The Swedish Gate
Freedom Monument
Latvian War Museum

ARSENALS – Fine Arts Museum
Riga Castle
St.-James-Cathedral
St. Mary Magdalene
Russian Theatre
Latvian National Opera
Latvian Museum of Natural History

Riga Cathedral
Museum of the History of Riga and Navigation
Pharmacy Museum
Porcelain Museum
St. John
Museum of the Occupation of Latvia
Mentzendorff House
St. Peter
Latvian Sports Museum

House of Dannenstern

Central Market

St. Francis

All-Saints-Church

Church of Jesus

Riga Ghetto and Holocaust Museum

The black cube next to it was actually built in 1970 as a museum for the red Latvian archers. Since 1993, however, it has been housing the Museum of Occupation, documenting the effects of National Socialism and Stalinism on defenceless Latvia. Between 1941 and 1991, 500,000 Latvians alone lost their lives. The building, known as the "black coffin", will soon be extended by a white annex. In the building there is a copy of the secret annex to the Hitler-Stalin Pact (see also page 85).

House of the Blackheads in Rīga

The new National Library, which Latvians call the "Palace of Light", is located directly on the riverbank. It was opened in 2014, when Rīga was the European Capital of Culture.

The city's founder, Bishop Albert von Buxhoeveden, was also responsible for the construction of the cathedral in 1211. This largest Baltic church was rebuilt several times in the following centuries and hardly any wlements remain from its original Romanesque style. Today, the tower helmet and interior design as well as the prospectus of the famous Walcker organ present themselves in Baroque style. On 13 January 1991, the population successfully resisted Soviet tanks on the cathedral square to demonstrate for their independence, and seven people lost their lives.

If you continue in this direction, you will reach the castle (Rīgas pils) after 200 metres. This has also been frequently rebuilt since the 14th century. Today it houses the museums of Latvian History and Foreign Art, as well as the President's office.

Although the medieval layout of the old town is still visible, there is only one fortification tower that has survived the times. It is the Powder Tower (Pulvertornis) at Smilšu iela, which is now part of the Latvian War Museum.

Those really interested in entertaining architecture will enjoy looking around the old town very much, and especially this street. However, in the new town - beyond the former fortifications - you will find an almost effervescent joy of design in the figurative Art Nouveau style. The most attractive buildings can be found in Elizabetes and Alberta iela.

Around 1900, ca. 800 Art Nouveau style houses were built in just a few years, many of them with elaborately decorated facades. Art nouveau buildings exist in many cities, but nowhere else can you find so many Art Nouveau buildings with such a lavish design in such a small space and with so many artistically playful facades. The architect and artist Michael Eisenstein, Sergei Eisenstein's father, who made film history with his film "Panzerkreuzer Potemkin", designed many Art Nouveau houses and received the nickname "the crazy confectioner".

Perhaps someone would like to go very high up: two kilometres south of the old town, on an island in the river Daugava, you can find the highest tower in the EU and the third highest in Europe. Its radio and television antenna reaches over 368 metres into the air. The viewing platform is not quite as high but at a height of almost 100 metres it still offers spectacular views.

There are many good eateries, which also are not too expensive, at the cathedral square (Doma laukums) and other places in the city centre. Especially suitable for foreign tourists are restaurants offering buffets, where visitors can choose what they would like to eat and also get a taste of the country's typical cuisine.

Overnight accommodation and bike service list

The following list includes accommodation in the following categories:

Categories

- 🅣 Tourist-Information
- Ⓗ Hotel
- Ⓗᵍ Hotel garni
- Ⓖʰ Inn
- Ⓟ Pension
- Ⓟᶻ Private room
- Ⓗᵒ Hostel
- Ⓜᵒ Motel
- Ⓝᶠ Naturfreundehaus
- Ⓐʰ Apartment Hotel
- Ⓑᵇ Bed and Breakfast
- Ⓑ Bungalow
- Ⓕʷ Vacation home (selected)
- Ⓑʰ Farm
- Ⓗʰ Hay Hotel
- Ⓢ Sonstiges
- Ⓜ Youth Hostel
- 🅐 Campground
- 🅐 Tent site

We have not attempted to list every possible place where visitors can spend the night, and listings should not be construed as any kind of recommendation. Because we wish to expand this list and keep it up-to-date, we welcome any comments, additions or corrections you may have. There is no charge for a single-line entry, for lack of space we cannot guarantee one.

Identification

I	Price Range	less than € 25,–
II	Price Range	€ 25,– to € 35,–
III	Price Range	€ 35,– to € 50,–
IV	Price Range	€ 50,– to € 70,–
V	Price Range	€ 70,– to € 100,–
VI	Price Range	over € 100,–
o.F.	no breakfast	
HP	with breakfast and dinner	
🛁	only room with shared bathroom	
2.5	distance to the route in kilometres	

Prices

These categories are based on the price per person in a double room equipped with shower or bath, with breakfast, unless otherwise indicated.

Distance

The blue number (2.5) at every accommodation shows the distance to the route in kilometres. Please note that this number refers to the linear distance, the difference in altitude and the actual distance covered is not included.

Updates

For further corrections concerning the overnight accommodation list see the LiveUpdate at www.esterbauer.com

bike workshop and rental

- 🔧 Bike workshop
- 🚲 Bike rental
- 🔌 E-Bike charging station

Storskog (Kirkenes) Ⓝ
Ⓟ Sollia Guesthouse, Storskog, ✆ 78990820, IV-V 0̲

Kirkenes Ⓝ
Ⓗ Barents Frokosthotell AS, Presteveien 3, ✆ 78993299 5̲
Ⓗ Scandic Kirkenes, Kongens gate 1, ✆ 78995900, V 4̲.̲5̲
Ⓗ Thon Hotel, Johan Knudtzens Gate 11, ✆ 78971050, IV-V 5̲

Neiden Ⓝ
Ⓟ 🅐 Neiden fjellstue AS, Gnr 8 Bnr 37 Øvre, ✆ 78996141, ✆ 97973080 0̲.̲5̲

Näätämö (Inari)
Ⓜᵒ Rajamotelli Näätämö, Sevettijärventie 12245, ✆ 045/8712408 0̲

Sevettijärvi (Inari)
Vorwahl: 040
Ⓟ Lodge Sevetin Rautu, Sevettijärventie 9040 B1, ✆ 1628779, III 🛁 0̲
Ⓟ Reindeer farm Toini Sanila, Sanilantie 36, ✆ 0290390, V 1̲
🅐 Peuralammen Camping, Sevettijärventie 9081, ✆ 4708845 0̲.̲5̲

Kaamanen (Inari)
Ⓟ Kaamasen Kievari, Kaamasentie 2855, ✆ 016/672713 1̲.̲5̲
Ⓑ Revontulen Tupa, Kaamasentie 2945, ✆ 040/4163437 2̲.̲5̲

Inari
Vorwahl: 016

ℹ Inari Customer Service Point , Inarintie 46, Siida,
  ✆ 040/1689668 ⓪

H Inari, Inarintie 40, ✆ 671026, IV-V ⓪⋅⁵

ℹ Inarin Kultahovi, Saarikoskentie 2, ✆ 5117100 ⓪⋅⁵

▲ Uruniemi, Uruniementie 7, ✆ 050/3718826 ⓪⋅⁵

Ivalo (Inari)

ℹ Ivalo Customer Service Point, Ivalontie 10,
  ✆ 040/1689668 ⓪⋅⁵

Saariselkä (Inari)

ℹ Saariselkä Customer Service Point Kiehinen, Kelotie 1,
  ✆ 040/1687838 ⓪

H Lapland Hotels Riekonlinna, Saariseläntie 13,
  ✆ 016/5594455 ①

H Santa's Hotel Tunturi, Lutontie 3, ✆ 016/68111 ①

Vuotso (Sodankylä)

Vorwahl: 040

P Purnumukka, Ajokastie 4, ✆ 0160568, ✆ 9118310 ①

B&B Ranta Äärelä, Sarvikotamaantie 432, ✆ 0632548 ③⋅⁵

B&B Vuotson Maja, Ivalontie 8775, ✆ 5339880, III ⓪

Peurasuvanto (Sodankylä)

B Peurasuvanto, Ivalontie 5086, ✆ 010/2305800 ⓪⋅⁵

Sodankylä

ℹ Tourist Information, Jäämerentie 3, ✆ 040/7469776 ⓪⋅⁵

H Karhu, Lapintie 7, ✆ 040/1228250 ⓪⋅⁵

Savukoski

H Samperin Savotta, Samperintie 34, ✆ 016/841351 ①

P Mrs Claus Tupa, Koskikatu 3, ✆ 016/841351 ①

P Teerenkieppi, Korvatunturintie 104, ✆ 040/0534686 ⑧

Salla

ℹ Tourist Information, Myllytie 1, ✆ 040/0269838 ⓪⋅⁵

H **Fw** Hioliday Club Salla, Revontulentie 2,
  ✆ 030/6865700 ⓪⋅⁵

B Isokelo vuokramökki, Tuntsanpahta 9,
  ✆ 0500/817529 ⓪⋅⁵

Kuusamo

Vorwahl: 030

ℹ Tourist Information, Torangintaival 2,
  ✆ 040/8608365 ⓪

H Holiday Club Tropiikki, Kylpyläntie 5, ✆ 6864400 ⓪⋅⁵

H Sokos Hotel Kuusamo, Kirkkotie 23, ✆ 010/7633620 ⓪

P Petäjäkylä, Petäjälammentie 6, ✆ 040/0587406 ⓪⋅⁵

M Kuusamo-opisto, Kitkantie 35, ✆ 050/4441157 ⓪

Suomussalmi

ℹ Tourist Office, Jalonkaarre 5, ✆ 08/61555544 ⑤

H Kylpylähotelli Kiannon Kuohut, Jalonkatu 1,
  ✆ 08/710770 ⑤

P Guesthouse Kuutamo, Kiannonkatu 6 C,
  ✆ 050/4622066 ⑤

Lentuankoskentie (Kuhmo)

Ht **▲** Lentuankosken leirintäalue, Lentuankoskentie 435,
  ✆ 040/7730050 ④

Kuhmo

H Kainuu, Kainuuntie 84, ✆ 08/6551711 ⓪

H Kalevala, Väinämöinen 9, ✆ 08/6554100 ⓪⋅⁵

Nurmijärvi (Lieksa)

P Jongunjoen Matkailu / Guesthouse, Kivivaarantie 21,
  ✆ 040/0949215 ②

Lieksa

ℹ Karelia Expert Tourist Service Ltd, Pielisentie 20,
  ✆ 040/0175323 ⓪

B Loma-Kitsi avoin yhtiö, Kitsintie 86 A, ✆ 040/0457015 ⓪

▲ **Ht** Leppee Oy, Timitrantie 25, ✆ 045/1237166 ②

Hattuvaara (Lieksa)

M Taiga Maja, Hattuvaarantie 277, ✆ 045/2707440 ①

Naarva

Fw Ulvovan Suden Majatalo / Guesthouse, Kivivaarantie 34, ✆ 050/3485605 ⑥

Möhkö

Vorwahl: 013

P Mantan Majatalo / Guesthouse, Möhköntie 210,
  ✆ 040/8616373 ①

AH Möhkön Rajakartano, Mustakorventie 11,
  ✆ 050/0649150 ⓪⋅⁵

▲ Möhkön Karhumajat Oy, Jokivaarantie 4, ✆ 844180 ⓪⋅⁵

Ilomantsi

Vorwahl: 040

ℹ Central Karelia Tourist Info, Kalevantie 13,
  ✆ 0240072 ③⋅⁵

H Pogostan Hovi, Kalevantie 12, ✆ 1964496 ③⋅⁵

B&B Kuuksenkaari, Kuuksenvaarantie 20 C,
  ✆ 050/5602844 ①

Bh Anssila farm, Anssilantie 7, ✆ 5431526 ④

Värtsilä (Tohmajärvi)

H Joki, Hopeakalliontie 3d, ✆ 040/0888681 ⓪⋅⁵

Tohmajärvi

P Jouhkolanhovi / Guesthouse, Jouhkolantie 41,
  ✆ 040/027881 ⑤

P Minimotel Tohmajärvi, Kirkkotie 5 C, ✆ 044/0964003 ⑦

Kitee

ℹ Kitee Tourist Info, Kiteentie 6, ✆ 040/1051021 ⓪⋅⁵

B&B Savikon Kartano, Savikontie 37, ✆ 040/0261552 ①⋅⁵

Puhos (Kitee)

H Pajarinhovi, Pajarinniementie 1, ✆ 020/7425770 ⑤

Kesälahti

ℹ Kesälahti Tourist Info, Pyhäjärventie 8,
  ✆ 040/1052008 ⓪

H Karjalan Kievari, Lappeenrannantie 18,
  ✆ 040/0260593 ②⋅⁵

Saari

H Fireman Center, Akapohjantie 25, ✆ 046/6219545 ④

Särkisalmi (Parikkala)

H Lohikontti, Melkoniementie 2, ✆ 054/83201

Parikkala

H Laatokan Portti, Kuutostie 722, ✆ 044/7227600 ⓪⋅⁵

Bh **B** Lehtolan Aitta ja Mökki, Vehkasuontie 84,
  ✆ 045/2604645 ①

Wolin ⓟⓛ

ℹ Informacja turystyczna, ul. Zamkowa 24, im Regional-
  museum, ✆ 913261763 ⑥⑥⑦

ℹ Informacja turystyczna, ul. Zamkowa 24, im Regional-
  museum, ✆ 913261763 ⑥⑥⑦

Simpele (Rautjärvi)

P Simmes Oy – Guesthouse, Reinikaisenkatu 6,
  ✆ 050/0853981 ①

Imatra

Vorwahl: 020

ℹ Imatra Base Camp, Virastokatu 2, ✆ 6177777 ⓪

H Cumulus Resort Imatran Valtionhotelli, Torkkelinkatu 2,
  ✆ 048117 ⓪

H Imatra Spa, Purjekuja 2, ✆ 7100500 ③⋅⁵

▲ Imatra Camping, Ottelukatu, ✆ 045/2550072 ②⋅⁵

Lappeenranta

Vorwahl: 020

🅘 Tourist Information, Brahenkatu 1, Shopping Center IsoKristiina, ✆ 05/667788 2.0

Lahtela (Hujakkala)

🅑 Lahtelan Maatilamatkailu, Lahtelantie 120, ✆ 040/7074991 0.5

Hujakkala

🅑🅑 Rajamaja, Väkeväläntie 400, ✆ 044/7772700 1

Miehikkälä

Vorwahl: 040

🅑 Kiisto Cottage, Tanssilavantie 40, ✆ 044/3595180, ✆ 044/5269338 1

🅑 Kyläseppä Cottage, Muurikkalantie 8, ✆ 044/3447449 0.5

🅑 Säästöpirtti Cottage, Niemenkankaantie 1, ✆ 050/3527490 1.5

Helsinki

Vorwahl: 09

🅘 Fremdenverkehrs- und Kongressamt, Pohjoisesplanadi 19, ✆ 31013300 0.5

🅗 Anna, Annankatu 1, ✆ 616621, III 1

🅗 Arthur, Vuorikatu 19, ✆ 173441, IV-V 0

🅗 Cumulus Kaisaniemi, Kaisaniemenkatu 7, ✆ /0200048107, III-V 0

🅕 F6 Oy, Fabianinkatu 6, ✆ 68999666, VI 0.5

🅗 Haven, Unioninkatu 17, ✆ 681930, VI 0.5

🅗 Helka, Pohjoinen Rautatiekatu 23, ✆ 613580 1

🅗 Holiday Inn Helsinki City Centre, Elielinaukio 5, ✆ /0200048103 0.5

🅗 Katajanokka, Merikasarminkatu 1, ✆ 686450 1

🅗 Kongressikoti, Snellmaninkatu 15, ✆ 040/7704400, II-III 0

🅗 Kämp, Pohjoisesplanadi 29, ✆ 576111 0.5

🅗 Lilla Roberts, Pieni Roobertinkatu 1-3, ✆ 6899880, VI 1

🅗 Omena, Lönnrotinkatu 13, ✆ /0600 555222, III 1

🅗 Park Hotel Käpylä, Pohjolankatu 38, ✆ 799755 3.5

🅗 Radisson Blu Royal , Runeberginkatu 2, ✆ 020/1234701 1

🅗 Rivoli Jardin, Kasarmikatu 40, ✆ 681500, V 0.5

🅗 Sokos, Kluuvikatu 8, ✆ 020/1234601, V 0.5

🅟 SweetDream Guesthouse, Hämeentie 21, ✆ 044/9868866 0.5

🅗🅞 CheapSleep , Sturenkatu 27b, ✆ 040/4838280, I 1

🅗🅞 Eurohostel, Linnankatu 9, ✆ 6220470 1

🅗🅞 Forenom, Haapaniemenkatu 7-9, ✆ 020/1983420, II 0.5

🅐 Rastila, Karavaanikatu 4, ✆ 31078517 0.5

Söderkulla

🅑🅑 Villa Sibbe, Joensuun raitti 58, ✆ 045/6165720, II 0.5

Porvoo

🅘 Tourist Information, Läntinen Aleksanterinkatu 1, ✆ 040/4899801 0

🅗 Pariisin Ville, Jokikatu 43 , ✆ 019/580131 0

🅑🅑 Old Town, Välikatu 10, ✆ 045/8512345, III-IV 0.5

Loviisa

🅗 Pilasterit, Sepänkuja 8

🅗 Ulrikanhovi, Kuhlefeltinkatu 35, ✆ 040/1837855 0

Siltakylä

🅗 Villa Vanessa, Siltakyläntie 272, ✆ 046/8121222, II 0

Kotka

Vorwahl: 044

🅗 Karhulan Hovi, Karhulan Hovin tie 1, ✆ 7333100, II-V 2

🅗 Kotkan Residenssi, Östringinkatu 10, ✆ 5230463, II 2.5

🅗 Kuninkaantien Majatalo, Kierikkalankatu 30, ✆ 040/5439141, III 0

🅗 Original Sokos, Keskuskatu 21, ✆ 010/7821000, V-VI 0.5

🅗 Santalahti, Mastotie 1, ✆ 05/2268010, III 2.5

🅟 Kuin Kotonaan, Porthaninkatu 24, ✆ 0921/1883267 0.5

Hamina

Vorwahl: 05

🅗 Haminan Seurahuone, Pikkuympyräkatu 5, ✆ 010/7635870, IV 0.5

🅗 SpaHotel, Sibeliuskatu 32, ✆ 3535555, IV 0.5

🅖🅗 Kallioranta, Norsviikintie 42, ✆ 040/5141052 1

🅐 Hamina Camping, Vilniementie 375, ✆ 040/1513446 0

Ravijoki

🅕🅦 Ravijoen Oravanpesä Apartments, Haakelintie 5, ✆ 041/4765994 0

🅑🅗 Harjun Hovi, Katariinankuja 19, ✆ 05/2295500 1

Virolahti

🅐 Hurpun leirintäalue, Hurpuntie 362A, ✆ 040/7018056 7

Vaalimaa (Virolahti)

🅐 Vaalimaa Camping, Hämeenkyläntie 153, ✆ 044/3571451 1.5

Vyborg (Выборг) 🆁🆄🆂

Vorwahl: 081378

🅘 Tourist Information Centre, Vokzalnaya Str., 13 (Вокзальная ул.), ✆ 34430 0.5

🅗 Atlantik (Атлантик), Podgornaya Str., 9 (Подгорная ул.), ✆ 24776 0

🅗 Druzhba (Дружба), Zheleznodorozhnaya Str., 5 (ул. Железнодорожная), ✆ 25744, 22383 0.5

🅗 North Crown Hotel (Северная Корона), Sbornaya Str., 2 (ул. Сборная), ✆ 22650 0.5

🅗 Sampo (Сампо), Vasilyeva Str., 11 (ул. Васильева улица, д.), ✆ 31496 0

🅗 Shel'f (Шельф), Primorskoye Shosse, 2Б (Приморское шоссе 2Б), ✆ 27027 0

🅗 Victoria Hotel Vyborg (Виктория), nab. 40th Anniversary of the Komsomol, 1 (наб. 40-летия ВЛКСМ), ✆ 52800 0

🅗 Vyborg (Выборг), Leningradsky Prospect, 19 (Ленинградский проспект д.19), ✆ 25675 0

🅗 braun-House Inn, Dimitrova Str., 4A (ул. Димитрова), ✆ 20893 0

🅟 Hotel on Water Korolenko, Zheleznodorozhnaya 5 (Железнодорожная ул.), at the quay behind Hotel Druzhba, ✆ 34478. Spend the night at the quay on a 1957 steamer in single and double cabins designed in the original style 0

Sovetsky (Советский) 🆁🆄🆂

🅗 Hotel Chaika (Чайка), Shkol'naya Str., 27 (ул. Школьная), ✆ 081378/57410 0.5

🅟 Kordon Kuz'micha (Кордон Кузьмича), Sportivnaya Str., 25 (ул. Спортивная), ✆ 0812/9992112 1

Primorsk (Приморск) 🆁🆄🆂

🅟 🅑 Manola (Манола), Beregovaya Str. 24 (ул. Береговая), ✆ 0812/7148873 3.5

Ozerki (Озерки) 🆁🆄🆂

🅑 Okunevaya recreation complex (База отдыха Окуневая), Okuneviy proezd 4 (Окунёвый проезд), ✆ 0812/7150500 0

Ⓑ Sea Home Cottages (Дом у моря), Morskoy proezd 1 (Морской проезд), ☎ 0812/7482990 ⓪

Roshchino (Рощино) Ⓜ

Ⓗ Raivola Hotel (Райвола), Pesochnaya Str., 1 (ул. Песочная), ☎ 0812/3225060 ⑧

Ⓑ Holiday Home Lesobitel, Yelovaya Al., 38 (Еловая аллея), ☎ 0911/2314178 ⑤

Komarovo (Комарово) Ⓜ

Ⓟ Komarovo Country-Club, Sovetskaya Str., 93 (ул. Советская) ⓵

Zelenogorsk (Зеленогорск) Ⓜ

Ⓗ Aquamarine (Аквамарин), Primorskoye shosse, 593 (Приморское шоссе), ☎ 0812/7022619 ⓪

Repino (Репино) Ⓜ

Ⓗ Repinskaya (Репинская), Primorskoye shosse, 428 (Приморское шоссе), ☎ 0812/4320530 ⓪

St. Petersburg (Санкт-Петербург) Ⓜ

Vorwahl: 0812

🅲 Tourist Information, Sadowaja Str., 14/52 (Садовая ул.), ☎ 2423909 ②⑤

Ⓗ Dostoevsky (Дом Достоевского), Kaznacheyskaya Str., 1 (Казначейская ул.), ☎ 9477656, III-IV ②

Ⓗ Galunov, Degtyarnaya Str., 1 (Дегтярная ул.), ☎ 6186188 ⓵

Ⓗ Indigo, Tchaikovskogo Str., 17 (ул. Чайковского), ☎ 4545577, III-IV ⓵

Ⓗ Ligotel, Ligovsky Ave, 55/4 (Лиговский пр.), ☎ 3201155, I-II ①⑤

Ⓗ Majestic Boutique, Sadovaya Str., 22 (Садовая ул.), ☎ 4488388, III-IV ②

Ⓗ Mokhovaya, Mokhovaya Str., 27/29 (Моховая ул.), ☎ 7407585 ①⑤

Ⓗ Obuhoff Village (Обухофф), Knipovich Str., 1 (ул. Книпович), ☎ 3251675 ①⑤

Ⓗ Okhtinskaya (Охтинская), Bolsheokhtinsky Prospekt, 4 (Большеохтинский пр.), ☎ 3331388 ⓪

Ⓗ Onix, Ligivsky Ave, 67/22 (Лиговский пр.), ☎ 4540413 ①⑤

Ⓗ Polosaty, Suvorovskiy Prospekt, 20 (Суворовский пр.), ☎ 0931/3615735 ①⑤

Ⓗ Pushka Inn, Moyka 14 (наб. реки Мойки), IV ②

Ⓗ Vodogray, Karavannaya Str., 2 (Караванная ул.), ☎ 5705737, II-III ②

Ⓗ Wynwood, Griboyedov Channel embankment, 18 (наб. Канала Грибоедова), ☎ 0911/2071820 ②

Ⓗⓞ BedandBike, Gorokhovaya Str., 43 (Гороховая), ☎ 9076409, I ②

Ⓗⓞ Chao, Mama, Grazhdanskaya Str., 27/30 (Гражданская ул.), ☎ 5700444 ②

Ⓗⓞ Chickadee, Lomonosova, 18- 4 (ул. Ломоносова), ☎ 0931/5796494 ①⑤

Ⓗⓞ Home Yoga, Zagorodnyy Prospekt, 17 (Загородный пр.), ☎ 0981/9796484

Ⓗⓞ Tanais, Nekrasova Str., 58 (ул. Некрасова), ☎ 5792731, I ①⑤

Ⓗⓞ Traveller's Palace, Mayakovskogo Str., 36 (ул. Маяковского), ☎ 2721628, I ①⑤

Ⓗⓞ Velohostel, Marata Str., 25a (ул. Марата), ☎ 0921/9348988, I-III ①⑤

Ⓗⓞ Zanevski, Zanevski Prospekt 9 (Заневский пр.), ☎ 0921/9036757 ⓪⑤

Peterhof (Петергоф) (St. Petersburg) Ⓜ

Ⓗ Aleksandriya, Sankt-Peterburgskoye Shosse, 134b (Санкт-Петербургское шоссе), I-II ⓪

Ⓗ New Peterhof, Sankt-Peterburgski Prospekt, 34 (Санкт-Петербургский пр.), ☎ 0812/3191010, III ⓪

Ⓗ Q Art Hotel, Zolotaya Str., 4 (Золотая ул.) ⓵

Gostilitsy (Гостилицы) Ⓜ

Ⓗ Mini Hotel Gostilitsy (Гостилицы, Мини-отель), Tsentral-naya Str., 1 (Центральная ул.), ☎ 0921/9464835 ⓪

Sergiyevskoye Ⓜ

Ⓟz Homestay Elena, Sergiyevskoye 43, ☎ 0905/2126487

Dubki Ⓜ

Ⓗ Dubki (Дубки), Dubki, 1A (Деревня Дубки), ☎ 0931/9789636 ⓪

Ivangorod Ⓜ

Ⓗ Vityaz, Kingiseppskoye Shosse, 7 (Кингисеппское ш.), ☎ 0813/7551661, I ⓪⑤

Ⓟ Guest House Kupecheskiy (Купеческий), Gagarina Str., 26 (Ул. Гагарина), ☎ 0921/5830218 ⓵

Narva Ⓢⓣ

🅲 Tourist Information, Peetri 3, ☎ 3599137 ⓪

Ⓗ Central, Sergei Lavretsovi 5, ☎ 3591333, I ⓪

Ⓗ Elektra, Paul Kerese 11, ☎ 7166651, I ⓪⑤

Ⓗ Europe, Roheline 8, ☎ 6638256, II ⓵

Ⓗ Inger, Aleksander Puškini 28, ☎ 6881100 ⓪

Ⓗ Vesta King Tulundusühistu, Lavretsovi 9, ☎ 3572404, I-II ⓪⑤

Ⓗⓞ Retro, Lavretsovi 8, ☎ 58305859 ⓪⑤

Ⓗⓞ Sparta, Hariduse 18b, ☎ 56075231, II ⓪

Sillamäe Ⓢⓣ

Ⓗ Krunk, Kesk 23, ☎ 3929030 ⓪⑤

Toila Ⓢⓣ

Ⓗ Toila Spa Hotel, Ranna 12, ☎ 3342900 ⓪⑤

Kunda Ⓢⓣ

Ⓗⓞ West-Wind Hostel, Ehitajate 7, ☎ 3221260 ⓵

Viinistu Ⓢⓣ

Ⓗ Viinistu Art Hotel, ☎ 55586984 ⓪

Pirita (Tallinn) Ⓢⓣ

Ⓗ Pirita Top SPA, Regati pst. 1, ☎ 6398600, IV-V ⓪⑤

Tallinn Ⓢⓣ

🅲 City Tourist Information, Niguliste 2, ☎ 6457777 ⓵

Ⓗ Barons, Suur-Karja 7, ☎ 6999700, IV-V ⓵

Ⓗ City Hotel, Paldiski maantee 3, ☎ 6600700, III ①⑤

Ⓗ City Hotel Portus, Uus-Sadama tn. 23, ☎ 6676600, III ⓪

Ⓗ Domina Ilmarine, Põhja pst. 23, ☎ 6140900, IV ⓪

Ⓗ Dzingel, Männiku tee 89, ☎ 6105201, II-III ⑥

Ⓗ Imperial, Nunne 14, ☎ 6274800, IV ⓪

Ⓗ Kreutzwald, Endla 23, ☎ 6664800, II-IV ②

Ⓗ Lillekula, Luha 18, ☎ 6271120, I ②⑤

Ⓗ Nepi, Nepi 10, ☎ 6551665, I ③

Ⓗ Old Town Maestros, Suur-Karja 10, ☎ 6262000, III-IV ⓵

Ⓗ Schlössle, Pühavaimu 13/15, ☎ 6997700, V ⓪⑤

Ⓗ Skåne, Kopli 2c, ☎ 6678300, I-II ⓪⑤

Ⓗ Sokos Hotel Viru, Viru Väljak 4, ☎ 6809300, IV ⓪⑤

Ⓗ St. Barbara, Roosikrantsi 2a, ☎ 6400040, III ①⑤

Ⓗ Stroomi, Randla 11, ☎ 6304500, I ⓪⑤

Ⓗ Susi, Peterburi tee 48, ☎ 6303300, III ②⑤

Ⓗ Tatari 53, Tatari 53, ☎ 6405150, II ②

Ⓗ Valge Villa, Kännu 26/2, ☎ 6542302, II-III ③

Ⓗ VanaWiru, Viru 11, ☎ 6691500, IV ⓪⑤

H Ülemiste, Lennujaama tee 2, ☎ 6032624, III 2.5
Gh Villa Lepido, Pärnu mnt. 364, ☎ 6701291, I 5
Pz Rex/Kodumajutus, Tartu mnt 62, ☎ 5078650 1.5
Ho Academic Hostel, Akadeemia tee 11, ☎ 6202275 3.5
Ho Mahtra, Mahtra 44, ☎ 6218828, I 4
BB Karjatare, Vaike-Laagri 4-9, ☎ 56203845, I 0.5
BB Oldhouse Trade, Uus 22, ☎ 6411464, ☎ 6411281 0.5

Laulasmaa (ST)
H Laulasmaa Resort, Puhkekodu tee 4, ☎ 6870800, IV 0.5

Nõva (ST)
Pz Roosi Turismitalu, Rannaküla küla Nõva vald, ☎ 5182718 0

Dirhami (ST)
P Guesthouse Dirhami, Noarootsi vald, ☎ 56825901 0.5

Linnamäe (ST)
Pz Kiige Turismitalu, Lääne-Nigula vald, ☎ 5094207 0.5

Padise (ST)
H Padise Manor , Padise vald, ☎ 6087877 0

Elbiku (ST)
B Roosta Puhkeküla, Lääne-Nigula vald, ☎ 4725190 0.5

Saare (Pürksi) (ST)
P Saare manor, ☎ 56242195 4

Haapsalu (ST)
i Haapsalu turismiinfokeskus, Karja 15, ☎ 4733248 1
H Baltic Hotel Promenaadi, Sadama 22, ☎ 4737250, II 2
H Fra Mare, Ranna tee 2, ☎ 4724600, III-IV 0.5
H Haapsalu Hotel, Posti 43, ☎ 4733347, III-V 1
H Kongo hotell, Kalda 19, ☎ 4724800, III-V 1
H Laine Sanatoorium, Sadama 9/11, ☎ 4724400, III-IV 1.5
H Päeva Villa Hotel, Lai 7, ☎ 4733672, II 1

P Bergfeldti Mudaravila, Suur-Liiva 15a, ☎ 4737436, II 1
P Hermannuse Maja, Karja 1a, ☎ 4737131, II 1.5
P Tokoi Külalistemaja, Suur-Lossi 24, ☎ 4735665 1.5
Pz Ungru kodumajutus, Ungru tee 4/3, ☎ 4735843 0.5
Ho Endla Hostel, Endla 5, ☎ 4737999 1
M Sport, Wiedemanni 15, ☎ 4735140 1

Suuremõisa (ST)
Ho Allika Hostel, Suuremõisa küla, ☎ 53631626, III 1

Kärdla (ST)
i Tourist Info, Hiiu tn 1, ☎ 4622232 0.5

Kassari (ST)
A Mesila talu, Kassari küla, ☎ 4652/03792
A Vetsi Tall, ☎ 4622550 12

Körgessaare (ST)
Gh Viinaköök, Sadame tee 2, ☎ 4693337 1.5
Fw Holiday Apartment Helena, Pargi tee 2-1, ☎ 404877837 1.5

Poka (Leisi)
Pz Niidi-Jaani talu, Poka küla, ☎ 5228524, I 1.5
A Mõisa, Parasmetsa küla, ☎ 5145/73257

Oitme (Leisi)
Pz Kongi talu, Oitme küla, ☎ 51998161 1.5
M Oitme matkamaja, Oitme, ☎ 5107253, I 1.5

Leisi (ST)
Pz A Adu-Jaani talu, Mätja küla, ☎ 4573653 6

Järveküla (ST)
Bh Ansu farm, Järveküla, ☎ 53964904 6

Hiievälja (Leisi)
Pz Välja Turismitalu, Hiievälja küla, ☎ 56699662, I 3.5
A Tamme, Hiievälja küla, ☎ 55632518 4

Selgase (ST)
Bh Värava, Selgase küla, ☎ 5251139 0.5

Panga (ST)
P A Panga puhketalu, ☎ 56692009 1

Kihelkonna (ST)
Pz Pühassoo, Neeme küla, ☎ 56645001

Loona (Kihelkonna)
H Loona Manor, Loona Village, ☎ 4546510 0.5

Lümanda vald
P Pilguse Mõisa Külalistemaja, Jõgela küla, ☎ 4545445, III 0.5
Pz Kuusiku talu kodumajutus, Viidu küla, ☎ 4576345
Pz Muha Ranna Puhketalu, Riksu küla, ☎ 426750 0
Pz Sepa-Jõe, Riksu küla, ☎ 4570386
A Kipi-Koovi, Kipi küla, ☎ 5130517 0
A Lümanda Söögimaja, Lümanda küla, ☎ 4576493 2.5

Mändjala (ST)
A Kämping Mändjala, Mändjala küla, ☎ 5029706 0

Nasva (ST)
H Nasva, Nasva küla, ☎ 4544044, II 1.5
BB Arina turismitalu, Ülejõe 3, ☎ 4544162 0

Kuressaare (ST)
i Tourist Information Center, Kuressaare town hall, Tallinna tn 2, ☎ 4533120 0
H Arabella, Torni 12, ☎ 4555885, II 0.5
H Arensburg, Lossi 15, ☎ 4524700, II-IV 0
H Ekesparre, Lossi 27, ☎ 4538778, IV 0.5
H Georg Ots SPA Hotel, Tori 2, ☎ 4550000, III 0
H Grand Rose, Tallinna 15, ☎ 6667018, III 0
H Johan, Kauba 13, ☎ 4540000, III 0.5

H Linnahotell, Lasteaia 7, ☎ 4531888, II-III 0
H Repo, Vallimaa 1a, ☎ 4533510, II 0.5
P A Kuus Sõlme, Roomassaare 7, ☎ 4538866, II 3.5
P Mardi, Vallimaa 5a, ☎ 4524633, ☎ 24644, II 0.5
P Seawolf, Tuule 3, ☎ 4554996, ☎ 48316, II 1
P Staadioni, Staadioni 4, ☎ 4533556, II 0.5
Pz Villa Smaragd, Uus-Roomassaare 5, ☎ 5247408 0.5
Pz Abaja Kodumajutus, Abaja 16, ☎ 4556/484914 0
Pz Central kodumajutus, Uus 22, ☎ 5089697 0.5
Pz Ida Kodumajutus, Ida 15, ☎ 4536775, ☎ 5235775 0.5
Pz Kiwi Villa, Kivi tänav 3, ☎ 5017378 1
Pz Kodumajutus Laura, Kohtu 2, ☎ 4554081, I-II 0
Pz Kraavi, Kraavi 1, ☎ 5092544, II 1
Pz Maria kodumajutus, Transvaali 23, ☎ 4556881 0.5
Pz Minesso Öömaja, Nooruse 8, ☎ 5088879, I 0.5
BB Anne ja Ülo Rooms, Tuule 11, ☎ 4556941
BB Helene Villa, Tuule 27, ☎ 4531800, I-II 1.5
BB Kodumajutus Transvaali 28, Transvaali 28, ☎ 5253415, I 0.5
BB Tuule, Tuule 1, ☎ 4533616 1
M SÜG Hostel, Kingu 6, ☎ 4554388 0.5
A Piibelehe Kodumajutus, Piibelehe 4, ☎ 4536206 0.5

Kaali (ST)
P Kaali Külastuskeskus, Pihtla vald, ☎ 45591184, II 2.5

Kõljala (ST)
A Kõljala puhkeküla, Kõljala külas, ☎ 56615095 1.5

Orissaare (ST)
i Tourist-Information Center, Sadama, ☎ 4545051 0
Pz Pühäristi, Ranna pst. 11, ☎ 4545149 0.5
Fw Raamat, Laheküla, ☎ 4528891 2.5
M Gümnaasium Hostel, Sadama 5, ☎ 4530276 0

Koguva (Muhu) 🛈

Pz Pärdi Talu, Koguva küla, ☎ 4548873
Pz Saadu talu, Koguva küla, ☎ 4548874
Pz Vanatoa Turismitalu, Koguva küla, ☎ 55587494 4̄

Liiva (Muhu) 🛈

▲ Aki körts-kämping, Liiva küla, ☎ 5148211 3̄

Salme 🛈

Pz Järve Turismitalu, Järve küla, ☎ 5016853, I 0.5

Mändjala 🛈

Pz Jassi Puhkemajad, Malle tee 38, ☎ 4531468, I-II 1̄

Paatsalu 🛈

Pz ▲ Paatsalu Puhkekeskus, Paatsalu küla, ☎ 5138000 1.5

Ermistu (Tõstamaa) 🛈

▲ Ermistu Puhkeküla, Ermistu küla, ☎ 56297627 2̄

Tõstamaa 🛈

Pz Sauli Äri, Varbla mnt. 8, ☎ 53468709 0̄
Pz Tõstamaa mõis (Manor House), Kalli mnt 13, ☎ 53468635 1̄

Seliste (Tõstamaa) 🛈

▲ Pz Jaaguranna Lillelanger, Seliste küla, ☎ 53466363 1̄

Pootsi 🛈

Pz Pootsi, Pootsi küla, ☎ 53546644 0̄

Lindi 🛈

Pz Sarnakörtsi talu, Lindi küla, ☎ 4467787

Papsaare 🛈

▲ Kullimänniku puhkeküla, Papsaare küla, ☎ 5653915 0.5

Pärnu

🛈 Turismiinfo, Uus tn. 4, ☎ 4473000 0.5
Ⓗ Ammende Villa, Mere pst. 7, ☎ 4473888, III-V 0̄

Ⓗ Delfine, Supeluse 22, ☎ 4426900, II 0̄
Ⓗ Emmi, Laine 2, ☎ 4476444, II-III 0.5
Ⓗ Koidulapark, Kuninga 38, ☎ 4477030, II-III 0.5
Ⓗ Legend, Lehe 3, ☎ 4425606, II 0̄
Ⓗ Parnu, Rüütli 44, ☎ 4478911, III 1̄
Ⓗ Scandic Rannahotell, Ranna pst. 5, ☎ 4444444, III 0.5
Ⓗ St. Peterburg, Hospidali 6, ☎ 4430555, IV 0.5
Ⓗ Strand SPA and Conference Hotel, A.H. Tammsaare puiestee 35, ☎ 4475370, II-III 0.5
Ⓗ Valli Hotel, Õhtu poik 4, ☎ 4420770, I-II 0.5
Ⓗ Viiking, Sadama 15, ☎ 4490500, IV 0̄
Ⓗ Villa Johanna, Suvituse 6, ☎ 4438370, II-IV 0̄
Ⓟ Laine, Laine 6a, ☎ 4439111, I 0.5
Ⓟ Netti, Hospidali 11-1, ☎ 5167958, II 0.5
Ⓟ Reldori, Lao 8, ☎ 4478400, II 1̄
Ⓟ Villa Artis, A. Adamsoni 1, ☎ 4471480, I-III 0.5
Ⓟ Villa Marleen, Seedri 15, ☎ 4420770, II 0.5
Pz Aleksandri, Vana-Rääma 8, ☎ 4432160 0.5
Pz Ene Villa, Auli 10a, ☎ 4425532, III-IV 0.5
Pz Freven Villa, Kooli 31, ☎ 56686545, II 1̄
Pz Green Villa, Vee 21, ☎ 4436040, IV 0.5
Pz Tulbi majutus, Tulbi 14, ☎ 4452/24828 0̄
Ho Terve, Ringi 50-3, ☎ 5298168 0̄
🏠 Anette, Tallinna mnt. 59, ☎ 55630169 1̄
🏠 Hommiku Hostel, Hommiku 17, ☎ 4451122, I 0.5
🏠 Lõuna, Lõuna 2, ☎ 4430943, I-III 0.5
🏠 Staadioni, Ranna pst. 2, ☎ 5253005 0̄
▲ Konse Puhkeküla, Suur-Jõe 44a, ☎ 53435092 1.5

Rannametsa 🛈

Pz Raiesmaa Talu, Rannametsa küla, ☎ 56625366 4.5

Uulu 🛈

Fw White House, Uulu küla

Häädemeeste 🛈

Ⓟ Valge, Pärnu mnt. 18, ☎ 4437368 0̄

Kabli (Häädemeeste) 🛈

Ⓗ Lepanina Hotel, Häädemeeste vald, ☎ 4465024, III-IV 0.5

Ainaži 🛈

Ⓗ Plavas, Valdemāra iela 121, ☎ 27555755, II-III 0̄

Salacgrīva 🛈

Vorwahl: 402

🛈 Tourismusbüro, Rīgas iela 10a, ☎ /64041254 0̄
Ⓗ Brīze, Valmieras iela 7, ☎ 64071717, I-IV 0.5
Ⓟ Kraukli, Limbažu raj., ☎ /26322316, ☎ /6431634 5̄
Ⓟ Svetupes, Salacgrīvas lauku ter, ☎ /64041469 7̄
Pz Purmali, Limbažu Pagasts
Fw Braslas, Salacrivas lauku teritorija, ☎ 6879331
Fw Korki, Salacgrīva rural area, Limbaži district, ☎ /29239788 0.5
🏠 High school dormitories, Pērnavas iela 31, ☎ /28703487 0.5
▲ Meleku licis, Meleki, ☎ /29284555 0̄
▲ Veczemju Klintis, rural area, ☎ /27852476 0̄
▲ Ⓟ Vējavas, Limbažu rajons, ☎ /64071667 0̄

Zvejniekciems (Saulkrasti) 🛈

▲ Jūras Priede, Upes iela 56a, ☎ 27 008 353 1̄

Tūja 🛈

Ⓟ Viesu Nams Jūras Bura, Jūras iela 41, ☎ 29847299 0̄

Jelgavkrasti 🛈

Ⓗ Pernigele, Liepupes pagasts, ☎ 29471933, I 0.5

Ⓟ Via, Liepupes pagasts, ☎ 402/0143, I
▲ Via, Liepupes pagasts, ☎ 402/0143

Saulkrasti 🛈

🛈 Tourist Information, Ainažu iela 10, ☎ 67952641 0̄
Ⓗ Minhauzena Unda, Ainažu iela 74, ☎ 67955198, III 0̄
Ⓗ Sunny Dune, Rīgas iela 28, ☎ 67951960, II-III 0̄
Ⓟ Baltas dujas, Zalā iela 2, ☎ 29735650 0̄
Ⓟ Pie Maijas, Murjaņu iela 3, ☎ 795/1372 0̄
Ⓟ Saulrieti, Raina iela 11, ☎ 67951400 0.5
Fw Aizvēji, Jūras Prospekts, ☎ 2654 7055, IV 0̄
Fw Mūsmājas, Saules iela 27, ☎ 26556518 0.5
🏠 Inčupe, Rīgas iela 82, ☎ 795/1247 0̄

Lilaste 🛈

Ⓗ Porto Resort, Medzābaki 2, ☎ 22722258 0.5
Pz Lilaste recreational complex, ☎ 67700358, I-II
▲ Lilaste recreational complex, ☎ 7700358, I-II

Trīsciems (Rīga) 🛈

Ⓗ Linga, Līču iela 2, ☎ 67348403, I 3̄

Rīga 🛈

🛈 Tourismusbüro, Rātslaukums 6, ☎ 67037900 0.5
Ⓗ Avitar, Krišjāņa Valdemāra iela 127, ☎ 67364444, III 0̄
Ⓗ Bellevue Park, Slokas iela 1, ☎ 67069000, II-III 2̄
Ⓗ Brigita, Saulkalnes iela 11, ☎ 67623000, I-II 4.5
Ⓗ Felicia, Stirnu iela 32b, ☎ 67599942, II 3.5
Ⓗ Grand Palace Hotel, Pils iela 12, ☎ 67044000, V-VI 0.5
Ⓗ Grīziņš, Pērnavas iela 32, ☎ 67279999, II 1.5
Ⓗ Gutenbergs, Doma laukums 1, ☎ 67814090, II-III 0.5
Ⓗ Helga, Elizabetes iela 22, ☎ 67243075, I-II 1̄
Ⓗ Hotel ABC, Šampētera iela 139a, ☎ 67892728, II 6̄
Ⓗ Hotel Valdemars, Krišjāņa Valdemāra iela 23, ☎ 67334462, II 0̄

[H] Hotel de Rome, Kaļķu iela 28, ☎ 67491500, IV-V 0.5
[H] Jakob Lenz, Lenču iela 2, ☎ 67333343, I-II 1
[H] Kert, Hospitāļu iela 17, ☎ 67373995, II-III 0
[H] Konventa Sēta, Kalēju iela 9/11, ☎ 67087507, II-III 0.5
[H] Laine, Skolas iela 11, ☎ 67289823, I 0
[H] Man-Tess, Teātra iela 6, ☎ 67216056, II-IV 0.5
[H] Marinas Nams, Ventspils iela. 63C, ☎ 67804244, II 4.5
[H] Nams 99, Stabu iela 99, ☎ 67310762, II 1.5
[H] Oskars, Krustabaznīcas iela 9, ☎ 67556955 1.5
[H] Radi un draugi, Mārstaļu iela 3, ☎ 67820200, I-II 0.5
[H] Radisson SAS, Kuģu iela 24, ☎ 67061111, III-IV 1.5
[H] Riga, Aspazijas bulvāris 22, ☎ 67044222, V
[H] Skanste, Skanstes iela 9, ☎ 67519921, II 0.5
[H] Tia, Krišjāņa Valdemāra iela 63, ☎ 67333918, I-III 0
[H] Valnis, Vaļņu iela 2, ☎ 67213785, II 0
[H] Veselība, Vairoga iela 32a, ☎ 67567498 🐾 2
[H] Viktorija, A. Čaka iela 55, ☎ 67014111, I-II 0
[H] Vilmāja, Ilmājas iela 12, ☎ 67873222, II 4.5
[H] Xdream, Artilērijas iela 34, ☎ 67312803, III 1.5
[H] ibis Styles, Katrīnas dambis 27, ☎ 67323130, II 2
[Ho] Amber Hostel, Miesniku 10, ☎ 22006446 4
[Ho] Funky Hostel, Barona iela 25, ☎ 29105939, II 0.5
[Ho] Knights Court, Bruņinieku iela 75b, ☎ 67311303, I 1.5
[Ho] Placis, Laimdotas iela 2a, ☎ 67551271 2
[Ho] Riga Hostel, Merķeļa iela 1, ☎ 67224520 1
[B&B] Liene, Avotu iela 75, ☎ 67314767, I-II 1.5
[B&B] Multilux, Kr. Barona iela 37, ☎ 67311602, II 0.5
[B&B] Riga, Ģertrūdes iela 43, ☎ 67278505, II 1
[B&B] „KB", Barona iela 37, ☎ 67312323, II 0.5
[m] Argonaut Hostel, Kalēju iela 50, ☎ 67220073 0.5
[m] Elizabeth´s Youth Hostel, Elizabetes iela 103, ☎ 27010611 1

[m] Friendly Fun Franks Backpackers Hostel, 11. Novembra krastmala 29, ☎ 25990612 1
[m] POSH Backpackers Latvia, Pūpolu iela 5, ☎ 67210917, I 1
[m] Profitcamp, Teātra iela 12, ☎ 67216361, I-II 0.5
[m] Riga Backpackers, Mārstaļu iela 6, ☎ 7229922 0.5
[m] Riga Old Town Hostel, Vaļņu iela 43, ☎ 67223406 1
[A] Kempings ABC, Šampētera iela 139a, ☎ 67892728 6
[🚲] Burusports, Gaujas iela 7, ☎ 67317782 0
[🚲] Fans Sport, Garozes 1, ☎ 67626012 4
[🚲] Citybike, Kalnciema iela 28, Gandrs, ☎ 6322358 2.5

Geographical index

Page numbers from page 193 refer to the list of accommodations